Methods of Theoretical Psychology

Methods of Theoretical Psychology

André Kukla

A Bradford Book
The MIT Press
Cambridge, Massachusetts
London, England

Set in Sabon by The MIT Press.
Printed and bound in the United States of America.

Library of Congress Cataloging-in-Publication Data

Kukla, André, 1942–
Methods of theoretical psychology / André Kukla.
p. cm.
"A Bradford book."
Includes bibliographical references and index.
ISBN 0-262-11261-2 (hc. : alk. paper)
1. Psychology—Philosophy. 2. Psychology—Methodology. I. Title.

BF38 .K84 2001
150'.1—dc21   00-048039

The distinction between a philosophical and a psychological theory is heuristic: a quick way of indicating which kinds of constraints are operative in motivating a given move in theory construction. In any event, that is the spirit in which the essays in this book are written; philosophical and psychological considerations are appealed to indiscriminately. I wish I could learn to be less discriminating still, for I am morally certain that real progress will be made only by researchers with access to an armamentarium of argument styles that considerably transcends what any of the traditional disciplines offer. That, despite frequent lapses into mere carnival, is what is hopeful about the recent interest in developing a cognitive science.

—Jerry Fodor (1981a, p. 19)

Contents

Preface

This book has its genesis in an *American Psychologist* article entitled "Nonempirical Issues in Psychology" (Kukla 1989). My aim in the article was frankly polemical. I wanted to convince psychologists that our discipline had suffered from a gross and systematic underestimation of the scope, variety, and import of theoretical work in the scientific enterprise. Most controversially, I tried to persuade my colleagues that there are many important theoretical issues the resolution of which does not call for empirical research: They require nothing but thinking. Naturally, I marshalled a series of example to make my point. For the sake of expository convenience, I located the various examples within a rough-and-ready taxonomy of theoretical activities. Half in jest, I called the result a "job description for armchair psychologists."

Then I got interested in the job description for its own sake. It seemed to me a worthy *metatheoretical* project to extend and clarify the rough-and-ready taxonomy, quite apart from its role in the polemical project that gave it birth. My endeavors along these lines appeared in a number of articles, the most substantial of which was "Amplification and Simplification as Modes of Theoretical Analysis in Psychology" (Kukla 1995a).

This book partakes of the spirit of both prior articles. Like the 1989 article, it is an attempt (more sustained) to persuade psychologists that they haven't given the theoretical side of psychology its due. Like the 1995 article, it is also a descriptive survey of the field. My treatment differs from other surveys of theoretical psychology, however. Other surveys (e.g., Marx and Hillix, 1973; Wolman 1981) divide the subject matter into distinct theoretical approaches. These books characteristically include a chapter on psychoanalytic theory, a chapter on S-R theory, and so on. In contrast, my book divides the field into *types of theoretical activities*. My book isn't really a work *in* theoretical psychology at all; it is a book *about* theoretical psychology. More precisely, it is an attempt to delineate the scope of a neglected but entirely legitimate area of specialization within psychology.

The audience that I had in mind when writing this book is the community of experimental psychologists. Here and there, however, I have included information that is common knowledge among psychologists. For example, no psychologist needs to be told what the law of effect is. Nevertheless, when I refer to the law of effect for the first time (in chapter 4), I introduce it with a paragraph of elementary explanation. The purpose of these elementary additions is to make the book accessible to non-psychologists who might have an interest in the topic. It also renders the book suitable for use as a primary text in an undergraduate course in theoretical psychology.

Here is a more complete list of the articles from which the material in this book derives:

"Nonempirical Issues in Psychology," *American Psychologist* 44 (1989): 785–794

"Is AI an Empirical Science?" *Analysis* 49 (1989): 56–60

"Clinical Versus Statistical Theory Appraisal," *Psychological Inquiry* 1 (1990): 160–161

"Evolving Probability," *Philosophical Studies* 59 (1990): 213–224

"Ten Types of Scientific Progress," in *Proceedings of the 1990 Biennial Meeting of the Philosophy of Science Association,* volume 1

"Theoretical Psychology, Artificial Intelligence, and Empirical Research," *American Psychologist* 45 (1990): 780–781

"Teaching Armchair Psychology," *International Society for Theoretical Psychology Newsletter* 7 (1991): 2–4

"Unification as a Goal for Psychology," *American Psychologist* 47 (1992): 1054–1055

"Amplification and Simplification as Modes of Theoretical Analysis in Psychology," *New Ideas in Psychology* 13 (1995): 201–217

"Is There a Logic of Incoherence?" *International Studies in the Philosophy of Science* 9 (1995): 59–71

"On the metametatheory of psychology: A reply to Dawson, Green, Mackay and Rozeboom," *New Ideas in Psychology* 13 (1995): 247–257.

Finally, a warm thanks to Dan Chiappe, Chris Green, and Elliot Paul, each of whom is a source of numerous substantive points scattered throughout the book.

Methods of Theoretical Psychology

1

The Enterprise of Theoretical Psychology

... the conceptual systems [of science] ... are bound by the aim to permit the most nearly possible certain ... and complete coordination with the totality of sense-experience. ...
—Albert Einstein (1951, p. 13)

1.1 Theoretical Psychology Defined

The epigraph above alludes to two mental processes that are essential to the scientific enterprise: observation and ratiocination. (Ratiocination is directed thinking, just as observation is directed perception.) If the aim of science is to coordinate conceptual systems with sense experience, then it is clear that scientists must allot some of their professional time to acquiring sense experiences and some to tinkering with concepts. The former is the observational side of science; the latter is its ratiocinative side. This much is universally acknowledged. There have been vast disagreements, however, concerning the proper roles of observation and ratiocination and concerning their relative importance. Roughly, *empiricism* is the tendency to emphasize the importance of observation and *rationalism* is the tendency to emphasize the importance of ratiocination. (These broad definitions will be refined in chapter 10.) Empiricists are of the opinion that the systematic acquisition of observational data is where the action is in scientific research. With the right sensory data, constructing and coordinating appropriate conceptual systems is thought to be relatively straightforward. Conversely, rationalists believe that the difficult problems and the major breakthroughs in science are played out largely in the conceptual arena.

The type of scientific work favored by empiricists is *empirical* work. By definition, an empirical project is one that requires observation at some stage. The type of scientific work favored by rationalists is *theoretical* work, a theoretical project being defined as one that does not require observation at any stage. The prototypical empirical project is the *experiment*, wherein conditions are systematically arranged for observing whether a particular phenomenon takes place. However, the realm of empirical investigations is broader than the realm of experimental studies. This is a lucky thing for sciences like extragalactic astronomy, where it would be difficult to arrange for phenomena to occur at our convenience. In addition to experimentation, there is a place in science for the empirical activity of *naturalistic observation*—the observation of phenomena as they occur in the world, independent of our control. There are also types of work whose empirical status is subject to debate. The most important example of this class in psychology is *introspection*, the systematic observation and description of the investigator's own mental states. A history of psychology could be written entirely in terms of the status granted to introspective reports. In the nineteenth century, introspection was deemed the only acceptable form of empirical work for a psychologist. During the first half of the twentieth century, it was almost universally condemned as unscientific. In recent years, psychologists probably have been more divided on this issue than ever before (Kukla 1983; Lyons 1986). I will have more to say about introspection below. Here my point is that scientists may very well disagree as to whether a particular activity is a legitimate instance of empirical work.

The prototypical theoretical project is the construction of a scientific theory explaining a set of data. The data themselves will have been obtained by empirical means, but constructing a theory to explain them is not another piece of empirical research. It is a project that requires nothing but thinking. Just as empirical work is a broader category than experimentation, theoretical work encompasses more than theory construction. Of the seven chapters in this book that deal with the varieties of theoretical projects, only one is devoted to theory construction. Not surprisingly, there are at least as many controversies concerning the boundaries of legitimate theoretical work as there are over the boundaries of the empirical. I will deal with these controversies in chapters 9 and 10.

I have defined *empirical* and *theoretical* as types of scientific activities. It seems a straightforward matter to use the same words to describe types of scientific *issues*, an empirical issue being one that is resolved by empirical means and a theoretical issue being one that is resolved by theoretical means. That would be ambiguous, however. Would it mean that an empirical issue is one that is *in fact* resolved by empirical means, or one that *should be* resolved by empirical means, or one that *can be* so resolved, or one that can be resolved *only* by empirical means? These notions are certainly not equivalent. Consider the famous problem of the seven bridges of Königsberg. Two islands in the river that passes through the city of Königsberg were connected by seven bridges as shown in figure 1.1. The question arose whether it was possible to cross all the bridges without crossing any single bridge twice. The experience of generations of townspeople provided strong empirical evidence for the proposition that no such path existed. The townspeople could therefore be said to have solved the problem of the seven bridges by empirical means. But in the early eighteenth century the great mathematician Leonard Euler was able to prove the same proposition mathematically. Bradley and Swartz (1979, p. 152) describe this episode as follows: "What was first learned experientially outdoors by tramping around the banks of the river Pregel . . . was later relearned by the powers of pure reason (presumably) in the comfort of Euler's study where he merely carefully and ingeniously thought about the problem." So is the problem of the seven bridges empirical, or theoretical? We can, of course, define our terms in any way we like. What matters is that we understand one another. According to common usage, any issue that can be settled by purely theoretical means is deemed theoretical, whereas an empirical issue is one that can be settled only by empirical means. The asymmetry built into these definitions is a bit confusing at first, but there it is. To say that an issue is empirical is to imply that it cannot be resolved

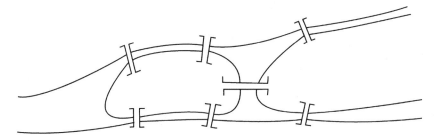

Figure 1.1
The seven bridges of Königsberg.

by purely theoretical means, but to say that an issue is theoretical does not rule out the possibility of an empirical resolution. With these definitions, the problem of the seven bridges turns out to be a theoretical problem that the townspeople had attacked by empirical means.

Both empirical and theoretical investigations have roles to play in the advancement of science. In some sciences (most notably physics), the preparation required for original empirical or theoretical work is so extensive that scientists must specialize in one or the other. Those who deal with the empirical side of their science are often called its *experimentalists*, after the most familiar (but not the only) form of empirical activity. Those who deal with the theoretical side of science are called, appropriately enough, its *theoreticians*. Thus, physicists are either experimental physicists or theoretical physicists. Despite their name, theoretical physicists do not spend all their time constructing new theories; they have a lot of other theoretical business to attend to. Also, under the definitions in the previous paragraph it is not strictly correct to say that theoretical physicists have exclusive rights over the theoretical issues of physics. Under my definitions of the terms, it is possible to seek a solution to a theoretical problem by empirical means. That is not what theoretical physicists do, however. Theoretical physics is the attempt to resolve theoretical issues in physics by theoretical means.

This book is about *theoretical psychology*, which stands in the same relation to psychology as theoretical physics does to physics. Only very recently has theoretical psychology developed, on the model of theoretical physics, into a distinct area of specialization within psychology. This is a story that should be told in some detail. It begins in ancient Greece.

1.2   Empiricism and Rationalism in the History of Psychology

As defined in section 1.1, empiricism and rationalism comprise a continuum of viewpoints rather than only two. Every region of this continuum has had its proponents at one time or another. At the very beginning of Western thought, we find Plato and Aristotle occupying positions near the extremes. According to Aristotle (1973, p. 235), "no one can learn or understand anything in the absence of sense." Plato, his teacher, had a different view about how we arrive at the truth. According to Plato (1961, pp. 48–49), he who wishes to obtain knowledge must proceed by "cutting himself off as much as possible from his eyes and ears . . . which prevents the soul from attaining to truth and clear thinking."

The same disagreement raged among twentieth-century fictional detectives. Inspector Maigret is a radical empiricist (Simenon 1971, p. 34):

"Do you think . . ."
"I don't think. You know that. I look."

Hercule Poirot is the complete armchair rationalist (Christie 1984, p. 103):

"Miller, the man who's on this case, is as smart chap. You may be very sure he won't overlook a footprint, or a cigar ash, or a crumb even. He's got eyes that see everything."
"So, *mon ami*," said Poirot, "has the London sparrow. But all the same, I should not ask the little brown bird to solve the case of Mr. Davenheim. . . ."
"You don't mean to say, Monsieur Poirot, that you would undertake to solve a case without moving from your chair, do you?"
"That is exactly what I do mean. . . ."

Ever since Plato and Aristotle, the history of Western thought has seesawed between empiricist and rationalist tendencies. Here is a brief recap of the most recent swings.

The seventeenth century saw the elaboration by Descartes, Spinoza, and Leibniz of what may be called *classical rationalism*. According to this doctrine, the properties of the natural world can all be discovered by pure reasoning, much as we discover the properties of mathematical objects. To the modern scientist, such a claim must seem utterly fantastic. Did the classical rationalists really believe that a process of pure reasoning could tell me whether I have any clean socks in my dresser drawer, or what the president of France ate for breakfast on December 11, 1983? The answer, at least in the case of Leibniz, is an unqualified Yes. Leibniz's chain of reasoning goes roughly as follows: First you prove that God exists and that He is both omnipotent and perfectly good. That the existence of God can be deduced like a mathematical proposition was a philosophical commonplace of Western philosophy in some eras; it survives in some circles even today. If one can get over this first hurdle, the rest of the job is easy. It follows from God's perfect goodness that He would have created the best world He possibly could. It follows from His omnipotence that He could have created any possible world. Hence, the world God created must in fact be the best of all possible worlds. But in order to establish whether I have any clean socks in my dresser drawer, I need only ask myself whether the best of all possible worlds is one in which there are clean socks in the drawer or one in which there aren't—and that task can, at least in principle, be accomplished entirely by a conceptual analysis of goodness.

In the eighteenth century, the European world largely abandoned classical rationalism for *classical empiricism*. The major figures in this movement were Locke, Berkeley, and Hume—all of them British. Here we already see a dichotomy between Continental and Anglo-Saxon thought—a dichotomy that has persisted throughout the modern era. Indeed, the transitions between rationalist and empiricist periods can for the most part, be described as changes in the geographical center of intellectual life between Continental Europe and the English-speaking countries. Locke (1706) provided the basic framework of modern empiricist thought. According to Lockean empiricism, the mind takes in sensory impressions whose causes originate in the outside world, and forms beliefs out of them by means of various mental operations. Without the sensory input, however, the mental operations are powerless to arrive at any truths about the world. Berkeley (1710) and Hume (1739) showed that the amount of knowledge that can be justified on the basis of an empiricist theory of knowledge is far less than Locke had supposed. Berkeley noted that one cannot conclude on the basis sensory evidence alone that there exists an outside world from which the sensations arise. According to Berkeleyan *idealism*, an empiricist can claim no more than that sensations come in regular and predictable patterns. Hume argued, further, that if all knowledge comes from experience we have no basis even for supposing that there are predictable patterns. (This important argument will be discussed in chapter 5.) According to Hume, empiricism entails that we can have no justification for adopting any belief that goes beyond what is currently being observed. In sum, Hume showed that classical empiricism leads to extreme skepticism about the possibility of human knowledge.

In the nineteenth century, the philosophical ball was returned to the Continental rationalists' court. Kant (1781) accepted the basic Humean conclusion that empiricism leads to skepticism. Whereas Hume had been content to settle for skepticism, however, Kant opted to repudiate empiricism. From the viewpoint of the modern empiricist Bertrand Russell, Kant's influence on philosophy was entirely retrogressive: "Hume, by his criticism of the concept of causality, awakened [Kant] from his dogmatic slumber—

so at least he says, but the awakening was only temporary, and he soon invented a soporific which enabled him to sleep again." (Russell 1945, p. 704)

I will assess the virtues and demerits of Kant's soporific in chapter 10. At present it is sufficient to say that Kant did not advocate a return to classical rationalism. He originated a subtler and altogether more plausible tradition of rationalistic thinking—one that has continued to influence the history of ideas. Indeed, in the English-speaking world, his influence is probably stronger now than ever before. Kantian rationalism concedes to skepticism that there is a great deal about the world that we can never know. Furthermore, it concedes to empiricism that much of what we do know can be acquired only by empirical means. However, Kantian rationalists insist that some of our most basic knowledge of the world does not come to us via the route of sensory experience. Kant refers to knowledge acquired by observation as "a posteriori knowledge" and to knowledge acquired in the absence of observation as "a priori knowledge." These terms provide a much-used alternative to "empirical" and "theoretical" in characterizing our knowledge-seeking activities. Unlike "empirical" and "theoretical," however, they are not used to characterize types of issues; the problem of the seven bridges of Königsberg (which happens to have been Kant's home town) can be resolved either by a posteriori or by a priori means, but in itself it is neither an a priori nor an a posteriori issue.

In the first half of the twentieth century, empiricism once again dominated the philosophical scene. Whereas Kantian rationalism had been a response to classical empiricism, this swing of the pendulum largely ignored its Kantian predecessor. Russell's assessment of Kant, quoted above, was characteristic of the period. Twentieth-century empiricism represented itself as a direct continuation of the program of Locke, Berkeley, and Hume, and so it was. Empiricists like Russell, the early Wittgenstein, and the members of the "Vienna Circle" made considerable headway toward solving various technical problems that had arisen in the course of elaborating the classical empiricists' program. This progress was made possible by the application to philosophical problems of sophisticated and powerful tools of symbolic logic that had been forged at the turn of the twentieth century (Whitehead and Russell 1910–1913). The use of logic was so central to the enterprise of these empiricists that this phase of philosophical history is often called the era of logical empiricism. (A more common name for the same school is "logical positivism.") There are, however, no special bonds between empiricism and logic. Rationalists can play that game too. Indeed they may find it even more congenial, since the pursuit of logic is an a priori activity. In any case, having introduced formal logic into philosophical discourse is probably the logical empiricists' most enduring contribution. However, logical empiricism was remiss in offering new solutions to the big problems of classical empiricism that had led to the Kantian analysis in the first place.

The recurrence of the big problems—particularly the problem of how to avoid skepticism—has led to the demise of logical empiricism and to a renewed appreciation for Kant. These developments are so recent that it is inappropriate to discuss them in a historical vein. The writing of this book is itself a part of what appears to be a new era of rationalistic thinking. The pendulum has begun to swing again. Evidence of the decline of empiricist sentiment has by now been noted in virtually every academic discipline, from physics (Bohm 1971) to jurisprudence and literary criticism (Michaels and Ricks 1980). Among philosophers of science, for whom these matters are of central professional concern, nearly everyone now seems to agree that the role of a priori knowledge in science was vastly underestimated by the logical empiricists of the previous generation.

How does the science of psychology fit into this picture? Psychology's formative years coincided with the hegemony of logical empiricism. Hence, it is not surprising that psychologists, as a whole, have been more empirically minded than most of their counterparts in other disciplines. The empiricizing tendency was considerably mitigated among European psychologists by their geographically determined inclination toward rationalism. But historical and geographical tendencies combined to produce an extraordinary peak of empiricist sentiment in early- to mid-twentieth-century North America. It is arguable that no group of scholars in any discipline has ever emphasized the empirical side of the pursuit of knowledge more exclusively than North American psychologists circa 1950. The representative psychologist of this era was B. F. Skinner, who argued that there are no theoretical issues in science (Skinner 1950). According to Skinner (1974, pp. 109–110), even problems of logic should be settled by doing experiments. Skinner was the anti-Plato.

Not all mid-century American psychologists were as extreme as the Skinnerians. But most of them were taught to regard "empiricist" as intrinsically complimentary, as in the phrase "a good empiricist." This attitude was less than optimal for the development of a strong tradition of theoretical thinking. Theoretical psychology was often called "armchair psychology." This was an appropriate and attractive name for the enterprise if uttered in the right spirit, but among experimental psychologists it was used as a term of derision. Like armchair adventure, armchair psychology was supposed to be a counterfeit of the real thing—an opinion that cannot easily be reconciled with the fact that the two greatest minds of the twentieth century, Albert Einstein and Hercule Poirot, chose to be armchair practitioners of their respective disciplines. Non-Skinnerians conceded the existence of theoretical issues in psychology; however, they tended to regard them as ancillary to the main business of science, which was to "collect data" by empirical research—for example, Christensen-Szalanki and Beach (1983, pp. 1400–1401) write: "It seem to us that psychologists should spend more time collecting data and less time advocating their favorite opinions." Many psychologists believed that theoretical issues were inevitably so trivial that experimentalists could handle the theoretical chores of psychology in their spare moments away from the laboratory (Longuet-Higgins 1981). Naturally, this opinion functioned as a self-fulfilling prophecy: Since most psychologists thought of theory construction as trivial, very few of them wanted to put a great deal of energy into it; as a result, only trivial theories were articulated. Just as naturally, students with strong theoretical interests tended to look in other fields for career satisfaction. In brief, psychology became almost completely bereft of a tradition of theoretical work.

This empiricist hegemony fell quite suddenly and unexpectedly, like the Berlin Wall, in the mid 1970s. Indeed, the past few decades have produced an unprecedented flowering of theoretical activity in psychology. The attention to theoretical issues in psychology doesn't yet begin to match the pervasive role of theoretical work in physics, but it is now quite comparable to biology in this respect. The change is, no doubt, related to the broad shift in the zeitgeist noted above. However, some special influences have been at work on psychology. Probably the important of these has been the impingement of other fields in which the importance of non-empirical issues was already taken for granted—notably linguistics, philosophy, and computer science. As a matter of fact, some of the very best recent work in theoretical psychology has come from non-psychologists, including Jerry Fodor (philosophy), Noam Chomsky (linguistics), and Allen Newell and Herbert Simon (computer science). Interest and criticism from non-psychologists have impelled psychologists to pay more attention to the neglected theoretical side of their discipline.

The main consequence for psychology of the new era of rationalism is that there now exists a subdiscipline of theoretical psychology with its own journals, professional associations, and conferences. This means, of course, that theoretical psychology now has a vocabulary, methodological precepts, a corpus of exemplary results, and controversies that are inscrutable to outsiders. A number of writers have suggested that one can no longer expect to make a theoretical contribution to psychology without special training in the field (Longuet-Higgins 1981; Mackay 1988). It seems to me that one cannot even *read* the contemporary theoretical literature without some special preparation. That's where this book comes in.

1.3   Plan of the Book

The traditional way to study theoretical psychology has been to take up one theoretical approach after another—behavioral, psychoanalytic, cognitive, and so on (Marx and Hillix 1973; Wolman 1981). But this book does not aim to impart a substantive knowledge of psychological theories, or even to engage in a critical analysis of selected theories. Its aim is to prepare the reader to evaluate the theoretical literature in any tradition. The good theoretician should be able to criticize and improve on psychoanalytic theory as readily as behavioral theory. The skills involved are the same. Discussing one specific theory after another is not the best way to acquire these skills. Instead of working through a list of theories, the material in this book is organized around various types of theoretical issues. The collection of all the issue types to be discussed may be regarded as an updated job description for armchair psychologists: These are the kinds of problems theoreticians may be called upon to resolve in their capacity as "consulting specialists." These issues cut across theoretical orientations. For example, in section 6.2, I will discuss the theoretical impact of arguments to the effect that a theory is internally inconsistent. The general form of such an argument, as well as its consequences for science, are pretty much the same whether the target theory is Freudian psychoanalysis or Skinnerian reinforcement theory. Specific theoretical issues will, of course, also be discussed, but these will function primarily as examples of certain types of theoretical problems and endeavors. In sum, this book is not an essay *in* theoretical psychology; it is an examination *of* theoretical psychology. Its aim is to impart the tools of the trade.

Most of the issues to be discussed have their counterparts in sciences other than psychology. The charge of internal inconsistency, for example, has been leveled at theories in physics and chemistry as well as in psychology. A similar book could have been written about the role of a priori analysis in science generally. There are two reasons, however, for relativizing the discussion to psychology. The first has to do with psychologists' need to know. Scientific training in psychology has emphasized the development of empirical research skills far more heavily than training in most other disciplines. Thus the ideas presented in this book will come as news particularly to students of psychology. Secondly (and, in light of the first point, ironically), it will be seen that psychology is a particularly promising arena for the exercise of a priori modes of research—far more so than, say, botany or endocrinology.

The next two chapters are devoted to background material in philosophy of language, logic, and philosophy of science that will greatly facilitate my theoretical discussions. Readers who are already familiar with the rudiments of these fields may skip this material. In chapter 4, I begin my compendium of theoretical issues in psychology with the most familiar of all theoretical tasks: theory construction. The reader should not be greatly disappointed if the first two or three substantive chapters deal with theoretical issues whose nature and scope are already well understood by many psychologists. Before the end of the book, I will be discussing ideas that call for drastic revision of received empiricist views.

2

Basic Tools

2.1 Primitive Terms

Certain logical and mathematical terms are so basic that they cannot be taught by means of explicit definitions. This is not a reparable deficiency of contemporary logic and mathematics. It is an unavoidable fact of conceptual life that every system of terms must contain some undefined elements. These are called the *primitive terms* of the system.

The need for primitives may be intuitively obvious to the reader. It will be instructive, however, to see how it is established on the basis of a priori reasoning. For one thing, it will make a good warm-up exercise for kind of mental work that will be engaged in below. In addition, the general patterns of argumentation involved are important in their own right, and will be used again in later chapters.

Suppose we try to define every term that we use. Let T1 be the first term to be considered, and suppose that it is defined by the term T2. T1 is the *definiendum*; T2 is the *definiens*. In general, we may very well use more than one term in the definiens. But we will certainly use *at least* one term, and that is all that is needed for the argument. T2 will, in turn, require the term T3 (and perhaps others terms) for its definition, T3 will require T4, and so on. There are two possible outcomes to this process. One possibility is that somewhere in the sequence of definitions we use a term in the definiens that has occurred previously—for example, T4, which is used in the definition of T3, turns out to be the same term as T2. In that case our system of definitions contains a *circularity*: T2 is defined by T3, and T3 is defined by T2 (= T4). If there is such a circularity, one cannot learn the system of terms as a whole by studying the definitions: To understand what T2 means one first has to understand the meaning of T3, and to understand T3 one first has to understand T2. For reasons that will be made explicit in the next paragraph, every dictionary that has ever been produced has contained circularities. If Martians encountered such a dictionary, they would be unable to use it, even if they could figure out that it was a dictionary. They would look up T2 and learn that T2s are T3s; then they would turn to T3, only to be informed that T3s are T2s.

The only way to avoid circularity is to use brand-new terms in every definition. But this leads to an *infinite regress*: To understand the definition of T157 one first has to understand what its definiens, T158, means; to understand the definition of T158, one has to be already acquainted with T159; and so on forever. Obviously, such a procedure cannot teach the meanings of any concepts, since there is no way for it to get off the ground. Any attempt to define every term must lead either to circularity or to an infinite regress. In the real world, such an attempt leads to circularity, since no one has enough time or paper to construct infinitely many definitions. This is why unabridged dictionaries can be contained in finite library rooms.

The conclusion is that you can't come to understand all the terms in your vocabulary by means of your having been given definitions for them. The terms for which you are not given a definition are the primitives. Since one must understand the primitives before one can profit from any subsequent definition, it becomes a problem to explain how we come to understand any terms at all. One possibility is that we learn the meanings of the primitives by being given examples of them: for example, that a child learns what a cat is by having cats pointed out. This procedure is called *ostensive definition*. There are well-known problems associated with the notion that we learn the primitives by ostensive definition. For one thing, we must assume that the child already understands that the activity we call "pointing to an example of the term T" is indeed an instance of pointing to an example of T: When you point to a cat and say "cat," how should the child know that you are not merely gratifying an aesthetic impulse by performing a little song and dance? Further, if the child does understand what you are trying to do, there is the problem of knowing how to generalize from a finite sample. The fact that a hundred cats (or indeed any finite number of cats) have been pointed to as examples of "cat" is consistent with infinitely many views as to what a cat is. For example, "cat" might refer to any four-legged creature. To be sure, any single candidate, such as "four-legged creature," can be ruled out by providing the child with a counterexample—e.g., pointing to a dog and conveying (somehow) the idea that *this* four-legged creature *isn't* a cat. But so long as the number of counterexamples remains finite (and it surely will), there will always be infinitely many candidates left. This observation will be established more firmly in chapter 4, where I will talk about the construction of theories to explain finite bodies of data. In chapters 6 and 7, I will discuss how the impossibility of explaining how primitive terms can be learned by ostensive definition has led some psychologists and some philosophers to postulate that we are born with certain ideas already wired into our mental apparatus (Fodor 1981b; Chomsky 1981b). For the time being, we can only hope that we understand our primitives in the same way.

2.2   Sets

The most basic of all mathematical concept is the concept of a *set*. It has sometimes been claimed that all other mathematical concepts can be defined in terms of sets. (See, e.g., Whitehead and Russell 1910–1913.) But "set" itself is always treated as a mathematical primitive. In lieu of being given an explicit definition, it can only chatted about until the learner recognizes which of his or her innate concepts corresponds to it.

The chat goes like this: A set is any collection of objects, entities, or processes whatever. The set of all national capitals is a set that contains Paris, Rome, and Ottawa, ... Alternatively, we can say that Paris, Rome, and Ottawa are *members* of the set of all capitals. Paris is also a member of the set of all cities whose name begins with the letter P. The set of all even numbers is an infinitely large set, one of whose members is the number 256. Two sets are identical just in case they have exactly the same members. The set of all positive integers that are both even and prime has only one member: 2. The set of all positive integers that are both even and less than 4 has the same single member. Therefore, these are two different ways of referring to one and the same thing, like "Beethoven" and "the composer of the Pastoral Symphony." When the members of a set are physical objects, it is important to distinguish the set from the corresponding physical heap. The set of all the squares on a particular chessboard is not simply the chessboard in its totality: The latter is a physical object, whereas the former is an abstract entity—a set. If the set of all the chessboard's squares were identical with the chessboard, then so would the set of all the chessboard's *halves*. But these two sets are demonstrably different: the first has 64 members, the second only two members. Sets can also be members of other sets. For instance, the set of all the squares on a chessboard is a member of the set of all sets containing 64 members.

Now that we know what a set is, we can start to give explicit definitions. To begin with, a set A is *included in* a set B if every member of A is also a member of B. From this definition it follows immediately that if A is included in B and B is included in A, then A is identical to B. Recall that A is identical to B just in case A and B have the same members. Thus, to show that A and B are identical sets we need show only that all the members of A are also members of B and that all members of B are also members of A. The first of these conditions is satisfied by the assumption that A is included in B, the second by the assumption that B is included in A.

The *empty set* is defined as the set that contains no members. We can speak of *the* empty set because it is easily proved that there cannot be two different empty sets. Suppose that A and B are both empty sets. Then there is nothing that is a member of A but not a member of B—for the simple reason that there is nothing that is a member of A. By the same token, there is nothing that is a member of B but not a member of A. That is, A is included in B and B is included in A. But then, by the proof given in the preceding paragraph, A must be identical to B. Thus, any two empty sets must be identical. (As an exercise, prove that the empty set is included in any and all sets.)

The *union* of sets A and B (written A $\cup$ B) is the set that contains every element that is either in A or in B. If A is the set (3, 6, 9, 12, 15) and B is the set (5, 10, 15), then A $\cup$ B is the set (3, 5, 6, 9, 10, 12, 15). The *intersection* of A and B (A $\cap$ B) is the set that contains all the elements that are both in A and in B. If A = (3, 6, 9, 12, 15) and B = (5,10,15), then A $\cap$ B is the set (15), which contains the number 15 as its only member.

It is useful to develop some facility in manipulating expressions dealing with unions and intersections of sets. For example, it should be clear that if A is included in B, then A $\cup$ B = B. If asked for a proof, one would say something like this: "Suppose A is included in B. Then every member of A is also a member of B. And then the set of elements that are either in A or in B is identical to the set of elements that are simply in B, since anything in A is automatically going to be in B too. But this is just to say that A ∪ B = B." Persuade yourself that the following principles are also true: (1) If A is included in B, then A ∩ B = A. (2) For any two sets A and B, A ∩ B is included in A ∪ B.

If A ∩ B is the empty set, then A and B have no members in common. In that case, A and B are said to be *mutually exclusive*. If the union of A and B is equal to some third set C, then A and B are said to be *exhaustive* of C— i.e., A and B, together, account for all the elements of C. A and B may be both mutually exclusive and exhaustive of C; that would mean that A and B correspond to a clean, non-overlapping partition of all the elements of C into two groups. It is often said that scientific category systems, such as the biologists' classification of living things into species, should be both mutually exclusive and exhaustive of all the entities dealt with by that science. If this condition is to be satisfied by the biological scheme, then every living thing must get assigned to some species or other (exhaustiveness), and no living thing can get assigned to two different species (exclusiveness).

2.3   Sentences and Terms

In the last analysis, the product of pure (as opposed to applied) scientific research is a set of declarative *sentences*—e.g., "Humans are descendants of non-human primates," "$F = ma$," "Organisms extinguish more slowly after partial reinforcement than after continuous reinforcement." By "declarative sentence" I mean a linguistic expression that is either true or false. Logicians say that sentences have *truth values*, the truth values being either truth or falsehood. To be sure, we do not always know what the truth value of a sentence is; we may not even have an opinion on the subject. But if we understand the language, we know of any sentence that it *has* a truth value—that it is either true or false.

Not all linguistic expressions have truth values. "Human," "primate," F, m, and a, for instance, don't have truth values. It makes no sense to ask whether "human" is true or false. These expressions are therefore not sentences. They are *terms*. Terms are expressions that name, refer to, or denote entities or classes of entities of any kind. The denotation of a proper name, such as "Sigmund Freud" or "World War II," is an individual entity—a person in the first case, an event in the second. The denotation of a common noun such as "human" is a *set* of individual entities—in this case, the set of all humans. When we say that Sigmund Freud is human, we are saying that he is a member of, or belongs to, the denotation of "human."

Note that the entities denoted by terms need not be physical objects. For one thing, the sets denoted by common nouns are not physical objects. The set of all humans is not itself a human, or anything else made out of matter—it is an abstract object, like a number. It is interesting to ponder the status of abstract entities—to ask whether such things as sets and numbers "really" exist. But let us forgo that pleasure here. Whatever their status may be, abstract entities are definitely permissible as denotations of terms. The term "3," for example, denotes a number just as surely as the term "Sigmund Freud" denotes a man.

Note also that the term "term" does not have the same denotation as the grammarian's term "word." Terms may be expressed by means of any number of words. "The country directly north of the United States" is a term that denotes the same entity as the single word "Canada."

What does it mean to say that terms *denote* entities? If anything is going to be primitive (and some things surely will be), then the relation of denotation between words and things is an excellent candidate. Consider what is involved in understanding an explicit definition. Suppose "bachelor" is defined as "unmarried adult male human being." To understand this as a definition, we have to understand that the definiendum, "bachelor," has the same denotation as the definiens, "unmarried adult male human being." That is, we have to understand what it is for a term to denote a thing. This is the situation with any proposed definition. Thus, one must understand the nature of denotation in order to understand any proposed definition of "denotation."

What is the denotation of the term "mermaid"? If there are no mermaids, one might be tempted to say that this term has no denotation. It turns out to be convenient, however, to ensure that every term has a denotation. Let us say that the denotation of "mermaid" is the empty set. This assertion ought not to be construed as a discovery about language, much less one about biology. Rather, it reflects a convention that facilitates certain types of discourse. This convention is akin to the decision to regard zero as a quantity. If someone has three apples and then loses three apples, what is the number of that person's remaining apples? We could say that there is no number of apples that this person has, but it is preferable to say that the number of his apples is zero. The reason for this preference is utilitarian: It makes applying the laws of arithmetic simpler. By the same token, the convention that terms like "mermaid" denote the empty set facilitates discussions about language and meaning.

If "mermaid" denotes the empty set, then so, of course, do "centaur," "square circle," and "female president of the United States before 1990." But these terms surely do not have the same meaning. Therefore, the meaning of a term is not the same thing as its denotation. To be sure, this particular example depends on our convention about terms that "really" don't name anything at all. But it is easy to devise other examples that make the same point. For instance, the terms "U.S. president before 1990 whose first name is Ronald" and "governor of California before 1990 whose last name is Reagan" certainly don't have the same meaning, although their denotations are identical. Another way to see that denotation and meaning are two different things is to realize that we can know the meaning of a term while being totally in the dark about its denotation. An example of this is the term "person who secretly listens to polka music and is never found out."

The most important thing to remember about terms is the observation with which we began: *Terms are neither true nor false.* This seems a simple enough point, but there is a surprising amount of confusion about it. New scientific theories routinely introduce new terms by means of which their new assumptions about the world are expressed. For instance, psychoanalytic theory introduced the terms "id," "ego," and "superego" and made the assumption that only the id exists at birth. S-R theory introduced "stimulus," "response," and "reinforcement" and assumed that every change in response tendency is due to reinforcement. Such new assumptions are, of course, either true or false. But we are frequently tempted to ask whether it is correct to talk about behavior in terms of id, ego and superego, or in terms of stimulus, response, and reinforcement. As we will see in chapter 9, it is certainly possible to evaluate the relative merits of systems of terms. But this evaluation is strictly in terms of how useful or convenient these systems are for achieving certain scientific purposes. It makes no sense to ask whether a particular terminology is true or false. One might as well ask whether English is true, or whether French might not be more correct. Sentences composed of English terms are true or false, as are sentences composed of psychoanalytical or behavioral terms, but the terms themselves have no truth values.

2.4   Propositions and Concepts

"Canada is in Europe" and "Europe contains Canada" are undoubtedly different sentences—the first begins with "Canada," the second with "Europe." Nevertheless, we have a strong intuitive sense that these two sentences "say the same thing." I will not, at this stage, try to clarify this intuition, but I will introduce some new terms for talking about it. When two different sentences say the same thing, let us say that they express the same *proposition*. The notion of a proposition is useful for stating the equivalence of sentences in different languages: "Canada est dans Europe" expresses the same proposition in French as is expressed in English by either of the two sentences above.

Similarly, different terms that have the same meaning are said to express the same *concept*. "Sibling" expresses the same concept as "brother or sister," and the same concept can be expressed in French by the term "frère ou soeur."

Now that I have made the distinction between sentences and propositions, and between terms and concepts, I will proceed to play fast and loose with it. I will routinely talk about, e.g., "the concept 'reinforcement,'" when I should say "the concept expressed in English by the term 'reinforcement.'" However, there will be occasions when the distinction matters; on such occasions we will have to be more careful. For instance, consider the theoretically important issue of how concepts are learned. As has already been intimated, some psychologists have argued that it is impossible to learn new concepts. It will not do to criticize this claim by noting that one can learn the new concept "sibling" by being told that a sibling is a brother or a sister: one can understand this definition only if one already has the concept "brother or sister," but the concept of a sibling is the *same* concept as the concept of a brother or a sister. More generally, definiendum and definiens are always expressions of the same concept. Thus, definitions do not teach us new concepts. What they teach us are new *terms* with which to express old concepts.

2.5   Necessary and Contingent Propositions

A very useful primitive for which there is no one-word expression in English is the concept of a *possible world*. Since it is a primitive, I cannot begin my discussion by defining it. I can only talk around the concept and hope that we all arrive at the same understanding of it. The actual world we live in is one of the possible worlds. But so is the world that is exactly like the actual world except that I am wearing a different shirt as I write these words. A more radically different possible world is one where the force of gravity is a function of the *cube* of the distance between two objects. On the other hand, there is no possible world in which bachelors are married, or black cats are not black.

The concept of a possible world can be used to clarify many other notions. For example, we saw in section 2.3 that the meaning of a term cannot be equated with its denotation. However, no positive suggestions as to what the meaning of an expression might be were provided. There is an intuitively appealing way to define "meaning" in terms of possible worlds. One can say that two terms have the same meaning just in case they have the same denotation, not only in the actual world, but in all possible worlds. This criterion gives us the right answer in the cases of "mermaid" and "centaur." It is true that the denotations of these terms are the same in this, the actual world—their denotations are both the empty set. But there certainly are possible worlds in which mermaids exist but centaurs do not, and vice versa. In these worlds, the denotations of the two terms are clearly different. In the possible world containing 34 mermaids and no centaurs, for instance, the denotation of "mermaid" is a set of 34 entities, whereas the denotation of "centaur" is still the empty set. Therefore, "mermaid" doesn't have the same meaning as "centaur." On the other hand, there is no possible world in which there exists an entity that is a sibling yet fails to be a brother or a sister. Nor are there possible worlds in which a brother or a sister fails to be a sibling. Therefore, "sibling" and "brother or sister" are synonymous.

The concept of possible worlds can also be used to draw an important distinction between necessary and contingent propositions: A *necessary* proposition is one that has the same truth value in every possible world, whereas a *contingent* proposition is true in some possible worlds and false in others. Thus, there are four basic types of propositions:

- necessarily true propositions, such as "Bachelors are unmarried" and "Black cats are black"
- necessarily false propositions, such as "Bachelors are married" and "Black cats are not black"
- contingently true propositions, such as "There are more than 100 bachelors in New York"
- contingently false propositions, such as "There are fewer than 100 bachelors in New York."

In chapter 8 we will see that it is often important to make clear whether our scientific assertions are to be understood as necessary or as contingent. If a proposition is necessary, it is generally a waste of time and effort to try to confirm it by empirical means. To confirm a proposition by empirical means is to look at the actual world in order to see whether the proposition is true therein. But if the proposition is necessary, it has the same truth value in the actual world that it would have in any other possible world we might imagine. Thus, looking isn't necessary; only the *contingent* propositions of science require experimental verification.

Suppose a certain proposition is true. How do you decide whether it is contingently true or necessarily true? Here is a partial answer: If you can describe a possible world in which the proposition is false, then you know it must be contingent. In the case of "There are more than 100 bachelors in New York," it is clear that there is a possible world in which everyone leaves New York because of some impending disaster. That is, there are possible worlds in which this sentence is false. Therefore the sentence is only contingently true. The philosophical literature is replete with elaborate possible-world constructions involving improbable extraterrestrials living on outrageously unlikely planets. We will encounter some of these ourselves in subsequent chapters. In many of these discussions, the envisioned scenario is so extremely unrealistic that it seems absurd to take such a possibility seriously. It must be remembered that the point of the construction is not to speculate about what might be the case but to establish that some proposition (perhaps a very mundane and universally accepted proposition) is contingent rather than necessary. The failure to envision a possible world in which some proposition is false doesn't yet establish that it is necessarily true. The failure may simply be due to limitations in our imaginative powers.

What if two individuals disagree as to whether something is a possible world? For example, suppose I construct a possible world in which there exist human beings with twelve arms, and you claim that such a world is impossible on the ground that possession of twelve limbs would be sufficient to establish that the creature in question is not a human being. This type of disagreement indicates that we attach different meanings to the same term. Perhaps one of us is right and the other is wrong, in the sense that one of us uses the term in conformity with common usage and the other deviates from common usage. But unless we are specifically interested in the issue of how the term is commonly used by speakers of English, it is pointless for me to insist that I am right and you are wrong. In regard to twelve-armed humans, I might as well grant you your usage and introduce a new term, "shmuman," which is stipulated to mean exactly the same as "human" except that there are no restrictions on the number of limbs possessed by shmumans. Then I could have my possible world populated with twelve-armed shmumans, and I could get on with whatever point I wanted to make.

One potential misunderstanding about the concept of a possible world should be cleared up. It might be argued that there are possible worlds in which bachelors are married after all—worlds in which people attach a different meaning to the term "bachelor." For instance, consider a world that is exactly like ours except that speakers of English use the term "bachelor" to mean any male adult under the age of 30. Isn't that a world that contains married bachelors? By the same argument, couldn't you even have a possible world in which black cats are not black (e.g., a world in which "not" means "very")? To be sure, there are possible worlds in which the *inhabitants* will correctly assert the sentence "Bachelors are married" or the sentence "Black cats are not black." But the *proposition* expressed by that sentence in the language of that possible world is not the same as the proposition expressed by the same sentence in the actual world. When we say that a sentence S is true in a possible world P, this claim is to be understood as meaning that the proposition expressed by "S" in *our* language is true in P. How do we know that this is a correct analysis of possible worlds? We know it because we *stipulate* that it is so. If someone does not go along with this stipulation and continues to insist that there are possible worlds wherein bachelors are married, then we will give up any proprietary claims to the term "possible world" and talk instead about *shmossible* worlds, which are very much like possible worlds except that we decide whether S is true in P by determining whether the proposition expressed by S in *our* language is true in P.

When we say of a proposition that it is true, without any references to possible worlds, what we mean is that it is true in this, the actual world; when we say that a proposition is false, we mean that it is false in the actual world. This point seems to generate an inordinate amount of confusion. The confusion is, I think, due to an erroneous tendency to think of the actual world as merely one of the possible worlds, and to forget that it is entitled to special privileges. After all, the actual world is the one and only world there is! Other possible worlds are merely unactualized possibilities. To say that I have a dog in the actual world is simply to say that I have a dog. To say that I have a dog in some other possible world is not to say that I have a dog in some remote location; it is merely to say that my having a dog is not a logical impossibility. True statements may very well be false in some possible worlds, and false statements may be true in some possible worlds. However, we should not lose sight of the fact that the aim of our scientific endeavors is not to discover what is true in some possible world but to discover what is true.

2.6   Logical Relations among Propositions

Two or more propositions are said to be *inconsistent* if there is no possible world in which all are true. "There are more than 100 bachelors in the world" is obviously inconsistent with "There are fewer than 100 bachelors in the world." Clearly, if the propositions of a scientific theory are inconsistent, then the theory cannot be true of the actual world—for the actual world is one of the possible worlds, and sets of inconsistent propositions are false in *all* possible worlds. In chapter 6, we will see that scientists sometimes inadvertently formulate theories that contain inconsistencies. When logical analysis uncovers the inconsistency, the theory is immediately shown to be false. Empirical research is irrelevant: There is no point looking at the actual world when we know that the theory is false in all *possible* worlds.

It is sometimes useful to distinguish two varieties of inconsistency. Two propositions are *contradictory* if there is no possible world in which they are both true and there is also no possible world in which they are both false. The first of these clauses describes the condition for inconsistency; the second adds another condition. Thus, all contradictory pairs of propositions are also inconsistent, but not all inconsistent propositions are contradictory. Contradictory propositions have *opposite* truth values in every possible world. An example is the pair "Snow is white" and "Snow is not white." Two propositions are *contraries* if there is no possible world in which they are both true but there *are* possible worlds in which they are both false. "World War I began in 1914" and "World War I began in 1915" are contraries: There is no possible world in which they are both true, but they are both false in the possible world in which World War I began in 1913.

A set of propositions is *consistent* just in case it is not inconsistent. Equivalently, a set of propositions is consistent if there *is* a possible world in which they are all true. The fact that a set of propositions is consistent does not, of course, entail that the propositions are true. Consistency requires that they be true in *some* possible world, but that world need not be the actual world. "The average bachelor is more than 7 feet tall" is consistent with "The average bachelor weighs more than 300 pounds," since there is a possible world in which the bachelors are enormous to this degree. Yet both propositions are undoubtedly false.

One proposition *implies* another if there is no possible world in which the first is true and the second is false. The proposition that all emeralds are green implies the proposition that all emeralds found in Africa are green, since the latter proposition will inevitably be true in any possible world in which the former is true. On the other hand, consider "All emeralds are green" and "All rubies are red." Both of these propositions happen to be true; however, there is no relation of implication between them, for there are possible worlds wherein one is true and the other is false. When one proposition implies another, it is often said that the first is a *sufficient condition* for the second and that the second is a *necessary condition* for the first. Thus, the fact that all emeralds are green is a sufficient condition for all

African emeralds' being green: The information that the former is true in some possible world is sufficient for us to conclude that the latter is also true in that world. Conversely, the fact that African emeralds are green is a necessary condition for all emeralds' being green: If the latter is going to be true in some possible world, it is necessary that the former also be true in that world. This use of the English word "necessary" is to be distinguished from its use in the preceding section, where necessary propositions were distinguished from contingent propositions. In section 2.5, the adjective "necessary" was used to designate a property of *single* propositions—namely, the property of being true in all possible worlds. In this section, the same word is used to designate a relation between *two* propositions—namely, the relation that holds when the second proposition implies the first.

Finally, two propositions are *equivalent* if the first implies the second and the second also implies the first. This definition comes to the same thing as saying that two propositions are equivalent if they have the same truth value in all possible worlds. "The average man is taller than the average woman" and "The average woman is shorter than the average man" are equivalent propositions. There are some possible worlds wherein "The average man is taller than the average woman" is true and some wherein this proposition is false. Similarly, there are some possible worlds wherein "The average woman is shorter than the average man" is true and some wherein it is false. But there is no possible world wherein either one of these propositions is true and the other is false.

It is instructive to explore the connections between these logical relationships and the notions of necessity and contingency introduced in the preceding section. For one thing, it follows from the several definitions I have given that a necessarily true proposition is consistent with any contingent proposition whatever: Let P be any necessarily true proposition, and let Q be any contingent proposition. To say that Q is contingent is to say that it is true in some possible worlds and false in some possible worlds. Let W be one of the worlds in which Q is true. To say that P is *necessarily* true is to say that it is true in *all* possible worlds. In particular, then, P is true in the world W. Thus, we have shown that there is at least one possible world—the world W—in which both P and Q are true. But this is exactly what it means to say that P and Q are consistent.

The use of symbols such as P and Q to stand for propositions requires some explanation. Everyone is already familiar with the use of variables to stand for numbers in algebra. When do we use numerical variables? Well, we know that $1 + 2 = 2 + 1$. We also know that $3 + 4 = 4 + 3$, and that $127 + 6 = 6 + 127$. In fact, we know infinitely many numerical facts of the same form. Obviously we can't list them all, but we can express our knowledge succinctly by saying that if x and y are *any* two numbers then it is invariably the case that $x + y = y + x$. In our discussions, the upper-case letters P, Q, R, and so on, are used in essentially the same way. The only difference is that they stand for arbitrary *propositions* instead of numbers. It is clear that "Snow is white" is inconsistent with "It is not the case that snow is white." It is equally clear that "Socrates is mortal" is inconsistent with "It is not the case that Socrates is mortal," that "New York is the capital of Honduras" is inconsistent with "It is not the case that New York is the capital of Honduras," and so on. More succinctly, we can say that, for any proposition P, P is inconsistent with the proposition that it is not the case that P.

To test your understanding of the concepts introduced thus far, try to prove the following:

• that any necessarily true proposition is equivalent to any other necessarily true proposition

• that any necessarily false proposition is equivalent to any other necessarily false proposition

• that any necessarily false proposition is inconsistent with any proposition whatever, including itself

• that any necessarily true proposition is implied by any proposition whatever

• that any necessarily false proposition implies any proposition whatever.

2.7   Deductive Arguments in Propositional Logic

The tools whereby theoreticians get their work done are *arguments*. An argument is a series of propositions satisfying certain requirements. The last member of the series is the *conclusion* of the argument; all the others are its *premises*. Arguments, like terms and concepts, are neither true nor false; they are either *valid* or *invalid*. At this juncture, I will define validity only for a special type of argument: the *deductive* argument. I will not keep using the qualifier "deductive," however. Until further notice, everything I say about arguments really applies only to *deductive* arguments.

An argument is valid just in case its premises imply its conclusion; otherwise it is invalid. Thus, valid arguments are "truth-preserving" in this sense: If the premises are true, then we can be sure that the conclusion is also true. The if-clause in the foregoing characterization should never be forgotten, however. An argument that is valid *and* has true premises is said to be a *sound* argument. If an argument is sound, we can be certain that its conclusion is true. But arguments may very well be valid even though their premises are false. Here is a simple example:

(A1)
Premise 1: Either snow is green or grass is red.
Premise 2: Snow is not green.
Conclusion: Grass is red.

In this case, both the first premise and the conclusion are false. Nevertheless, the argument is valid. What does it mean to call the argument valid? It means that in every possible world in which the premises *are* both true, the conclusion is also true.

An argument may also be *invalid* even though all its premises and its conclusion are true, as in the following:

(A2)
Premise: Snow is white.
Conclusion: Grass is green.

What makes this argument invalid is that the truth of the conclusion is not logically implied by the truth of the premise—an infinitely brilliant logician could not, on the basis of the premise alone, reason his or her way to the conclusion.

We have just seen examples of a valid argument with false premises and a false conclusion and of an invalid argument with true premises and a true conclusion. As an exercise, one might construct a valid argument that has false premises and a true conclusion. In fact, it is possible to construct both valid and invalid arguments with every combination of truth and falsehood among premises and conclusions except one. The only impossibility is a valid argument with true premises and a false conclusion (otherwise validity would not be truth-preserving).

To show that an argument is invalid, we need only invent a possible world in which the premises are true and the conclusion is false. It does not matter how outrageously improbable this world may be; if it is at all possible, the truth of the premises alone does not ensure the truth of the conclusion. For example, the invalidity of (A2) is established by the fact that there are possible worlds in which snow is white but grass isn't green.

Showing the validity of an argument is a more involved matter. It is obviously not enough to fail at the attempt to construct a possible world wherein its premises are true and its conclusion is false. Such a failure could be due to weaknesses in our powers of imagination rather than to the invalidity of the argument. In logic courses, one learns basic rules of inference that tell what types of conclusions can validly be drawn from certain types of premises. I will not touch upon the deep philosophical question of how basic inference rules are themselves to be justified. My subsequent theoretical analyses will rely largely on logical intuition, just as generations of scientific theorists and mathematicians had to do before the relatively recent advent of formal logic. But intuition can be considerably sharpened at very little cost by a brief study of some elementary logical rules.

The proposition "It is not the case that P" is called the *negation* of P. Since there will be numerous occasions to speak of the negations of propositions, it is convenient to introduce an abbreviation for the cumbersome phrase "it is not the case that." The negation of any proposition P can be written as ~P. If P stands for the proposition "Snow is white," then ~P stands for the proposition "It is not the case that snow is white"—in more colloquial English, "Snow is not white." Similarly, I will use the ampersand to abbreviate "and." P & Q (read "P and Q") is called the *conjunction* of P and Q. The English word "and" is often used to conjoin concepts, as in "John and Mary are here." The logic symbol &, however, is to be used only to connect two propositions. It is often called, reasonably enough, a *propositional connective*.

We will need three other propositional connectives. The *disjunction* of two propositions P and Q is the proposition "P or Q," which will be written P ∨ Q. The English connective "or" can be understood in two ways. Suppose it is claimed that either John is in New York or Mary is in New York. If we discover that John is in New York and Mary is in Los Angeles, or that John is in Los Angeles and Mary is in New York, we will concede that the disjunctive claim is true. If it turns out that John and Mary are both in Los Angeles, then the claim is surely false. But what if they are both in New York? Proper English usage in this case is not entirely determinate. In any case, there is no point arguing about such an issue. All that matters is that we come to an agreement. If we say that "P or Q" is true when P and Q are both true, then we are using "or" in its *inclusive* sense; if we say that one or the other of the two propositions must be false for their disjunction to be true, then we are using "or" in its *exclusive* sense. In conformity to standard logical nomenclature, the logical symbol ∨ will be used to refer to inclusive disjunction.

The *conditional* proposition "if P, then Q" will be symbolized by P → Q. The notion of implication introduced in the preceding section is *one instance* of the if-then relationship: If P implies Q, then the proposition P → Q is certainly true. But P → Q is a much broader notion than "P implies Q." If P describes a state of affairs that *causes* the state of affairs described by Q, then P → Q will be true, even though P may not logically imply Q. For example, the following proposition is true: *If* you drop an object from a height of 5 feet above the surface of the earth, *then* the force of gravity will cause the object to fall. However, it is certainly not the case that dropping an object logically *implies* that it will fall to the ground, for there are possible worlds in which gravity doesn't exist. In fact, logicians use the conditional in such a way that P → Q is true *unless* P is true and Q is false. Thus, a logician will say that "If snow is white, then grass is green" is true. This extremely broad usage occurs only occasionally in English. When people say things like "If he wins the race, then I'm a monkey's uncle," they don't mean to assert that there is either a logical or a causal connection between winning the race and being a monkey's uncle. Their claim is presumably to be considered true so long as it isn't the case that he wins and I'm not a monkey's uncle. Nevertheless, there is no denying that there are many instances of P → Q that would be considered true by logicians but would be condemned as false (or as nonsense) by customary English usage. The "→" relation is often called *material implication*, to distinguish it from the narrower *formal implication* that was introduced in section 2.6. The if-clause of the conditional is its *antecedent*; the then-clause is its *consequent*.

Finally, the *biconditional* P ↔ Q is true just in case both conditionals P → Q and Q → P are true. The relation between the biconditional (or *material equivalence*) and the *formal equivalence* described in section 2.6 obviously parallels that between material and formal implication. Specifically, P and Q are logically, or formally, equivalent if they have the same truth value in all possible worlds. However, to be materially equivalent, they need only have the same truth value in this, the actual world. The material equivalence between P and Q is often expressed as "P if and only if Q," or as "P just in case Q."

Now I am ready to state some basic inference rules. In the following, I separate the premises of the arguments from their conclusion by a straight line. I also give the traditional name of each rule.

Modus ponens (MP)

P → Q

P

———

Q

For obvious reasons, this rule is sometimes referred to as the rule of affirming the antecedent. Recall that a rule such as MP is a schema that tells us that we can substitute *any* proposition for P and Q. Thus, modus ponens is the justification for concluding that Socrates is mortal from the premises "If Socrates is a man, then Socrates is mortal" and "Socrates is a man," and also the justification for concluding that grass is red from the premises "If snow is green, then grass is red" and "Snow is green." P or Q may also be a proposition formed by joining several other propositions with propositional connectives. Thus, the following argument is an instance of modus ponens:

If snow is white and grass is green, then I'm a monkey's uncle.
Snow is white and grass is green.
Therefore, I'm a monkey's uncle.

Modus tollens (MT)

P → Q

~Q

———

~P

MT is also called the rule of denying the consequent.

MP and MT are to be carefully distinguished from the two common-est *fallacies* of deductive logic: the fallacies of affirming the consequent and denying the antecedent. To commit a fallacy is to mistake an invalid argument for a valid one. The fallacy of affirming the consequent looks as follows:

P → Q
Q
___
P

The following would be an instance of affirming the consequent:

If he didn't study, then he failed the exam.
He failed the exam.
Therefore he didn't study.

The flaw in this argument, of course, is that the premises leave open the possibility that he might also have failed the exam for some reason other than not studying—e.g., on account of dying. The fallacy of denying the antecedent is

P → Q
~P
___
~Q

as in the following example:

If she studied, then she passed the course.
She didn't study.
Therefore she didn't pass the course.

(Of course, she might not have studied, but might still have passed the course by sheer luck, or by cheating.)

The remaining rules scarcely require explanation.

Simplification (S)

P & Q
___
P

Q & P
___
P

It might seem redundant to list both forms of the simplification rule. But I am trying to be entirely explicit. Certainly the order of propositions matters for *some* connectives: P → Q is not at all equivalent to Q → P. But order doesn't matter for conjunctions.

Conjunction (C)

P

Q
_____

P & Q

Addition (A)

P
_____

P ∨ Q

Disjunction (D)

P ∨ Q

~P
_____

Q

Chain Rule (CR)

P → Q

Q → R
_____

P → R

Transposition (T)

P → Q
_____

[~Q] → [~P]

Note the use of brackets in the conclusion to the transposition rule. If we were simply to write ~Q → ~P, we would not know how to read this expression. One possibility would the one that we actually have in mind: that the negation of Q (materially) implies the negation of P. But another possibility is that the first negation sign applies to the entire remainder of the expression. In that case, ~Q → ~P would be read as asserting the negation of the claim that Q implies the negation of P. Brackets or parentheses indicate the intended reading. If we wanted to assert the second reading, we would write ~[Q → ~P].

Double Negation (DN)

P
___

~~P

~~P
___

P

DeMorgan's Law (DM)

~[P & Q]
___

[~P] ∨ [~Q]

~[P ∨ Q]
___

[~P] & [~Q]

The process of deriving conclusions from premises by means of constructing deductively valid arguments is called *deduction*. As we will soon see, the enterprise of science involves the construction of other kinds of arguments too. These arguments must be considered deductively invalid. But to say that an argument is deductively invalid is not yet to say that it is good for nothing. Deductive invalidity simply means that the truth of the premises does not *guarantee* the truth of the conclusion.

The deductive rules of inference given above are trivial when looked at one at a time. Yet arguments based entirely on these rules may very well lead to non-obvious conclusions. This possibility arises because of the cumulative character of deduction: Once a conclusion has been derived from a set of premises, it is permissible to employ that conclusion as an *additional* premise for further deduction. That is, if we can deduce conclusion C1 from premises P1 and P2, and if we can then deduce C2 from premises P1, P2, *and* C1, then we can say that C2 follows deductively from P1 and P2. A deduction may involve such a long chain of reasoning that if we look at the initial premises alone and the *final* conclusion their relationship may not be intuitively evident. It is instructive to look at an example of a slightly more intricate piece of deductive reasoning. (This one will come up later in my discussion of the disconfirmation of theories.) Suppose that we want to show that the three premises [T & I] → P, I, and ~P together lead to the conclusion ~T. The argument is as follows. (Next to each line of the argument I indicate the previous lines and the inference rule used to obtain that proposition.)

1. [T & I] → P   Premise
2. ~P   Premise
3. ~[T & I]   1, 2, MT
4. [~T] ∨ [~I]   3, DM
5. I   Premise
6. ~~I   5, DN
7. ~T   4, 6, D

One instance of this argument form is the argument according to which a theory is false if it makes a prediction that turns out not to take place even though the initial conditions required for a proper test are in place. Let T be a theory (e.g., the theory that all green-eyed people are jealous), let I be the initial condition for a test of T (e.g., that the subjects are green-eyed), and let P be the prediction from the theory (e.g., that the subjects will be jealous). *If* the theory is true and the initial conditions obtain, *then* the prediction will be true (this is the first premise and the first line of the argument). Suppose that the prediction turns out *not* to be true (this is the second premise and second line of the argument). It follows that the conjunction of theory and initial condition is false (line 3), which by DeMorgan's Law is equivalent to saying that *either* the theory is false *or* the initial conditions do not obtain (line 4). But in this case, it is assumed that the initial conditions did obtain (premise 3, line 5), which is the same thing as saying that it is not the case that the initial conditions *did not* obtain (line 6). Thus, by the rule of disjunction, we know that the theory is false (line 7).

2.8   Conditional and Indirect Proof

The type of argument illustrated at the end of the preceding section is called a *direct proof*. The form of a direct proof is as follows:

1.
2.
.
.
.
n. P.

Lines 1 to n – 1 contain either premises or propositions that can be obtained from previous lines by means of the inference rules. The result is a proof of the claim that P follows from the premises.

There are two other patterns of argumentation that make the job of deduction much easier: *conditional proof* and *indirect proof*. Conditional proof may be undertaken when the proposition to be proved has the form of a conditional. In conditional proof, one is permitted to treat the antecedent of the conditional as an additional premise to the argument. If one can then arrive at the consequent, the conditional is considered to be proved. The form of a conditional proof is

1. P
2.
3.
.
.
.
n. Q.

Here, the lines 2 through n − 1 are either premises or propositions that are obtained from previous lines (including line 1) by means of inference rules. The result is *not* a proof of Q, because the argument makes use of the assumption P, which is not one of the premises. What the argument proves is that the conditional P → Q follows from the premises.

Consider once again the premises that (1) if some particular theory T is true and the initial condition I obtains, then the prediction P follows [T & I → P] and (2) the initial condition does obtain (I). Let us show by conditional proof that *if* the prediction turns out to be false then the theory is false [~P → ~T].

1. ~P   Assumption for conditional proof
2. [T & I] → P   Premise
3. ~[T & I]   1, 2, MT
4. [~T] ∨ [~I]   3, DM
5. I   Premise
6. ~~I   5, DN
7. ~T   4, 6, D

The unfamiliar formal presentation ought not blind us to the fact that we routinely use conditional proof in everyday argumentation. When we try to persuade someone of a conditional assertion (e.g., if interest rates go down, the stock market will rise), we characteristically begin by *supposing* that the antecedent is true (e.g., that interest rates *will* go down) even though we may know that it is in fact false. We then show that the consequent would then follow (e.g., that the market would go up). The result, of course, is not a proof that the market will go up but a proof of the conditional assertion.

Indirect proof proceeds by assuming the *negation* of what one is trying to prove and then arriving at a contradiction therefrom. Its form is

1. ~P
2.
3.
   .
   .
   .
m. Q
   .
   .
   .
n. ~Q.

In this pattern, lines 2 through n may be either premises or propositions that are obtained from previous lines (including line 1) by the application of inference rules. For any proposition Q, Q and ~Q are, of course, contradictories: There is no possible world in which both are true. Thus, the fact that we obtain both Q and ~Q from the assumption that indicates that ~P must be false—i.e., that P is true. Indirect proof is also called *reductio ad absurdum*, since it reduces the assumption that ~P is true to the absurdity that Q and ~Q are both true.

Here is an indirect proof of the claim that ~P follows from the premises P → Q and Q → ~P:

1. ~~P   Assumption for indirect proof
2. P   1, DN
3. P → Q   Premise
4. Q   2, 3, MP
5. Q → ~P   Premise
6. ~P   4, 5, MP.

This completes the indirect proof of ~P, since the assumption of its negation (~~P) has led to a contradiction—namely, P on line 2 and ~P on line 6. The fact that the contradiction involves the very proposition we are trying to establish is an incidental feature of this particular example. The proof would be just as valid if we had established some altogether different proposition, R, and its negation, ~R.

2.9   Deductive Arguments in Quantifier Logic

There are many valid arguments that cannot be justified by the inference rules described in section 2.7. Here is a simple example:

All mammals are animals.
All dogs are mammals.
Therefore all dogs are animals.

Unlike the arguments considered in the preceding section, the propositions that make up this argument cannot be regarded as composites made out of smaller propositions. If we tried to symbolize the argument with propositional variables, we would have to use a different one for each proposition. The end result would look as follows:

P
Q
—
R

This pattern can hardly be regarded as universally valid. If it were, then any proposition would follow from any other two propositions! Nevertheless, there is a universal pattern that the argument does follow. It is valid for the same reason that the following argument is valid:

All humans are music lovers.
All children are humans.
Therefore all children are music lovers.

If we try to indicate what the two arguments have in common, however, we find that we need to introduce variables that range over *concepts* rather than propositions. The universally valid form of argument of which our two arguments are instances is

All Ys are Zs.
All Xs are Ys.

All Xs are Zs.

This inference rule produces valid arguments no matter what concepts are substituted for X, Y, and Z, but obviously it opens an entirely new chapter in the study of logic. The preceding section dealt only with the logical properties of the propositional connectives. This topic is called, aptly enough, *propositional logic*. But now we have broached the subject of *quantifier logic*, which is the study of the logical properties of claims about whether all, some, or no entities fall under certain concepts.

Propositions that assert something about *all* members of a class are called *universal propositions*, and the concept "all" itself is the *universal quantifier*. Propositions that assert something about *some* members of a class (e.g., "Some humans are music lovers") are *existential propositions*, and the concept "some" is the *existential quantifier*. There is no special name for propositions that tell us that something is true of *no* members of a class, nor is there a special name for the quantifier "no" or "none." This is because propositions using the quantifier "no" can always be rewritten as equivalent propositions that use only "all" or "some." For instance, the proposition "No snakes are mammals" is the same as the proposition "It is not the case that some snakes are mammals."

In modern logic courses, quantifier logic is studied after propositional logic. Historically, however, it was studied first. In fact it was studied by Aristotle some 2500 years ago. What goes under the name of traditional or Aristotelian logic concerns itself exclusively with quantifiers. Aristotle considered exhaustively all possible *syllogisms* (arguments containing two premises, three concepts, and the quantifiers "all," "some," or "none'). Most of these combinations are invalid; for example,

All Xs are Ys.
Some Ys are Zs.

No Zs are Xs.

Aristotle was able to pick out and give names to all the valid syllogisms. The modern treatment of quantifiers is both more powerful and more elegant. (One expects some progress to have been made in 2500 years!)

Instead of a lengthy enumeration, modern quantifier logic specifies a relatively small number of inference rules from which all the valid syllogisms can be derived. Furthermore, the rules enable us to derive many patterns of valid reasoning about quantifiers that do not fit the Aristotelian syllogistic framework. I will not, however, be able to do justice to this topic here. When it comes to arguments involving quantifiers, we will have to rely on logical intuition.

3

Theories and Data

In this chapter I present a conceptual framework for talking about theories and their relation to data. This subject is beset on all sides with controversies. Fortunately, the day-to-day work of the theoretical scientist remains largely unaffected by these disagreements. This means that we can afford the luxury of ignoring most of the controversial issues. However, it is useful to have a definite vantage point from which to discuss the varieties of theoretical work. I will therefore adopt a specific viewpoint without a persuasive demonstration of its superiority over its rivals.

The viewpoint to be adopted is called *Bayesianism* after the eighteenth-century mathematician Thomas Bayes, who proved a theorem about probabilities that has a central role in this approach. (Bayes's theorem will be discussed in section 5.3.) Bayesianism is a species of the more general view known as *probabilism*. The latter perspective supposes that it makes sense to ascribe probabilities to scientific theories, so that we can say, e.g., that the probability is very high that the theory of evolution is true, whereas the probability of the phlogiston theory of heat is close to zero.

The vast majority of scientists and philosophers of science are probabilists. But there are dissenters who claim either that it makes no sense to ascribe probabilities to contingent universal statements, or that the probabilities of all contingent universal statements is zero, or that scientists simply do not ascribe discrete probabilities to their theoretical views. (See e.g. Glymour 1980; Laudan 1977; Thagard 1988.) Bayesianism is currently the most popular brand of probabilism. Its definition will be given in chapter 4.

I choose probabilism and Bayesianism largely for the sake of facilitating discussion. Most of what will be said about the nature and varieties of theoretical issues could be reformulated, with minimal change of content, in such a way as to make it compatible with any currently respectable position in the philosophy of science.

3.1   Data

The best way to understand the nature of scientific theories is to contrast them with *data*. Data are propositions that are known to be true solely on the basis of observation. Merely looking at the world is enough to acquire the datum that this rose before me is red. No process of reasoning is required. On the other hand, mere looking will not tell me that the rose is made out of atoms. This is a conclusion to which I come as a result of a long chain of reasoning. That is, the claim that this rose is made out of atoms is not a datum. Data are *given* to us by the world, without our having to do any inferential work.

Actually this notion of the "given," which is what "data" literally means, is far from unproblematic. Before I detail its problems, however, let me be clear about its intended role in our epistemic (knowledge-seeking) enterprises. One way to arrive at new knowledge is by reasoning on the basis of prior knowledge. The vast majority of our opinions are of this type—e.g., that Moscow is the capital of Russia, that humans existed in the eighteenth century, that the inhabitants of a street I have never visited in my home town wear clothes, or that I would be seriously hurt if I shot myself in the head. Nevertheless, it cannot be the case that *all* my opinions are inferences from other opinions, on pain of an infinite regress. For instance, I may conclude that someone is in the basement on the ground that there are voices emanating from there. But where does this prior knowledge that there are voices in the basement come from? Perhaps this item is itself an inference based on prior knowledge: I may believe that there are voices emanating from the basement because someone whom I consider to be reliable tells me so. Eventually, however, I must arrive at a proposition that is not itself derived from any earlier belief. Such a proposition is simply "given": I know that someone told me about the voices because I *observed* the telling, I was *there* when the telling took place. Reasonable individuals might disagree as to what is legitimately given to us, but there is no way to avoid appealing to *something* given in rational discourse. Explanations have to stop somewhere. This analysis does not show us that explanations have to stop at what is observed with our five senses, however. Some have claimed that the role of the given can be played by intuitive hunches—that the cycle of explanations stops when we say that we just have a strong feeling that something is so. Also, certain propositions might be given to us in the sense that we are wired from birth to assent to them uncritically. These possibilities will be discussed again. The point of the foregoing analysis is not to establish the necessity for observational data but to elucidate their role in rational discourse. The citation of data is the point (perhaps one point among several) where asking for evidential grounds stops.

Now for the difficulties. Suppose I see a dog in the room and say "There is a dog in the room." This announcement seems like a very good candidate for datahood. But isn't what I see also compatible with the proposition that the creature is a mechanical robot with the outer form of a dog? Wouldn't I have to examine its internal physiology before I could say that I know it is a dog? Without such an examination, isn't my opinion that it is a dog based on the prior knowledge that such doglike robots have not yet been built? If this is so, then my claim that there is a dog in the room isn't directly "given" after all. For that matter, what about the possibility that my vision of a dog is a hallucination? Perhaps the only items of knowledge that are given to me are descriptions of my sensations—statements about shapes and colors that would remain true even if my experiences were hallucinatory. This view, called *phenomenalism*, had a fair number of proponents in the 1930s and the 1940s. (See Price 1950.) According to phenomenalists, the only data are "sense data," such as "I have a visual impression of a greenish oblong blob." Any belief about the physical world—indeed, even the belief that the physical world exists—was considered to be an inference *based on* sense data. Berkeley's *idealism*, discussed in chapter 1, was an early form of phenomenalism. Unlike Berkeley, most twentieth-century phenomenalists thought that the inference to the physical world was a very good one. Their point was not that we should be skeptical about its existence, but that we should realize that its existence was not *given* to us by direct observation. Phenomenalism itself was rejected when it was realized that the phenomenalists' style of argumentation could be turned against sense data as well as against any other observational claims. For example, when I say that the oblong blob that I see is greenish, isn't this claim dependent on my trusting that I remember correctly what the word "greenish" refs to? And doesn't my faith in my own memory on this matter depend on a wide array of evidence?

To make a long philosophical story short, nobody has ever succeeded in delineating an absolute criterion for datahood. Nevertheless, an appeal to something given at some point cannot be circumvented. How are we to get around this impasse? The most popular view nowadays is that what counts as data can only be specified *relative to a theory*. That is, each theory carries with it a specification of the types of claims that may be regarded as given, as opposed to the types of claims that require us to give reasons. The specification is to some extent arbitrary; nevertheless, it must be made. This view has far-reaching implications. For one thing, if each of two competing theories specifies a different set of propositions as potential data, then the choice between them cannot be made on observational grounds. Data that confirm or disconfirm one theory may not even be data relative to the other theory. This issue will come up again.

There is a long tradition, among phenomenalists and non-phenomenalists alike, of supposing that data are *incorrigible*: What is given to us was thought to be known with absolute certainty and to be beyond the reach of revision. This view is incompatible with the current treatment of the subject. The current view is that there is a possibility for error with any type of claim. Even if we merely describe how things appear to us in the phenomenal language of colored blobs, it is possible that we are misapplying a phenomenal concept. The consequences of giving up the incorrigibility of data are also enormous. One of them is that when theory and data conflict it is not a foregone conclusion that the theory has to give way. We may decide that the *data* have to be revised. For all that, most of the subsequent discussions will be based on the presupposition that data *are* known to be true with absolute certainty.

It might seem scandalous to base our analysis on an assumption that is firmly believed to be false. Actually, it is common scientific practice. Scientists trying to understand and predict physical systems routinely assume that surfaces are frictionless, that vacuums are perfect, that gases are composed of perfectly elastic particles, and so on, even though their own theories tell them such states of affairs never exist in the real world. These *idealizing assumptions* are considered to be legitimate when two conditions are satisfied: (1) that the idealizing assumption greatly simplifies the analysis of the situation, so that one can think about it more easily, and (2) that there is good reason to believe that the neglected factor is so insignificant that its omission will not make any substantial difference to one's conclusions about the problem at hand. Of course, we may be mistaken about the second condition—our idealizing assumption may lead us to make drastic errors. One can only do one's best. In any event, the assumption that observational data are known to be true with certainty is intended to be this kind of idealization and to facilitate discussion of many topics without greatly distorting the results.

Setting these perplexities aside for the moment, let us distinguish two types of propositions that fail to qualify as data:

• There are universal propositions that generalize over all time or all space, such as "All emeralds are green" or "$F = ma$." Such a statement is never "given" to us in its entirety, because we can never be finished observing all time or all space. Having observed a million emeralds and found them all to be green, we may agree that it is overwhelmingly likely that all the emeralds that ever were, are, or will be are green. But we certainly cannot say that this is a fact we have personally observed. By the same token, "$F = ma$" is supposed to hold true for all particles, at any time and any place.

• Propositions may be ineligible for datahood because they refer to entities or processes that are unobservable in principle. These are the types of non-data that may be specified differently by different theories. Traditional examples of unobservable entities include the forces, fields, and fundamental particles of physics, the social classes, roles, and statuses of sociology, and the unconscious mental processes of both psychoanalysis and cognitive science. Evidently, "$F = ma$" is ineligible for datahood on both counts.

These types of non-data play crucial roles in science. The next two sections are devoted to them.

3.2   Laws of Nature

It is often said that collections of data per se do not yet constitute a science—they are merely *natural histories*. On this account, science begins when we formulate *laws of nature* that purport to be true of all space and time. For my part, I do not think there is much to be gained by attempts to legislate the use of the word "science" (except in the practical sense that groups who manage to attach the label "science" to their activities stand a much better chance of obtaining financial support for their work; this is why we have library science, actuarial science, police and fire science, and the like). It is undeniable, however, that much of the excitement about science over the last few hundred years has centered on its claim to have discovered universal principles, or "laws."

The word "law" has a descriptive sense and a prescriptive sense. A law in the descriptive sense tells us how the world *is*; a law in the prescriptive sense tells us how the world *should be*. This book is concerned exclusively with descriptive laws. It should be noted, however, that prescriptive laws also play an important role in the science of psychology. Theories of mental health and of rational decision making are prescriptive through and through.

Propositions that have the right form to be descriptive laws of nature are often called *nomological* or *nomic* propositions, whether they are true or false. Every nomological statement has the form of a universal proposition referring to all time and all space. Once again, "$F = ma$" is supposed to hold everywhere in the universe and at every moment of its history. However, not all universal propositions are nomological. Suppose we find out that all the coins that were ever in George Washington's pockets were made of silver. Now that George Washington is dead, we can safely assume that no additional coins are going to find their way into any of his pockets at any time in the future. Thus, the following universal proposition is quite likely true:

(1) All the coins in any of George Washington's pockets are made of silver.

In this statement, the use of the grammatical present tense is to be understood as referring to all times, past, present, and future, as in "gold *is* a metal." Now consider another universal statement:

(2) All objects released 3 feet above the earth's surface fall down.

Propositions (1) and (2) appear to be very similar in logical form. Yet intuition ascribes very different sorts of logical consequences to them. These differences are most strikingly brought out by the counterfactual inferences we are willing to license from each proposition. A counterfactual statement is a statement about what the world would be like if some proposition, which happens to be false, were to be true. For example, consider the copper penny that I currently have in my pocket. Suppose that I keep it in my pocket for a week and then melt it down, thereby ensuring that it will never be released 3 feet above the earth's surface. Nevertheless, on the basis of (2), you would probably be willing to assent to the following claim:

(3) If my penny were to be released 3 feet above the earth's surface, it would fall to the ground.

But you would probably *not* be willing to go along with the same type of inference from (1):

(4) If my penny were to be in George Washington's pocket, it would be made of silver.

That is to say, you (and I) suppose that proposition (2) sustains counter-factual inferences whereas proposition (1) does not. Our denial of the valid-ity of the move from (1) to (4) is tantamount to denying that the true universal statement about coins in George Washington's pockets is a law of nature.

But what is the basis for this distinction? Intuitively, we sense that the truth of (1) is merely *coincidental*, whereas (2) is true by virtue of a *causal connection* between an object's being released and its falling to the ground. George Washington might have happened to have copper coins in his pocket, but the released coins *had* to fall. The necessity expressed by this "had to" is not logical necessity, however. It is certainly not a logical con-tradiction to suppose that a coin released 3 feet above the ground hovers like a helicopter. Evidently, we are invoking a notion of *causal necessity* that is weaker than logical necessity but more demanding than simple contingent truth. There are many possible worlds in which released coins do not fall, but there is a significant class of possible worlds—the *nomologically* pos-sible worlds—in every one of which released coins always fall. Laws of nature are universal propositions that are true in all nomologically possi-ble worlds

But all this is merely terminological. To be told that it is true in all nomologically possible worlds does not help us to understand what a law is; it merely provides us with another way of talking about the law. In fact, it turns out to be extraordinarily difficult to clarify what is meant by the concept of nomologicality. It is true that nomological statements sustain counterfactual inferences. But this truth does not help us to understand what is meant by a law. If we were asked to explain when counterfactual inferences may be sustained, we would have nothing more to say than that they apply to laws. Nevertheless, the connection between laws and counterfactuals is worth noting. It provides a quick and easy way to establish whether a particular proposition plays the role of a law in our thinking: Simply check to see whether you are willing to grant its counterfactual implications. By this test, we discover that proposition (2) above is nomological but that (1) isn't—for us. Passing this test does not establish that (2) is a *true* law of nature, or that (1) *isn't* a law of nature. It merely clarifies our own opinion.

And on what should we base this opinion? Well, if it is true that the coin in my pocket *would* fall to the ground if it were dropped, then I can *make* it fall to the ground by the simple expedient of dropping it. More generally, if we arrange for the antecedent of a counterfactual to become true, then the consequent will follow. However, if we try to play that game with a non-nomological generalization, the only thing we accomplish is to falsify the generalization: You can't turn copper into silver by stuffing pennies into George Washington's pocket. In textbooks on methods of experimental research, the distinction between nomological and non-nomological generalizations is often referred to as a distinction between "causal" and merely "correlational" relations. The advantage of the experimental method over naturalistic observation is precisely that it enables us to ascertain whether a generalization is causal or merely correlational. Indeed, an experiment may be defined as an arrangement whereby the antecedent of a counterfactual is satisfied, whereupon we can observe whether the consequent falls into line.

3.3   Theoretical Terms, Theoretical Statements, and Theories

Many laws postulate the existence of entities or processes that cannot, even in principle, be observed. A few examples: the force of gravity, electrons, the aether, phlogiston, weather fronts, unconscious mental processes, intelligence, character traits, social classes, the justice system, nations, gross national products. The terms that denote these entities are *theoretical terms*, whereas *observation terms* denote the entities that can be observed directly. *Theoretical statements* are statements involving at least one theoretical term; *observation statements* are those whose only non-logical terms are observation terms. These distinctions inherit all the perplexities involved in the definition of "data." If we know what data are, we can say that every datum is an observation statement. Not every observation statement is a datum, however. For one thing, there may be laws that attribute observable properties to observable entities. "All emeralds are green" is a plausible candidate. Such a law would satisfy the definition of "observation statement," but, being a universal proposition, it could never be a datum. Furthermore, even a spatio-temporally restricted observation statement might not be a datum, simply because no one had ever made the relevant observation. For example, consider the claim that an emerald at a certain location is green. If someone travels to that location to have a look, and if that person does indeed find a green emerald there, then the claim would have to be admitted into humanity's stock of data. But if nobody ever goes to check, then it will never become a datum. It will still be an observation statement, however, by virtue of the fact that it makes no reference to any entities or processes that are unobservable (as opposed to merely unobserved).

By definition, theoretical statements can never be data. Their truth can be established only by a process of inference. In this regard, they are like scientific laws. In fact, they may very well be scientific laws. For example, "$F = ma$" is a law by virtue of being a counterfactual-sustaining universal proposition, and it is a theoretical statement by virtue of referring to theoretical entities. Such a law is often called a *theoretical law*. One might suppose that laws like "All emeralds are green," which refer to observable entities, would be called "observation laws." But no—they are *empirical laws*.

To make the terminological jungle even worse, there is the ubiquitous term "theory." In ordinary language, a theory is any hypothesis that falls short of being established beyond reasonable doubt, as in "I have a theory that the butler did it." In scientific discourse, a theory is often taken to be a collection of interrelated laws. Sometimes it is stipulated that at least some of these laws have to be theoretical laws. But the usage is far from being standardized. Some writers have extremely specific notions in mind for the word "theory," and some have rather general notions. In this book, I will opt for an omnibus definition. I will take a theory to be any description of an unobserved aspect of the universe, whether the aspect is observable in principle or not. Both theoretical and empirical laws qualify as theories on this account. But so do particular observation statements such as "The butler did it," so long as no one observed whether the butler did it. (What is a theory for the detective may very well be a datum for the butler.) This broad usage has scientific credentials; the "big bang" theory of the origin of the universe, for instance, is a description of a particular state of affairs. In sum, a theory is any proposition that goes beyond the data. This notion is loosely connected to the ordinary-language conception of a theory as an uncertain hypothesis, since we are generally more uncertain about claims that refer to matters that we have not ourselves observed. But there is nothing in the *definition* of a theory that prohibits us from feeling as confident as we like about the truth of a theory. Indeed, since even data cannot be established with absolute certainty, it is possible that we might ascribe a higher probability to some theories than to some data.

3.4   The Instrumentalist Account of Theoretical Entities

The status of theories about the unobserved but observable ("The butler did it," "All emeralds are green") is clear enough: They are our best guesses as to what we *will* observe or *would* observe under appropriate conditions. But what about theories that refer to theoretical entities? Why would anyone feel impelled to postulate anything about a realm that is unobservable in principle? There are two broad categories of replies to this question. *Realists* say that our observational capacities reveal only certain portions of the universe to us, and that we must rely on a process of inference to learn about what is going on in the rest of the world. For realists, theoretical statements are claims about those hidden realms. Hence, they are either true or false descriptions of the world. *Instrumentalists* say that theoretical entities are convenient fictions devised to facilitate one pragmatic purpose or another. For example, one may find it useful or illuminating to think of mental processes as a series of operations carried on by homunculi ("little men") in one's head that pass messages and instructions to one another. But the use of such a model does not commit one to the view that there really are little men in people's heads. Evidently, one can take an instrumentalist stance toward some theoretical entities and a realist stance toward others. One might believe in the reality of electrons but not of homunculi. Some empiricists have been across-the-board instrumentalists, maintaining that all theoretical entities are fictional. According to this view, the only entities one may justifiably believe in are those that can be observed.

The difference between realism and instrumentalism is well illustrated by the different attitudes toward the unconscious held by Sigmund Freud and Pierre Janet. Freud conceded that many aspects of the psychoanalytical theory of the unconscious had been anticipated by Janet. However, he complained that Janet had "expressed himself with exaggerated reserve, as if he wanted to admit that the unconscious had been nothing more to him than a form of words, a makeshift, *une façon de parler*—that he had meant nothing real by it. . . I think he has unnecessarily forfeited much credit." (Freud 1917, p. 296) In modern terminology, Freud took a realist view of the unconscious, whereas Janet was an instrumentalist. With his talk of forfeiture of credit, Freud hints at the interesting thesis that only a realist can lay claim to the discovery of a theoretical entity.

Let us examine the instrumentalist view of theoretical statements more closely. If theoretical entities are convenient fictions, for what purposes are they convenient? A number of proposals are to be found in the instrumentalist literature. The most unsatisfactory of these is that theoretical laws serve to "generate data." The idea seems to be something like the following: Theoretical laws have certain observational consequences. By formulating the law, we encourage empirical research to establish whether the expected observational consequences are true. The result is an increase in our observational knowledge. On this view, the theoretical law itself has no intrinsic value. It serves only to instigate research. Expressions of this view abound in the psychological literature. Here is a version taken from a widely used textbook of personality theories (Hall and Lindzey 1978, p. 12):

We have now seen, in general terms, of what a theory consists. The next question is, What does it do? First, and most important, it leads to the collection or *observation of relevant empirical relations not yet observed.* The theory should lead to a systematic expansion of knowledge concerning the phenomena of interest and this expansion ideally should be mediated or stimulated by the derivation from the theory of specific empirical propositions (statements, hypotheses, predictions) that are subject to empirical test. . . . The theory can be seen as a kind of proposition mill, grinding out related empirical statements. . . .

This conception of the theory as proposition mill is untenable for two reasons. First, if theories were nothing more than devices for motivating empirical research it would be impossible to explain where they get their motivating power from. What would be the advantage of deriving an empirical hypothesis from a theory over, say, testing hypotheses in alphabetical order? Second, if the valued outcome is nothing more than the acquisition of empirical data, then we need not look for *any* systematic method of generating data. Obtaining new data is the easiest thing in the world. We are swimming in an infinite sea of data. We could record the license plate numbers of all the automobiles that go past a certain point for a week, and then do the same thing at another point for the following week. One could keep tabs on every item of clothing that one put into a washing machine. One could count the number of cracks in specified sidewalks. There is no need for elaborate proposition mills. To be sure, theories dictate certain directions that empirical endeavors are to take. But if the only goal of science is to pile up large quantities of data, there is no reason to value theory-directed empirical discoveries over other types. Indeed, there is no point to making theoretical statements at all. This is a conclusion that some psychologists have not been hesitant to accept—see for example, Skinner 1950.

A second instrumentalist suggestion is that the function of theories is to *summarize* large collections of data in a convenient and easily accessed form. This is certainly a correct characterization of some statements that appear to refer to unobservable entities. Consider the following claim:

(5) The average person has 1.87 children.

One might very well accept the truth of this statement without supposing that the universe contains a peculiar being who manages to produce fractional offspring. Our view is rather that the statement about the average person is a convenient abbreviation for a much longer conjunction of statements about particular persons of the ordinary variety, each of whom has an integral number of children. Another way to put the same point is to say that (5) is *reducible* to a longer proposition in which the term "average person" no longer appears. The reduction sentence of (5) is something like this: If you add up the number of children that each person has and divide by the number of persons, the result is 1.87.

But proposition (5) is not yet a theory. Theories invariably have implications that go beyond the data that give rise to them. This is why they can be used to make predictions. Having observed a million emeralds and found them all to be green, we may theorize that all emeralds are green. This hypothesis does more than summarize the data. It also leads to the prediction that the next emerald to be discovered will be green. If our only concern about theories were that they provide us with a correct summary of a body of data, there would be no reason to prefer "all emeralds are green" over the theory that the first million emeralds to be observed were green but all the rest will be blue.

A third formulation of instrumentalism concedes that theoretical statements do more than summarize bodies of data but holds onto the view that they can be reduced to observation language. It is conceded that the abbreviated observation statements may be not only data but also *empirical generalizations* (like "All emeralds are green") that make predictions about all time and space. According to this view, it is still true that theoretical statements are introduced only for the sake of convenience. In principle, we could express anything of substance without them; however, they help us to save time and paper.

Until the 1960s, it was widely believed that all theoretical terms could be reduced to observation terms in this way. The possibility of translating theoretical talk into observation language without loss of content was the central tenet of the logical positivists. In psychology, the *logical behaviorists* claimed that talk about unobservable mental processes could be translated without loss into talk about observable behavior. The following is from Skinner 1953 (p. 162):

When the man in the street says that someone is afraid or angry or in love, he is generally talking about predispositions to act in certain ways. The "angry" man shows an increased probability of striking, insulting, or otherwise inflicting injury and a lowered probability of aiding, favoring, comforting, or making love. The man "in love" shows an increased tendency to aid, favor, be with, and caress and a lowered tendency to injure in any way. "In fear" a man tends to reduce or avoid contact with specific stimuli—as by running away, hiding, or covering his eyes and ears; at the same time he is less likely to advance toward such stimuli or into unfamiliar territory.

Naturally, logical behaviorists espoused an instrumentalist view of mental processes. However, it has by now become clear that most of the interesting theoretical terms in science cannot be translated out in the manner of "the average person." In the case of logical behaviorism, one finds that every attempt to translate a mentalistic concept into behavioral language involves a surreptitious reference to other mentalistic concepts. It is simply not true that the expression "in love" is used as an equivalent to "having a tendency to be with and caress," or anything of the sort. Sadly, the person caressing you might be doing it for money instead of love. Nor can this problem be resolved by specifying the behavioral requirements for love in greater detail. If you pay some individuals enough money, or threaten them with dire enough punishment, they will manifest any behavioral tendency you like. There is no getting around the fact that it is part of the meaning of the word "love" that the person "in love" *wants* to be with you and caress you. But "want," of course, is not a behavioral term. The same problem arises again if we try to specify a behavioral equivalent for wanting. We cannot say that to want something is to display an increased tendency to get it, for such a relation will obtain only on the condition that we believe that we have the ability to produce the desired outcome (or else we would not even try). But belief is a mentalistic concept. And so it goes.

There are similar stories to be told about the theoretical entities in other sciences, such as the forces and subatomic particles of physics. The attempt to define them in terms of the observable movements of macroscopic objects through space and time failed just as completely as the logical behaviorist program. It seems that every science has its irreducible theoretical terms. For all that, it should not be forgotten that *some* theoretical terms, such as "average person," can be reduced. Some individuals prefer to restrict the expression "theoretical term" to the irreducible variety. MacCorquodale and Meehl (1948) coined the name *intervening variables* for the reducible theoretical terms and the name *hypothetical constructs* for the irreducible ones.

The failure of reductionism robs instrumentalism of a simple and powerful argument. But it does not yet compel us to become realists. In contemporary theoretical psychology, Daniel Dennett (1971) has continued to favor an instrumentalist stance toward mentalistic concepts even though he acknowledges that these concepts cannot be defined in behavioral terms. His position is that the theoretical apparatus of mentalistic psychology is useful for making predictions about behavior even though the mental processes postulated by such a theory do not exist. The same option is available with regard to any set of theoretical statements. The idea is based on the logical possibility that all the observational consequences of a theory T might be true even though T itself is false. (For example, physicists now believe that Newton's laws of motion are false; nevertheless, Newton's laws continue to be used to make predictions in circumstances where they are known to give the same answers as the currently favored theory of relativity, on the rationale that the same answer is obtained in either case and using Newton's laws requires less computational effort.) Thus, it could be rational to *use* a theory we believe to be false for the purpose of making predictions. If we followed such a strategy, we would be taking an instrumentalist stance toward the theory we were using. By extension, we could adopt this attitude toward *all* theories, claiming only that we believe in the observational consequences of some theories but not in any of the theories themselves.

The impossibility of reducing a set of theoretical statements to observation language does not mean that we are forced to employ the statements in our scientific work. We can also take the view that the theoretical statements in question are neither literally true (contra realism) nor particularly useful (contra instrumentalism). Their irreducibility can be taken as an indication that we should stop using these concepts altogether. This is *eliminativism*. Just as with realism and instrumentalism, one may espouse eliminativism with respect to some theoretical concepts and not others. The main spokesperson for the elimination of mentalistic concepts has been Paul Churchland, according to whom we can "look forward" to a day when everybody has been "persuaded" by science to "give up" all this talk about "beliefs" and "desires," much less being "in love" (Churchland 1981). In the scientifically correct world of the future, courting couples will whisper direct descriptions of their neurological and endocrinological states into each other's ears.

In psychology, the debate among instrumentalists, realists, and eliminativists with respect to mental processes is still a live issue. But an across-the-board eliminativism with respect to all theoretical entities is out of the question. It would gut the physical sciences of almost everything in them that has proved interesting or useful.

3.5   The Realist Account of Theoretical Entities

For a realist, the point of making theoretical claims is quite simply that one hopes they are true. Science is in the business of discovering what the world is like, and our best guess at the moment is that the world contains various entities and processes that we are unable to observe. These unobservable portions of the universe are described by theoretical statements.

Why should we believe the realists? The most famous recent argument for realism is Hilary Putnam's (1975) *miracle* argument. According to Putnam, realism is the only hypothesis that can explain why it is that our scientific theories work. If there really weren't any subatomic particles of the type postulated by physics, then the enormously impressive predictive success of physics would have no explanation at all. It would be a miracle. The standard instrumentalist reply to this argument is to claim that there are always indefinitely many theories that have exactly the same observational consequences as any given theory. In particular, there are going to be indefinitely many alternative theories that make the same observational predictions as the true theory (if there is a true theory). Evidently, these alternative theories manage to predict successfully without themselves being true. Therefore, the miracle can happen—the predictive success of a theory is not a reason to conclude that the theory is true.

The main argument for instrumentalism is the argument from the *underdetermination of theories by data* (van Fraassen 1980). The premise of the argument is once again the claim that every theory has empirically equivalent rivals that make the same predictions. It follows that we can never have adequate empirical grounds for believing in any single theory, and therefore we should be instrumentalists.

The realist retort to the underdetermination argument is that, although there may be indefinitely many empirically equivalent theories, these theories are not all equally good, and we should adopt the best one. This realist reply presupposes two things. First, realists need a rule that allows them to ascertain which is the best of a set of empirically equivalent theories. Since all the theories in the set make the same predictions, the tie-breaking rule has to be a *non-empirical* criterion. What does such a criterion look like? A good example is the criterion of *simplicity*: Of two theories that have the same observational consequences, we should prefer the simpler one. Second, realists need to *justify* the rule they use to break empirical ties between theories. If the rule is to adopt the simpler of two theories, we need to be able to say why such a rule should be obeyed. Why should we prefer the simpler theory? Isn't it possible that the universe is a very complex place? The role of simplicity in science will be discussed in chapter 9. For now, it functions only as an example of the type of non-empirical consideration to which the realist must appeal in order to reply to the underdetermination argument. The instrumentalist defense of the underdetermination argument characteristically takes the form of claiming that the nonempirical criterion for theory evaluation alluded to by the realist (e.g., simplicity) has no justification.

It would be inappropriate to try to settle the realism-instrumentalism issue in this book. In order to facilitate discussion, I will adopt the convention of talking like a realist from this point on. Most of what I have to say is also compatible with one form or another of instrumentalism. Where the distinction makes a difference, I will point it out. In any case, whether one opts for realism or instrumentalism, it is clear that theoretical statements have an intrinsic value in science over and above the value ascribed to the data.

4

Constructing and Evaluating Theories

4.1 The Construction of Scientific Theories

Constructing theories is the most familiar of all theoretical tasks. There are a number of prevalent misconceptions about it, however. One of these is that it is the *only* theoretical task. Subsequent chapters will bear ample testimony to the inadequacy of this view. It goes without saying that theory construction is an a priori activity. To be sure, theories have to be tested by empirical research. This subject will be taken up in the next chapter. But before empirical tests can be performed, we must have a theory to test. Data do not yield up theories of themselves, nor do theories emerge simply because more data have been added to the lot. There is no alternative but to sit down in one's armchair and *invent* a theory. This much is universally understood.

It is hardly necessary to provide an example of theory construction in psychology—every reader could supply his or her own. Nevertheless, some of the features of this theoretical activity will be easier discuss if we have a concrete example to refer to. I have chosen one of the most influential events in the history of psychological theory: Edward Lee Thorndike's (1898) formulation of the *law of effect*. The intellectual background of Thorndike's work was the monumental debate in the late nineteenth century over the Darwinian doctrine of evolution. Evolutionists could point to an impressive array of evidence relating to the continuity of physical structures between species. Anti-evolutionists, however, pointed to the putative discontinuity of mental abilities between humans and nonhuman organisms. The early response of Darwinians was to cite anecdotal evidence of intellectual achievement in various animals. Thorndike's aim was to bring the power of the experimental method to bear on the issue.

Thorndike's method was to place cats in variously constructed "puzzle boxes," where they had to perform some specific action, such as pressing a lever, in order to get out and be rewarded with a small amount of food. Upon obtaining this reward, a cat would be returned to the box for another trial. The data showed that the amount of time from insertion into the box until escape gradually diminished with continued trials (figure 4.1). That is, the cat *learned* to escape. Thorndike argued that these data could not be explained by the hypothesis that the cats had used a process of reasoning to figure out the requirements of the task: If the cats had come to understand the solution at some time during the continued trials, the data should have shown a sudden drop in latency rather than the gradual decrease that was actually observed.

If not intellectual understanding, then what? Here is the theory that Thorndike constructed. He assumed that stimuli and responses are connected by *S-R bonds* that can vary in *strength*: The stronger the bond between a particular stimulus S and a particular response R, the more likely is the organism to emit R when in the presence of S. This property of S-R bonds is not yet a contingent scientific hypothesis—it is a part of the *definition* of an S-R bond. Thorndike's scientific hypothesis—the law of effect— has two clauses: (1) that when a response R is emitted in the presence of S

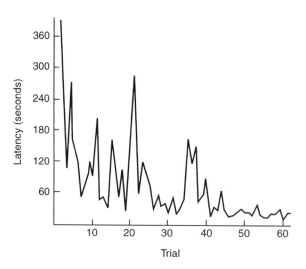

Figure 4.1
Learning curve of one of Thorndike's cats (after Thorndike 1898).

and is immediately followed by a reward the strength that particular S-R bond increases, and (2) that when R is emitted in the presence of S and is *not* immediately followed by a reward the strength of the S-R bond decreases.

It should be clear how the law of effect provides a theoretical explanation of the latency data. In the beginning of the experiment, the strength of the bond between the stimulus of the puzzle box and the response that leads to escape is very low. Thus, the cat is likely to emit responses other than the "correct" one. Since these are not followed by reward, the strength of their bond with the stimulus situation of the puzzle box diminishes. This means that the tendency to emit these incorrect responses will be diminished on subsequent trials. Eventually, as one response in the puzzle box follows another, the correct response does get performed. When it takes place, it is immediately followed by the reward of food, whereupon the strength of *its* bond to the stimulus situation is increased. Thus, on the next trial, there is a somewhat smaller likelihood of the cat's emitting some of the incorrect responses and a somewhat greater likelihood of its emitting the correct response. It follows that the time elapsed before the correct response is emitted will probably be somewhat less than on the first trial. The whole process repeats itself on the following trial, leading to a further diminished latency on the trial after that, and so on. Eventually, the strength of the association between the stimulus and the correct response is so much greater than that of all the other bonds that the correct response is emitted first every time. In this way, the law of effect explains the observed fact that the latency of escape from the box gradually diminishes to a minimal value.

The formulation of the law of effect is obviously *not* an empirical accomplishment. Empirical work provided the data on latency; however, the data make no mention of S-R bonds or their strength, nor could further empirical research ever yield up a data set in which the strength of S-R bonds makes an appearance. This theoretical notion transcends any possible data. It had to be invented.

4.2   The Interplay between Theory Construction and Theory Evaluation

Having constructed a theory, or several competing theories, we obviously want to know how good our constructions are. This is the task of *theory evaluation*.

The results of empirical tests have an enormous bearing on our evaluation of a theory's merits. The nature and the import of these empirical tests will be discussed in the next chapter. There are two reasons, however, why at least some aspects of theory evaluation must be based on non-empirical, a priori analyses. One of these reasons is practical; the other is logical.

The practical reason is that it is a practical impossibility to lavish the costly resources of time, effort, and money involved in empirical research on every theory that anybody might think up. Evidently, we must have some evaluative standards that a theory is required to pass before it is deemed worthy of empirical testing; otherwise we could not function as scientists in the real world. Applying these standards to candidate theories is another type of theoretical work.

The logical reason stems from the oft-cited fact that every theory has indefinitely many theoretical rivals that provide alternative explanations for the same data. This is the section in which this claim will finally be demonstrated. Before the demonstration, however, I will cite one more consequence of the result to come. If every theory T1 has a rival T2 that explains the same data, then our preference for T1 (or T2, as the case may be) cannot be explained by its superior fit with the data. If we are ever going to prefer one theory over its rivals, it must be because of its possession of a greater amount of some theoretical virtue other than empirical success. To be sure, any specific rival T2 may be ruled out if further empirical work turns up new data that T1 can explain but T2 cannot. But if it is true that there are multiple theories that can explain *any* set of data, T1 will never be the only theory that explains the data, no matter how vastly the data set is expanded. Thus, if we are ever to favor a single theory, it must be on the basis of an a priori evaluation.

It might occur to the reader that the first two theoretical tasks—theory construction and theory evaluation—can be run together: Once we know what the a priori principles of evaluation are, can we not use this knowledge to construct theories that will automatically receive high marks? Whether this is so depends on the nature of our evaluative measure. Our rules for evaluating theories *might* be such that they provide us with a recipe for constructing theories that automatically receive high marks. But then again they might not. To take an utterly contrived example of the first sort, suppose that the only theoretical virtue is brevity: The shorter the statement of the theory in standard English, the better. In that case, we can do better than to think up theories ad libitum and submit them for evaluation. We can assure ourselves of constructing the most excellent theory right from the start by means of the following procedure. First, rank-order all possible strings of letters by their length, and within a given length by alphabetical order. (I will ignore niceties about punctuation marks, capitalizations, spaces, and so on.) The resultant ordering will look like this: a, b, c, ..., z, aa, ab, ..., zz, aaa, aab, ..., and so on. Second, take the strings in order and ascertain whether each expresses a theory. The first theory encountered by this procedure is bound to be the best, or at least tied for the best with others of the same length that come later in alphabetical order. Perhaps the best theory there can be is "Ants act." In this case, the manner of the theory's construction automatically provides us with its evaluation. There is no need for a separate evaluative stage.

However, there are conceivable modes of evaluation that will not yield up an algorithm for optimal theory construction. Suppose that the only theoretical virtue is the degree to which a theory is approved by an individual designated as the Theory Oracle. In this case, it is clear enough how to go about settling the claims of competing theories: Simply submit them to the Theory Oracle for approval. But knowing how to evaluate the theories does not of itself give us a clue as to how to go about constructing them. In this scenario, we have no alternative but to separate the processes of theory construction and theory evaluation. First we have to think the theories up, using whatever partial and imperfect insights we may have into the psychology of the Theory Oracle. Then we send them in.

What is the actual situation with scientific theories? Are there rules for the construction of optimal theories? This question has traditionally been discussed in terms of the distinction between the "context of discovery" and the "context of justification" (Reichenbach 1963). To "discover" a theory is to construct it; to inquire into its degree of "justification" is to evaluate it. The principles of evaluation are referred to as a "logic of justification." The question now becomes whether there is such a thing as a "logic of discovery"—whether there is a set procedure that one ought to follow in constructing new theories, or whether anything goes in the construction stage. The lesson of the last three paragraphs was that the existence of a logic of discovery depends on the nature of our logic of justification.

One proposal for a logic of discovery is utterly discredited but still has a grip on some social scientists: Baconian inductivism. Francis Bacon, after whom the procedure is named, was a late-sixteenth-century precursor of the classical empiricism that was to sweep the philosophical world a century later. His ideas were avant-garde in 1600, but there has been some progress since then that we should all know about. According to Bacon and his contemporary inductivist disciples, scientific research is entirely a matter of gathering data and arranging them in a systematic order. For example, all the information we have about gems and stones might be placed in a bin labeled "lapidary science." Within this bin there would be subcompartments for data relating to the various specific gems—"rubies," "emeralds," and so on. And within "emeralds" we might classify data according to the types of properties they refer to. One subcategory would consist of data relating to the weights of various observed emeralds. Using E1, E2, E3, . . . , and En to refer to the n emeralds we have data on, this subcategory might contain the following items:

E1 weighs 7 carats
E2 weighs 15 carats
E3 weighs 11 carats

.

.

.

En weighs 4 carats.

The rest of the inductivist story is easily told: We merely look for repeating patterns in the data. For example, if we look at the "emeralds, color of" subcategory we are liable to find

E1 is green
E2 is green
E3 is green

.

.

.

En is green.

This is exactly the kind of thing we are looking for. When such a pattern is discovered, we hypothesize that future data will conform to the same pattern. That is to say, we formulate the theory that all emeralds are green.

Future empirical research may confirm or fail to confirm this theory, but it is the best theory that we can possibly construct with the data we have at hand.

If this inductivist story were correct, the enterprise of theory construction would amount to no more than the shuffling and reshuffling of data sets. Perhaps some individuals would be quicker at discovering patterns than others, but one could always compensate for a lack of quickness by patience and perseverance. The important point is that the best theory would always emerge from consistent application of an entirely mechanical procedure. All the action in science would be in the data-gathering phase. It is easy to understand why scientists who believe in inductivism (and who also believe that theory construction is the only theoretical task) would be inclined to say that experimentalists can handle the theoretical chores of science in their "spare moments away from the lab" (Longuet-Higgins 1981, p. 200). However, the inductivist account of theory construction is subject to devastating criticisms.

First, inductivism accounts for, *at most*, the acquisition of *empirical laws* like "All emeralds are green." There is no chance that an inductivist methodology can lead us to *theoretical laws* like "$F = ma$" or Thorndike's law of effect. The reason is simple. Theoretical laws make reference to theoretical entities, and data do not. Thorndike's "S-R bond" is a theoretical term; we will never obtain behavioral data that make reference to S-R bonds. Therefore, no generalization over behavioral data could ever yield the law of effect.

In addition, inductivism does not even account for the construction of empirical laws. There are various ways to make this point. I will adapt a famous argument put forth by Nelson Goodman (1954): Inductivism fails because there are always infinitely many empirical laws that satisfy its requirement, regardless of what the data may say. Consider the data that emeralds E1, . . . , En are all green. According to inductivism, these data should lead us to formulate the theory that all emeralds are green. But the same data can be transformed into another set of true observation statements that generate an entirely different empirical law. Let us define the term "grue" as follows:

An object is grue if it satisfies either of the following conditions: (i) It is first observed before the year 2100 and found to be green. (ii) It is not observed before the year 2100 and it is blue.

Now, emeralds E1, . . . , En all satisfy this definition. They are all grue. Thus, by the simple expedient of redescribing the data, the inductivist strategy gives us the alternative empirical law "All emeralds are grue." These two laws are not equivalent: If all emeralds really are grue, then the first one to be observed after December 31, 2099 will turn out to be blue. Furthermore, we can construct indefinitely many "gruish" theories about emeralds using different colors and different dates for the Big Switch. For example, emeralds E1, . . . , En are also gred, where "gred" is defined as "first observed before February 23, 2163 and found to be green, or first observed after that date and found to be red." Also, it is clear that these constructions do not depend in any way on our starting with a patterned set of data. There are also infinitely many laws that fit our data on emerald weights to perfection. One of these is the disjunctive claim that all emeralds weigh exactly the same as one of the emeralds that we have already weighed—i.e., "All emeralds weigh either 7 carats or 15 carats or 11 carats or . . . or 4 carats." Another is the law that all emeralds have one of the observed weights if their weight is measured before the year 2100, and that they uniformly weigh 3 kilograms otherwise. Evidently, the inductivist recipe for theory construction leads to infinitely many theories of any finite set of data. (This is also the frequently promised demonstration of the principle that there are infinitely many theories for any set of data; the critique of inductivism is that it fails to eliminate any of the infinitude.) This infinitude of theories cannot, of course, all be submitted to further empirical test. We must deploy other evaluative tests to narrow down the candidates. But then inductivism does not provide a recipe for constructing optimal theories. The inductivist strategy may find its place as a *part* of a more complex logic of discovery, but it cannot be counted on to produce good theories on its own. Inductivists will protest that they never had it in mind that such bizarre constructions as "All emeralds are grue" should be considered on the same footing as "All emeralds are green." But this is merely to concede that inductivism is incomplete: In addition to the inductivist procedure, inductivists need to rely on some a priori principles that rule out the bizarre theories that they never had in mind to consider.

The failure of inductivism is not a devastating indictment of empiricism generally. In fact, one could still reasonably call oneself an empiricist even if it were to turn out that there is no systematic way of constructing theories by performing operations on data sets. Suppose that the best theories emerge when we forget all about the data and get drunk. It seems to me that this state of affairs should not greatly discomfit empiricists. After all, we are not talking about the decision to accept a theory as true. The only question is how to come up with promising candidate theories. The heart of the empiricist doctrine is the view that data are preeminent in determining which theories to accept. If need be, empiricists can afford to give up the idea that the data also dictate which theories they ought to consider in the first place.

Is there a logic of discovery that succeeds where inductivism fails? This question can only be answered relative to a logic of justification. We have seen that some justificatory principles, such as the brevity rule, enable us to construct an algorithm for discovery, whereas others, such as the Theory Oracle principle, do not. To which type does our actual justificatory procedure belong? At present there are numerous candidates for a logic of justification. None of them has generated a logic of discovery. The situation is not as desperate as with the Theory Oracle, however. In the case of the Theory Oracle, it is pretty clear that a logic of discovery is not going to be forthcoming. In regard to the current logics of justification, the possibility for a corresponding logic of discovery is open to debate. Perhaps we will have a mechanical procedure for generating theories some day. There are a number of research groups working along these lines (Holland et al. 1986; Langley et al. 1987). For the time being, however, there is no substitute for spinning theories off the top of one's head. C. S. Peirce (1901) called this "first starting of a hypothesis and the entertaining of it" by the name of *abduction*. The abduction of scientific theories is, for now, an essential and entirely intuitive stage of scientific research. By "intuitive" here, I mean that the agent does not know what procedure is being followed in arriving at a judgment, or even whether any systematic procedure is being followed at all.

The phenomenon of abduction presents us with a curious problem. The range of theories we might abduce is literally infinite. This point was already made in my discussion of inductivism. But I have in mind here a much broader set of theories than the infinite set allowed by inductivist procedures. I am talking about the set of all theories that can be formulated in our language. This set includes some theories that make "All emeralds are grue" seem positively reasonable—for instance, that quasars are made entirely of peanut butter, or that every time someone says "Manitoba" somewhere an elf breaks cleanly in two. There are also logically contradictory theories, such as that quasars are made entirely of peanut butter and not made entirely of peanut butter. Regardless of what principles of theory evaluation we eventually settle on, it is clear that all but a minute subset of these theories will be judged to have no redeeming value whatever. But then the chance of abducing a theory at random that turns out to be good is essentially nil. It does not help to assume that we can spot a good theory as soon as we see one. If we have to reject an infinitude of clunkers in real time, then we will never get to see a good theory, even if the evaluative stage takes no more than a nanosecond. Readers familiar with the literature of artificial intelligence will recognize this difficulty as a manifestation of the frame problem (see section 5.6 below). Peirce (1901, pp. 237–238) was already aware of it:

By what process of thought were [good theories] ever brought to mind? A chemist notices a surprising phenomenon. . . . Why does he then not note that this phenomenon was produced on such a day of the week, the planets presenting a certain configuration, his daughter having on a blue dress, he having dreamed of a white horse the night before, the milkman having been late that morning, and so on? . . . How was it that man was ever led to entertain [the] true theory? You cannot say that it happened by chance, because the possible theories, if not strictly innumerable, at any rate exceed a trillion . . . and therefore the chances are too overwhelming against the single true theory ever having come into any man's head.

In this passage, Peirce underestimates the difficulty. In fact, the possible theories *are* literally innumerable. The problem is how to account for the fact that we ever manage to entertain good theories in the first place.

According to Peirce, the only way out of this difficulty is to suppose that our abductive mechanism has an innate capacity to "zero in" on the truth. The hypotheses that pop into our heads must be preselected for fruitfulness even before they go through a process of evaluation. Nature must have designed us to have an "instinct" for the truth. This idea has currently been revived and given an evolutionary rationale. The basic tenet of "evolutionary epistemology" is that natural selection will favor organisms whose guessing strategy leads to success. As will be seen in chapter 9, this line of reasoning has a number of serious problems Yet I confess that I see no alternative resolution.

4.3 Truth

I have been speaking incessantly of "good" theories and "bad" theories. The time has come to say what makes a theory good.

For scientific realists, the most important characteristic of a theory is its truth value. This may seem so obvious as to be scarcely worth mentioning, but in fact truth plays no role in instrumentalists' evaluations of theoretical laws. Instrumentalists do not believe that any theoretical laws are literally true. They are looking for other virtues, such as computational simplicity or the capacity to make correct observational predictions. Realists may also be interested in some of these other virtues, but they will consider the importance of other virtues to be either derivative (the other virtue is important because it is indicative of truth) or secondary (the other virtue is very nice, but it cannot be purchased at the expense of truth). In what follows, I will be taking a realist perspective.

Much as realists would like their theories to be true, in practice they must be willing to settle for something substantially less. Every scientific theory ever proposed has turned out to be false in the long run, and most scientists expect that their current theories will eventually suffer the same fate. Nevertheless, theories are not all equally off the mark. They differ in how plausible they are in relation to everything else that we believe. Accordingly, the operative criterion for theory evaluation is not *truth per se* but *the probability of truth*. Of two theories T1 and T2 that are equally virtuous in other respects, the one with the higher probability is to be preferred.

How is the probability of a theory ascertained? In subsequent chapters I will discuss rational principles for *altering* probabilities to accommodate new empirical and theoretical discoveries. But all these principles presuppose that the theory has a *prior* probability assignment. Where does the first probability assignment come from? If we have just abduced a new theory, how do we assess its initial degree of plausibility? The commonest view among contemporary probability theorists is *Bayesianism*, or *personalism*, according to which probabilistic reasoning must begin with a purely subjective assignment of prior probabilities. Having abduced a theory for the first time, we have to decide how plausible it is without the guidance of any explicit principles. Every individual's opinion is as good as every other individual's, in the sense that nobody has any arguments to wield against those who disagree.

Why should we be Bayesians? No reason in the world. If we can specify rational grounds for fixing the values of prior probabilities, then by all means we should do so. But such grounds have been very difficult to come by. Bayesianism is a default position. Thus, long as we cannot specify how to assign priors, we have no choice but to be Bayesians. This state of affairs accounts for the fact that there are competing theoretical schools among scientists who have access to the same data. The existence of such differences does not necessarily indicate that someone is being irrational. The competing groups may simply have begun with different prior probabilities. Fortunately, the principles of rational probability change entail that different prior probabilities will converge to the same value as they are altered to accommodate new evidence (unless they are initially equal to 0 or 1).

There are some rational constraints on prior probabilities, however. The main one is that our probability assignments taken as a whole must obey the axioms of the probability calculus:

(P1) $0 = p(A \& \sim A) \leq p(A) \leq p(A \lor \sim A) = 1$,

(P2) $p(A \& B) + p(A \lor B) = p(A) + p(B)$.

In P1 and P2, A and B stand for any propositions whatever. P1 states that the probability of any contradiction is 0 ($0 = p(A \& \sim A)$), that the probability of any logically necessary tautology of the form $A \lor \sim A$ is 1 ($p(A \lor \sim A) = 1$), and that the probability of any proposition whatever lies between 0 and 1 ($p(A \& \sim A) \leq p(A) \leq p(A \lor \sim A)$). From these axioms, it can be proved that the probability of any necessary falsehood of any form is 0, and that the probability of any necessary truth of any form is 1. It can also be shown that

(P3) $p(A) + p(\sim A) = 1$.

The proof of P3 is easy. Substituting $\sim A$ for B in P2, we get

$p(A) + p(\sim A) = p(A \& \sim A) + p(A \lor \sim A)$.

But by P1, $p(A \& \sim A) = 0$ and $p(A \lor \sim A) = 1$. Thus,

$p(A) + p(\sim A) = 0 + 1 = 1$.

An assignment of probabilities that satisfies P1 and P2 is said to be *coherent*; an assignment that violates the axioms is said to be *incoherent*. The irrationality of incoherence is dramatically illustrated by the *Dutch book theorem.* This theorem establishes that if our probability function is incoherent then we will be prepared to accept certain wagers we are bound to lose no matter what happens. The shortest proof on record is the "Two Minute Dutch Book Theorem" (van Fraassen 1989, pp. 159–160). Using coherence as a constraint on our prior probabilities, we know that if we assign a probability of 0.8 to theory T then we must assign a probability of 0.2 to the hypothesis that T is false. If we think that T is very likely to be true, then we are committed to the view that ~T very likely to be false. But this still leaves quite a bit of leeway. The requirement of coherence falls far short of fixing a unique probability function.

A few additional constraints on priors have occasionally been contemplated. None of them, however, is as neatly and as definitively justifiable as the requirement of coherence. The main candidate is the principle of *strict coherence*, according to which one may never assign a probability of 0 or 1 to any contingent statement. Its rationale is that it is reasonable to remain at least a little open-minded about every contingent issue. As was mentioned above, strict coherence is required if investigators with divergent prior probabilities are to converge upon reception of identical evidence. Also, there is a modified Dutch book theorem that applies to strict coherence. If our probabilities violate strict coherence, then we will be prepared to accept bets we cannot win but may lose (Salmon 1988).

The advice always to keep an open mind on all matters sounds innocuous enough. Unfortunately, it runs afoul of the fact that there are infinitely many matters. For example, there are the infinitely many gruish laws that are compatible with our data on emeralds. Consider an infinite subset of these laws that are mutually exclusive, such as the following:

(T1) Emeralds are green until January 1, 2100, and blue thereafter.
(T2) Emeralds are green until January 2, 2100, and blue thereafter.
.
.
.

Since T1, T2, . . . are all mutually exclusive, coherence (not strict coherence) requires that the sum of their probabilities be no greater than 1. (The proof requires a slight extension of our axiom system to enable it to deal with infinite disjunctions.) But if the probability of each theory has to be greater than 0, how are we to keep the sum of the probabilities within finite bounds?

Perhaps we could assign smaller and smaller probabilities to successive theories, so that their infinite sum would converge to a number less than or equal to 1. For example, suppose that $p(T1) = \frac{1}{2}$, $p(T2) = \frac{1}{4}$, $p(T3) = \frac{1}{8}$, and so on. Then

$$p(T1) + p(T2) + p(T3) + \ldots = \tfrac{1}{2} + \tfrac{1}{4} + \tfrac{1}{8} + \ldots ,$$

which is a sum that never exceeds 1. But of course this strategy is utterly arbitrary. Why should we suppose that it is any more or less likely that emeralds will turn blue on December 11, 2319, than on May 1, 7007? In fact, any such assignment would violate another reasonable probabilistic principle: the *principle of indifference*, according to which one must assign identical probabilities to hypotheses unless one can point to a reason for doing otherwise.

The requirement of strict coherence is routinely violated in scientific practice. Researchers *do* assign probabilities of 0 to logically possible theories. Their minds are closed to certain possibilities. Maybe this is the only way we can get on with the business of doing science. The violation of strict coherence has extraordinary consequences, however. It means that two groups of scientists who close their minds to different possibilities will never be able to reach agreement, even if they both accept the same data and acknowledge the same rules of theory evaluation. The historical studies of Thomas Kuhn (1962) on the existence of "paradigms" and those of Imre Lakatos (1978) on the "hard core" of scientific research programs suggest that this is precisely the situation in science (as well as in every other department of life). This important subject will be discussed at length in chapter 10.

Empiricists will want to protest that formal considerations such as coherence and strict coherence are merely ancillary factors in the determination of prior probabilities. What matters most in assessing the plausibility of a theory is to be found in its relation to established *data*. The first question to be asked here is whether "established data" (i.e., reports of prior observations) should be assigned a probability of 1. To do so is to violate strict coherence. I have already noted that no statement is ever so close to the "given" that it can be regarded as incorrigible. But I have just noted that scientists routinely violate the requirement of strict coherence. In fact, scientific inferences are routinely (though not invariably) made on the assumption that the truth of certain observational statements is known with certainty. With this idealizing assumption in hand, the data certainly do have an effect on prior probabilities. In particular, if D is a datum and if a theory T logically implies ~D, then the probability that T is true must be 0. This conclusion follows from a general principle of probability theory, provable from axioms P1 and P2, which we will have many occasions to use:

(P4) For any propositions A and B, if A implies B, then $p(A) \leq p(B)$.

Now, if we assign probability $p(D) = 1$ to the datum D, it follows from P3 that $p(\sim D) = 0$. But if T implies ~D, P4 gives us $p(T) \leq p(\sim D) = 0$. Thus, the data can be used to eliminate any theory that is incompatible with them from further consideration. If we take the more realistic view that $p(D)$ is merely close to 1, then $p(\sim D)$ must be close to 0, from which it follows by P4 that $p(T)$ is also close to 0.

Now, it is not practical to ascertain whether a particular theory is compatible with all the data about the universe that are at our disposal. There are simply too many such data. In practice, a new theory is checked for consistency with a selected subset of data. There is no principled way to select this subset, for in principle any contradiction with established data is as significant as any other. In practice, the theory tends to be checked against data that previously figured in the evaluation of competing theories of the same domain (Laudan 1977). This primary set of data against which a theory is evaluated for consistency will be called the theory's *initial domain*. If the theory turns out to be consistent with its initial domain, we will say that it has *prior adequacy*. The initial domain is always drastically smaller than the set of all established data. Thus, it is always possible that we will discover, somewhere down the line, conflict between a theory that had passed the test of prior adequacy and a datum that had been known all along but had not been included in the initial domain. (This possibility creates opportunities for a certain type of a priori theoretical endeavor—see chapter 6.)

It is important to understand that the use of data in establishing prior adequacy does not impose any new constraints on our freedom to assign prior probabilities any way we like. The entire procedure is merely a special case of the coherence requirement. The fact that the data are observation statements does not figure in the rationale. The same role could be played by a theoretical statement. If we assume that a theory T2 bas an enormously high probability, then any theory T1 that implies ~T2 must also be assigned a probability near 0. The idea of prior adequacy is not essentially an *empirical* criterion at all. The requirement is simply that new theories not contradict established knowledge. Theories about which we feel confident can play the role of "established knowledge" just as well as observational reports about which we feel confident.

Suppose that the initial domain D comprises the data that emeralds E1, ..., En are all green. The following theories all satisfy the criterion of prior adequacy:

(T1) All emeralds are green.

(T2) All emeralds are grue.

(T3) Every time someone says "Manitoba," somewhere an elf breaks cleanly in two.

One wants to say here that, given the data contained in D, T3 is not even in the running. To be sure, T3 does not contradict anything in D; but neither is it *relevant* to anything in D. This intuition about relevance turns out to be extremely difficult to make explicit. What is it about T1 and T2 that makes them relevant to D? Well, they both logically *imply* D, whereas T3 does not. Shall we then require that theories be dropped from further consideration unless they imply their initial domains? This criterion is undoubtedly too severe, for a theory may appear to be very probable in the light of data that cannot be deduced from it. For example, consider the domain D1, consisting of the single fact that a very trustworthy and knowledgeable person has said that all emeralds are green. The theory T1 that all emeralds are green does not imply D1, yet it seems entirely reasonable to ascribe a fairly substantial prior probability to T1 on the basis of D1. Thus, we cannot say that T3's failure to imply D is a sufficient ground for outright dismissal.

Can we at least justify the intuition that T3 is not a good bet? We might contemplate the adoption of a principle like the following: If T1 implies D and T3 does not imply D, then, considering only the information contained in D, we should assign a higher probability to T1 than to T3. However, the adoption of this principle leads directly to incoherence: Let T1 and T3 have the stipulated properties, and define T4 as the conjunction of T3 and D. In this case, we have

(T4) Every time someone says "Manitoba," somewhere an elf breaks cleanly in two, and furthermore emeralds E1, E2, . . . , En are all green.

This theory trivially implies that emeralds E1, . . . , En are green. Thus, by our purported principle, p(T4) should be greater than the probability of any theory that does not imply D. But T3 is such a theory. Thus, p (T4) > p(T3). Since T4 just is T3 & D, we have p(T3 & D) > p(T3). On the other hand, T3 & D implies T3. It follows by P4 that p(T3 & D) ≤ p(T3), which contradicts the previous conclusion. That is to say, the adoption of this new rule would result in incoherence. Thus, theories that imply the initial domain may or may not have higher prior probabilities than theories that do not imply it. Bayesians patiently await the next proposal for a rational constraint on the assignment of prior probabilities. In the meantime, there is no substitute for massive deployment of our intuitive faculties. It bears repeating that "intuition" in this context does not necessarily refer to a special faculty, distinct from the process of reasoning, for arriving at judgments. For all we know, an intuition may be such a special faculty; but it may also be unconscious reasoning. Only further work will tell.

4.4   Generality

If probability were the only epistemic value, we would never go beyond the data. Any theory constructed on the basis of the data constitutes an epistemic risk. This is an elementary consequence of probability theory. Since T & D implies D, p(T & D) ≤ p(D). Thus, so far as the probability of being correct is concerned, there is never any advantage to constructing a theory. However, theorizing trades off a certain amount of epistemic security for an increase in the breadth of one's knowledge, for the conjunction T & D gives us more information than D alone. Let us try to make this concept of informativeness a bit more precise.

Let us say that a proposition A answers the question whether B just in case either B or ~B can be deduced from A. Thus, the proposition "All emeralds are green" answers the question whether emerald E26 is green. So does the proposition "No emeralds are green." Now, a theory T1 is more informative than T2 if T1 answers more questions than T2 does. Equivalently, it is sometimes said that T1 is more *general* than T2, or that T1 has a larger *scope* than T2. Clearly, theorizing increases the scope of our belief system, for T & D will obviously answer every question that D answers and more. More generally, T1 will have at least as large a scope as T2 whenever T1 implies T2. Suppose, for example, that T1 is "All emeralds are green" and T2 is "All African emeralds are green." Then T1 implies T2, and it is clearly the case that T1 is the theory of larger scope: "All emeralds are green" answers every question that "All African emeralds are green" answers and more. For example, T1 answers "What color are Asian emeralds?" but T2 doesn't.

Judgments of relative scope are straightforward when one theory implies the other. But if the theories are logically independent, the comparison is extremely problematic. We cannot simply count up consequences, since every proposition has infinitely many consequences. "All emeralds are green," for instance, has the consequences that any emerald found on January 1, 2100 will be green, that any emerald found on January 2, 2100 will be green, and so on. At present, there is no known rule for determining which of two arbitrarily selected theories has the larger scope. Yet such judgments are made by scientists all the time. Whatever its shortcomings may be, psychoanalysis is generally conceded to have enormous scope; there is a psychoanalytic answer to virtually every psychological question. On the other hand, William Sheldon's (1942) theory of the relation between body type and personality is thought to be a relatively narrow theory. Yet both psychoanalysis and Sheldon's theory have infinitely many consequences. The *variety* of the consequences that follow from psychoanalysis, as compared to the homogeneity of the consequences that can be drawn from Sheldon's theory, is often pointed to as an indication of scope. But this notion of variety is itself intuitive.

We have now encountered three distinct places in the enterprise of science where scientists have to proceed intuitively, without the guidance of explicit rules: There are no rules for abducing theories from data sets, no rules for determining the prior probabilities of new hypotheses, and no rules for measuring the scope of theories. Contemplation of this state of affairs is a useful corrective for the prevalent idea that "the scientific method" refers to a cookbook that gives explicit instructions for what to do in every eventuality.

Ideally we would like to have a theory with maximal scope and maximal probability—a theory that answers every question and whose truth is absolutely certain. This goal is, of course, utopian. In practice, we must settle for as much of both properties as we can get. How much certainty should we be willing to give up in order to increase the breadth of our knowledge? The question is poorly posed. There is no rule concerning the relative weights of probability and scope in theory evaluation, nor is it appropriate to look for such a rule. What we need to know is how much certainty we *do* give up for any proposed increase in breadth. And that is the state of our knowledge. The result of scientific work is not necessarily a single "best" theory that consigns all others to oblivion. It is more generally a set of theories, each of which has an associated probability and scope. Scientific work is largely a matter of performing operations, both empirical and theoretical, that increase either the probability or the scope of some theory. It is entirely reasonable, and indeed quite common, for a scientific community to work toward improving the status of several competing theories at once. It is true that, if asked to make the best prediction we can about some observable phenomenon, we have to make it on the basis of the most probable theory. Suppose that T1 is more probable but less informative than T2. Suppose also that T1 answers the question whether P in the affirmative, whereas T2 answers the question whether P in the negative. Then if we are asked whether P, we maximize our chance of being right by answering in accordance with the more probable theory, T1. This does not mean, however, that science should "adopt" T1 and forget all about the less probable T2. Both theories may be worthy of further investigation.

An increase in either theoretical virtue is a scientific advance if the amount of the other virtue does not diminish. It is trivially easy to increase the amount of either virtue if we are oblivious to what happens to the other. Given any theory T, we can increase the scope of our theory by conjoining to it an arbitrary hypothesis H. Any H that is not a logical consequence of T will suffice. But, though T & H answers more questions than T, it is also less likely to be true. Similarly, we can always increase the probability of a theory by deleting one of its principles, but the remaining theory will then answer fewer questions. When the amount of one virtue goes up at the cost of a decrement in the amount of the other, it is a judgment call whether, in the balance, science has progressed. But an increase in either virtue that leaves the other unaffected is an unambiguous case of progress.

Discussions of scope almost always emphasize a theory's ability to establish whether *observation statements* are true or false. Suppose that T1 and T2 answer exactly the same observational questions, but that T1 answers more *theoretical* questions. Should T1 be considered a better theory than T2 on the grounds of its greater informativeness? If we had T2, would anything be gained by the introduction of T1? In sum, should the capacity to answer theoretical questions count in our assessment of a theory's informativeness? Instrumentalists, of course, will answer in the negative. However, even many realists believe that, if two theories have identical observational consequences, the one making *fewer* claims about the realm of theoretical entities is the better theory. The justification for this opinion is probabilistic: It is supposed that the richer theory, by virtue of making more claims about the world, is bound to be less likely. This is, of course, true, but it begs the question about informativeness that we are in the midst of trying to sort out. The tacit assumption is that only answers to observational questions count in the measurement of scope—that an increase in informativeness about theoretical entities can never compensate for a loss of probability. It seems to me that scientific realists cannot afford to take this principle for granted. But it is undeniably the current scientific practice to consider only the observable consequences of a theory as constitutive of its scope. A theory is not regarded as having been improved if it yields new theoretical consequences but not new observational consequences. Having registered a rationalist qualm about this practice, I will bow to empiricist orthodoxy and redefine the scope of a theory as the amount of observational information that it specifies. This issue will have to be brought up again, however.

4.5   Other Theoretical Virtues

Are there any other theoretical virtues besides probability and scope? Well, we have a choice between saying that probability and scope are the only virtues and saying that there are indefinitely many virtues. Let us take as an example a frequently discussed candidate for a third virtue: simplicity. It is often said that, all else being equal, we should prefer the simpler of two theories. The concept of theoretical simplicity will be examined at length in chapter 9. For the moment, let us pretend that we already know what it means to say that a theory is simple. Now what do we want simplicity for? Theoretical preferences may be divided into *derivative* and *intrinsic* preferences. To say that a preference is derivative is to say that it can or should be justified on some other basis. The amount of variety in a theory's consequences is clearly a derivative virtue. It was mentioned above that variety is often used as an index of scope. It has also been claimed that greater variety in a theory's tested consequences produces a greater probability that the theory is true (Horwich 1982). Similarly, to say that simplicity is a derivative virtue is to say that our preferences for simple theories can or should be justified on some other basis—for example, on the basis that simpler theories are likelier to be true. In that case, of course, we are not dealing with a third virtue at all; we are dealing with a new criterion for the possession of an old virtue. To treat simplicity as an intrinsic virtue is to say that we should prefer simple theories simply because they are simple. The issue at hand concerns the status of an intrinsic preference for simplicity. Is such a predilection rationally well founded?

Well, the rationality of a preference can only be assessed relative to a purpose. There is a sense in which an intrinsic preference for simple theories is beyond reproach: If I announce that it is my intention to find the simplest theory for a particular domain, then my subsequent theoretical activities are rational to the extent that they further this aim. Who are we to say that others should *not* seek to simplify their theories? By the same token, however, there is nothing to stop anyone from seeking to construct *complex* theories, or *funny* ones. There's no arguing about taste. Similar remarks apply to other candidates for an intrinsic third virtue. We can construct theories for any purpose we want—to gratify our aesthetic sense, to increase our dominion over nature, to scandalize the bourgeoisie, to make a decorative wallpaper pattern. This latitude is not peculiar to theories. We can also use tables and chairs any way we want—as doorstops, objets d'art, and so forth. But just as the essential virtue of a chair is to provide a place to sit, so is the essential virtue of a theory to answer a lot of questions correctly.

5

Deriving and Testing Empirical Hypotheses

5.1 The Varieties of Empirical Projects

For any theory T, let T* be the set of all the observational consequences that follow from T. If T is "All emeralds are green," one element of T* is "The next emerald to be discovered will be green." We say that T is *empirically adequate* if every member of T* is true. The empirical adequacy of a theory does not yet establish its truth, since a true conclusion may be derived from false premises. In fact, supposing that T is empirically adequate, one can always construct another theory that is both empirically adequate and false. For let T be empirically adequate, and let P be any proposition such that neither P nor ~P leads to any new observational consequences when conjoined with T. Then both T & P and T & ~P are empirically adequate. At least one of them, however, must be false. Thus, empirical adequacy is not a sufficient condition for the truth of T. But it is a necessary condition, for a theory that has false consequences must itself be false.

Consider a theory T that contains at least one law. Since T has an infinite number of observational consequences, empirical work can never fully establish that T is empirically adequate. The criterion of empirical adequacy functions only as an ideal. T's *confirmational status* is defined as $p(T*)$, the probability that all its observational consequences are true. Since two mutually inconsistent theories may both be empirically adequate, it is clear that $p(T*)$ is not always identical to $p(T)$. Factors other than confirmational status enter into the determination of theoretical probabilities. However, since T implies T*, P4 tells us that $p(T) \leq p(T*)$. A theory T's confirmational status sets an upper limit to the probability that can rationally be ascribed to T.

Much of the activity of science is a matter of performing operations, both empirical and theoretical, that alter the probabilities of various theories. Some of these operations affect $p(T)$ by means of an effect on $p(T^*)$: We ascribe a new probability to T because there is a change in its confirmational status. An operation that increases $p(T^*)$ is called a *confirmation* of T. An operation that decreases $p(T^*)$ is a *disconfirmation* of T. Radical empiricists sometimes suppose that the only way to affect theoretical probabilities is by empirical research. This is an indefensible position. There are both empirical and theoretical methods of affecting a theory's confirmational status. In fact, there are also theoretical methods of altering the likelihood of a theory's being true without affecting its confirmational status. These methods will be discussed in chapter 6. *Empirical* confirmation and disconfirmation will be discussed in this chapter. This activity is, of course, largely in the experimentalist's domain, but the theorist has an important role to play here.

We have seen that some empirically inclined instrumentalists suppose that the sole purpose of theories is to generate data. Rationalistic realists sometimes suffer from the opposite affliction: They tend to think that the only reason for doing empirical work is to confirm or disconfirm theories. This view is as one-sided as that of their intellectual opponents. Certainly confirming or disconfirming theories is an important type of empirical work. In fact, it is probably the most important type. It must be acknowledged, however, that there also exists a relatively atheoretical type of empirical work, exemplified by the activities of the natural historian. In this kind of work, one collects data that seem to be intrinsically interesting even though they do not speak to any theoretical issue. Perhaps it is thought that these data are likely to concern future theorists. Of course, even natural history is impossible without the deployment of some conceptual structure. At the very least, we need a system of categories that tells us how to code the data. But it is undeniable that data have been recorded and published without reference to any substantive theoretical issue.

There is also a type of empirical research that has the effect of altering the *scope* of a theory without necessarily having any effect on its confirmational status. This category includes the empirical task of determining the value of a theoretically important but unspecified constant. We may have a theory that says that there are electrons and that electrons have a mass but does not specify a value for that mass. The number is to be determined by empirical research. This research will not provide additional confirmation for the theory, for it is undertaken with the assumption that the theory is correct. But it enables the theory to make predictions that were previously beyond its scope. After ascertaining the mass of the electron experimentally, we are in a position to calculate the gravitational force between two electrons. In psychology, an example of the same type of work is the attempt to discover the temporal interval between unconditioned and conditioned stimuli that leads to classical conditioning (Spooner and Kellog 1947). There are also empirical discoveries that diminish the scope of a theory, such as the discovery that previous measurements of a theoretical constant have to be discarded because they were obtained by means of an improperly constructed instrument.

I have mentioned these empirical projects here in order to avert the false impression that all empirical work is an attempt to confirm or disconfirm a theoretical hypothesis. However, the rest of the book will be concerned exclusively with the confirmatory or disconfirmatory effect of new data.

5.2 Empirical Confirmation: The Hypothetico-Deductive Account

There are several conflicting accounts of the process of empirical confirmation. Most of them can be regarded as variants or more precise specifications of the classical *hypothetico-deductive* (H-D) account, an account that is due largely to Hempel (1965). The H-D account runs like this. From a theory T, we *deduce* an observational consequence P that was not in T's initial domain and whose truth value is not yet known. P is a *prediction* from the theory T. Having obtained P, we arrange to observe whether P is true. This may involve actively setting the stage (as in an experiment) or passively waiting for circumstances to produce P or its negation (as in naturalistic observation). Both experimentation and naturalistic observation are, of course, empirical activities. If P is observed to be true, we conclude that T is confirmed—that $p(T^*)$ and $p(T)$ must both be increased. This claim is a preliminary statement of the principle of *induction*, which may also be described as follows: The probability of a universal proposition goes up every time one of its instances is found to be true. Induction, deduction, and abduction are the three categories of ratiocination that have roles in scientific work.

It is important to distinguish the process of confirmation from the process (discussed in the preceding chapter) of assigning prior probabilities to theories. Suppose that T1 entails 99 observation statements in its initial domain, and that it has led to one correct prediction. Suppose also that another theory, T2, entails one observation statement in its initial domain and has led to 99 correct predictions. Each of the theories accounts for 100 facts, but they do so in significantly different ways. On the basis of its more extensive initial domain, we may be impelled (but are not logically compelled) to ascribe a higher *prior* probability to T1 than to T2. Whatever these initial assignments may be, however, T2 must be considered far better *confirmed*. Derivations of data in the initial domain do not count as confirmations because theories are *designed* with their initial domains in plain view. The theory can be tinkered with until it entails its initial domain.

How do we justify our belief in induction? Why should the observation of a *consequence* of T produce an increase in our confidence that T is true? That inference is not deductively valid. Indeed, from a deductive standpoint, it is an instance of the well-known fallacy of affirming the consequent. For any observational consequence of T, there are possible worlds wherein the observational consequence is true but T itself is false. This leads to an old joke about the two parts of logic: the deductive part, where the fallacies are explained, and the inductive part, where they are committed. Let us examine the problem of induction in the relatively simple case of an empirical law. (Everything that will be said applies equally to theoretical laws.) We might take "All emeralds are green" as an example; however, since we are doing theoretical psychology, let us consider a theory which says that rats perform some response R under some condition S. Suppose that 1000 rats are tested under condition S and that they are all observed to perform response R. Since each of these 1000 bits of data is an observational consequence of the theory, the H-D account stipulates that each one produces an increment in the probability that the theory is true. After the thousandth case, we should have an enormously high degree of confidence in the truth of the theory, as a result of which we should be willing to bet a lot of money on the hypothesis that the 1001st rat to be tested under condition S will also do R. Our question is: Why? Why does the observation of 1000 rats doing R make it any more likely that the 1001st will do the same thing?

In one of the most influential analyses in the history of philosophy, Hume (1739) approached the problem of induction by asking what we would have to know in order to establish that our inductive inference is valid. In other words, what sort of hypothesis would complete the following argument?

1. In the past, rats have always performed R under condition S.
2. ?
3. Therefore, rats always do R under condition S.

The missing principle, which Hume calls the Principle of the Uniformity of Nature, is evidently something like "Regularities observed in the past will continue to occur in the future." Now, there are various ways in which this principle might be modified and refined. For one thing, the H-D account stipulates that the principle, as well as the inductive conclusion (3), should be probabilistic rather than absolute. With a number of refinements of this kind, the Principle of Uniformity would eventually begin to look like one or another of the modern theories of *statistics*, which are elaborate systems for drawing inferences about the unobserved portions of the universe (the *population*) on the basis of the observed portions (the *sample*). But the problem of justifying our belief in these statistical theories is essentially the same as that of justifying the Principle of Uniformity in its crudest form. For the sake of simplicity, let us therefore stick with the nonprobabilistic version.

According to Hume, the problem of justifying inductive inference is equivalent to the problem of justifying our acceptance of the Principle of Uniformity. Hume does not provide a proof that such a justification is impossible, but he notes that all the prima facie candidates for a justification are logically defective. For example, it is natural to suppose that the evidence for the validity of inductive reasoning is its impressively successful history: Attempts to formulate scientific theories on the basis of observed regularities have resulted in a vast increase in our capacity to predict future events. But the fact that inductive reasoning was successful in the past gives us no reason to believe that it will continue to be successful for even a moment longer—unless we assume the very principle whose truth we are trying to establish. The defective argument can be represented as follows:

1. In the past, previously observed regularities have continued to occur in (what was then) the future.
2. ?
3. Therefore, regularities observed in the past will continue to occur in the future.

Obviously, the missing premise that would complete this argument is identical to the conclusion. Presenting an argument whose conclusion is identical to one of its premises is called *begging the question*. If question-begging arguments were permitted, we could prove all manner of wondrous things. For example, here is a proof that cabbages are kings:

1. Cabbages are kings.
2. Therefore, cabbages are kings.

Since Hume's day, there have been increasingly subtle attempts to provide a non-question-begging justification for our inductive practices. All of them, however, have eventually been shown to be defective for one reason or another (Salmon 1966). In fact the situation has only gotten worse, for now we know that even if Hume's problem could be resolved we would still have Goodman's (1954) "grue" problem to contend with before our inductive practices could be justified. (See section 4.2.) We will return to this dilemma in chapter 10. For now, let us follow the example of all scientists in all fields and all eras and simply ignore the problem.

Some lesser difficulties with the H-D account can be dealt with more productively. For one thing, the H-D account does not tell us by how much to change p(T) as a result of a given confirmation. It is clear, however, that not every confirmation is as good as every other. Suppose that a prediction from a theory is judged to be extremely likely irrespective of whether the theory is true or false. In that case, its confirmation doesn't increase our confidence in the theory as much as the confirmation of a novel and counterintuitive prediction. We would not lend much greater credence to a psychological theory on the basis of its correctly predicting that most individuals will choose to accept a cash prize rather than be tortured to death. The more counterintuitive the confirmation, the more it adds to the theory's confirmational status. To this day, Einstein's prediction of the bending of light around the sun has been the only empirical confirmation of the theory of general relativity. But this prediction was so unexpected that it bestowed an enormously high confirmational status on the theory. In psychology, Leon Festinger's (1957) theory of cognitive dissonance was influential largely because of its counterintuitive prediction that subjects would show more attitude change when given *fewer* inducements to do so. (I will have more to say about dissonance theory in section 6.7.) There is nothing in the H-D account that explains the greater confirmational effect of novel predictions.

Also, not all theories can be allowed to benefit equally from a single confirmatory event. For any observational prediction D, there are infinitely many mutually exclusive theories from which D can be derived. The argument that establishes this claim is the same as the argument (set forth in the preceding chapter) that establishes that there are infinitely many theories that account for any set of data. Only the sequence of events is different. In this case, the empirical discovery that D is true simultaneously confirms the entire infinitude of theories that predict it. But these theories cannot all be assigned the same probability, since the sum of their probabilities cannot be allowed to exceed 1. The H-D account does not tell us how the confirmatory effect is to be apportioned.

Still another shortcoming of the H-D account is that observational data may confirm a theory even though they fail to be logical consequences of the theory. A similar point was made in the preceding chapter concerning prior probabilities. It was noted that one might reasonably assign a higher prior probability to a theory in light of data that were not deducible from the theory. The point here is similar; once again, only the temporal order of events has been changed. Suppose we have this theory that all emeralds are green, to which we have already ascribed a certain prior probability. Afterward, we observe several new emeralds, and they all turn out to be green. According to the H-D account, each of these observations confirms our theory. But the theory is also confirmed by the observation that *other* trustworthy individuals with normal color vision report seeing green emeralds. Yet the latter data concerning the verbal behavior of others are not logical consequences of the theory that emeralds are green. In section 5.4 we will see that observational data are rarely, if ever, strict logical consequences of our theories. (The reason for this state of affairs has thus far been suppressed for pedagogic purposes.) This means that this particular shortcoming of the H-D approach is especially severe.

A famous dilemma for the H-D account is known as the "ravens paradox" (Hempel 1965). Consider the following theory:

(1) All ravens are black.

The H-D account stipulates that (1) is confirmed every time we observe a black raven, since every sentence of the form "Raven X is black" is a logical consequence of the theory. But "All ravens are black" is logically equivalent to (2).

(2) All non-black things are non-ravens.

According to the H-D account, (2) is confirmed by every one of its instances, i.e., every observation of a non-black non-raven. In particular, (2) is confirmed by the observation of a white handkerchief. But (2) is the same theory as (1) expressed in a different logical form. Thus, the observation of a white handkerchief confirms the theory that all ravens are black. But this conclusion is, to say the least, rather difficult to accept. It certainly does not square with accepted scientific practice.

These and other difficulties with the H-D account have led to various modifications. One of the most widely accepted is *Bayesian confirmation theory*.

5.3   Empirical Confirmation: The Bayesian Account

As its name implies, Bayesian confirmation theory is an outgrowth of the Bayesian approach discussed in chapter 4. The main feature of this approach is its assumption that the rational assessment of hypotheses can begin only *after* we have assigned prior probabilities to them. The prior assignment itself is entirely subjective. Bayesian confirmation theory is an attempt to specify how prior probabilities should be altered as our information about the world changes.

Before presenting the theory, I must define the concept of *conditional probability*. For any two propositions A and B, the conditional probability of A on B is given by (3).

(3) $p(A \mid B) = \dfrac{p(A \,\&\, B)}{p(B)}$.

Intuitively, $p(A|B)$ is the probability of A *if B is assumed to be true*. The formal definition given in (1) tells us that the conditional probability of A on B is very high if $p(A \,\&\, B)$ (the probability that both A and B are true) is almost the same as $p(B)$ (the probability that B alone is true). In the extreme case, $p(A|B) = 1$ if the conjunction A & B is exactly as likely as B alone. This is necessarily the case if B logically implies A. Conversely, the conditional probability of A on B is very low if the probability that A and B are both true is much lower than the probability that B alone is true. In the extreme case, $p(A|B) = 0$ if the conjunction of A and B is impossible. This is necessarily the case if B implies ~A, or vice versa.

Reversing the roles of A and B in the definition of conditional probability, we get

(4) $p(B \mid A) = \dfrac{p(B \ \& \ A)}{p(A)}$.

Multiplying both sides by $p(A)$ and flipping the equation left to right yields

(5) $p(B \ \& \ A) = p(A)\,p(B \mid A)$.

Since B & A is the same proposition as A & B, we can rewrite (5) as

(6) $p(A \ \& \ B) = p(A)\,p(B \mid A)$.

Now divide both sides by $p(B)$:

(7) $\dfrac{p(A \ \& \ B)}{p(B)} = \dfrac{p(A)p(B \mid A)}{p(B)}$.

But by definition (3) the left-hand side of (7) is equal to $p(A|B)$:

(8) $p(A \mid B) = \dfrac{p(A)\,p(B \mid A)}{p(A)}$.

This important result is known as *Bayes's theorem*. The theory known as "Bayesian confirmation theory" was devised long after Thomas Bayes's time. However, the theory has been given his name because of the crucial role played in it by his theorem.

Now suppose that we have assigned a prior probability $p_1(T)$ to theory T. How is this probability affected by the discovery of a new datum D? The basic principle of Bayesian confirmation theory is that the new (or *posterior*) probability of T, $p_2(T)$, should be equal to the old conditional probability of T on D:

(9) $p_2(T) = p_1(T \mid D)$.

It follows from Bayes's theorem that

(10) $p_2(T) = \dfrac{p_1(T)p_1(D \mid T)}{p_1(D)}$.

This expression specifies a value for the new theoretical probability in term of three prior probabilities: our prior opinion of how likely the theory was $(p_1(T))$, our prior opinion of how likely D was before we found out that it was true ($p_1(D)$), and our prior opinion of the conditional probability of D on T ($p_j(D|T)$). The rule for probability change expressed by (10) is often called *conditionalization*.

It is important to understand that the conditionalization rule is a new probabilistic principle (Hacking 1967). It does not follow from the basic axioms of probability theory, and its violation does not make us incoherent. There are strong arguments in its favor, however. Just as incoherence renders us liable to a Dutch book, the violation of the conditionalization rule renders us liable to a "dynamic Dutch book," which is almost as bad (Skyrms 1987). The import of the dynamic book theorem is that if we follow any strategy for changing our probabilities other than conditionalization, it is possible for a bookie to construct a *series* of conditional bets that will result in our surely losing money in the end. (A "conditional bet" has the form "Accept bet A if P turns out to be true, and accept bet B otherwise.")

What is the relationship between conditionalization and the H-D account? The latter amounts to the claim that $p_2(T) > p_1(T)$ if T implies D. This limited principle falls out as a special case of the Bayesian theory, for, if T implies D, then $p(D|T) = 1$, from which it follows from (10) that

(11) $p_2(T) = \dfrac{p_1(T)}{p_1(D)}.$

But $p_1(D) < 1$, since it represents our assessment of the likelihood of D *prior to* our discovering that it is true. Thus, $p_2(T) > p_1(T)$. The Bayesian analysis goes far beyond this simple conclusion, however. Unlike the H-D account, it tells us by how much to change $p(T)$. In particular, it provides an explanation for the greater confirmatory effect of novel predictions. An "obvious" prediction D is one that we believed was quite likely to be true regardless of whether the theory turns out to be true—that is to say, $p_1(D)$ is close to 1. But if $p_1(D)$ is almost 1, then, by (11), $p_2(T)$ will not be much bigger than $p_1(T)$. This is why a theory would gain very little in credibility by correctly predicting that humans would choose cash over death. On the other hand, a novel prediction is one where $p_1(D)$ is very small. In that case, $p_2(T)$ will be much bigger than $p_1(T)$.

The conditionalization rule also accounts for the fact that not all theories benefit equally from a specific confirmatory event. Suppose that T1 and T2 both imply D, and that an experiment confirms the prediction D. Formula

(11) tells us that the posterior probabilities of T1 and T2 will be determined by their prior probabilities as well as by the prior probability of D. In particular, if T1 was deemed to be much more plausible than T2 before their confirmation, it will continue to be more plausible afterward. This analysis accounts for the fact that extremely implausible hypotheses are not easily rendered plausible by empirical research, even if that research confirms the theory's predictions. The classic example is the hypothesis of extrasensory perception, to which most scientists ascribe a vanishingly small prior probability. Bayesian confirmation theory tells us that it may be rational to refuse to be persuaded that ESP exists even in the face of overwhelmingly confirmatory evidence. If the ESP hypothesis correctly predicts experimental results that had a prior probability of one in a million, but if the hypothesis itself had a prior probability of one in a trillion, we would still think that there is only one chance in a million that the hypothesis is true. This is not, of course, an argument against ESP. It is only an argument vindicating the rationality of those who refuse to accept it. Conversely, it would be rational to embrace the ESP hypothesis on the flimsiest evidence if our prior probability were high enough. Bayesianism is a very democratic theory. In the most extreme case, a theory that is assigned a probability of 0 will not benefit from any confirmation. No matter how many of the theory's observational consequences turn out to be true, and no matter how counterintuitive they are, the posterior probability of the theory will always remain at 0. Thus, investigators who begin with different ideas about what is impossible will never come to agree, no matter what the evidence says—not by the process of Bayesian conditionalization, anyway. The consequences of this state of affairs will be discussed in chapter 10.

The foregoing analysis forms the basis for a devastating critique of the methodology of null-hypothesis testing (Bakan 1966; Meehl 1967). In social psychology, most attempts to confirm theories rely on the procedure of deriving from the theory a prediction that one experimental group will differ from another with respect to some dependent variable. The theory is considered to be confirmed if the "null hypothesis" that the two groups do not differ turns out to be false. One problem with this procedure is that every null hypothesis is almost surely false, regardless of whether the theory being tested is true, for the chance that any two groups will prove to be exactly equal on any measure (be it IQ, anxiety, yearly income, or height) is vanishingly small. It is only a matter of running enough subjects until our statistical test reports a significant difference. That is to say, if T implies D, where D is the proposition that the null hypothesis is false, then $p_1(D)$ is about equal to 1. But then, by (11), it follows that the posterior probability of our theory, $p_2(T)$, is about the same as its prior probability, $p_1(T)$. The rejection of the null hypothesis is too overwhelmingly probable for its occurrence to have any confirmatory effect.

A partial reply to this criticism is that social-psychological theories usually predict the *direction* of the difference between two groups, which gives the null hypothesis a probability of about $\frac{1}{2}$ instead of 1. This is still a very weak test, but at least it is something. But even this weak confirmatory effect cannot automatically be credited to the theory we are interested in. It must be shared by all the theories that make the same prediction, in proportion to their prior probabilities. In social psychology, however, it is almost always a trivial matter to generate numerous alternative theories that are reasonably plausible and make the same prediction as the one being tested. This state of affairs renders null-hypothesis testing nearly useless for the purpose of confirming theoretical hypotheses. Yet it is fair to say that this procedure has carried almost the entire burden of theoretical progress in social psychology. These criticisms have been circulating for several decades without having any noticeable effects on the confirmational practices of the field. According to Meehl (1990, p. 230), social psychologists as a whole have reacted with "a mix of defense mechanisms (most predominantly, denial) so that they can proceed as they have in the past with a good scientific conscience." Meehl continues:

I cannot strongly fault a 45-year-old professor for adopting this line of defense, even though I believe it to be intellectually dishonest, because I think that for most faculty in social psychology the full acceptance of my line of thought would involve a painful realization that one has achieved some notoriety, tenure, economic security and the like by engaging, to speak bluntly, in a bunch of nothing.

Now let us return to the comparison between the Bayesian and H-D approaches. The former also allows for the confirmatory effect of data that are not strictly logical consequences of the theory. To say that T is confirmed by the datum D is to say that T is more likely once D is known than it was before—i.e., that $p_2(T) > p_1(T)$. By (10), this condition is met whenever

(12) $\dfrac{p_1(D \mid T)}{p_1(D)} > 1.$

Equivalently, D confirms T if $p_1(D|T) > p_1(D)$. The case where T implies D is the best possible one, for then $p_1(D|T)$ has the maximal value of 1. But it is clear that there can be a confirmatory effect even if $p_1(D|T) < 1$.

There is no doubt that Bayesianism represents a major advance over the H-D account. Its successes have made it a popular confirmation theory among statisticians and philosophers of science. However, there are problems for which it has not yet yielded up any easy solution. The ravens paradox is one of these. Another is the confirmatory effect of a *variety* of evidence as compared to relatively homogeneous evidence. As was mentioned in chapter 4, a theory is considered to have greater scope if it predicts a heterogeneous variety of phenomena. It is also frequently claimed that the theory gains in credibility if a variety of predictions is confirmed. Newtonian physics became enormously credible on the basis of its correctly predicting such widely disparate phenomena as the motions of the planets, the tides, the paths of projectiles, the periods of pendulums, and the actions of springs and balances. It is not clear whether a Bayesian analysis can encompass the effect of variety, or explain the ravens paradox. There have been attempts to construct Bayesian solutions to these and other difficult problems in confirmation theory (e.g., Horwich 1982). At the same time, some investigators have been pursuing entirely different approaches to confirmation theory (e.g., Glymour 1980). For present purposes, however, the Bayesian theory is good enough. It provides a framework that will prove adequate for the rest of my discussion.

5.4   Empirical Disconfirmation

The acquisition of a new datum D *disconfirms* a theory T if the new empirical knowledge renders the theory less probable than it was before. According to Bayesian theory, this happens just in case $p_1(T|D) < p_1(T)$. As in the case of confirmation, it is not necessary for there to be a deductive relation between the theory and the datum. In the special case where D is observed to take place and T implies ~D, both Bayesian theory and H-D theory stipulate that $p_2(T) = 0$. Indeed this result is an elementary consequence of the propositional inference rule of modus tollens: If T implies ~D and if D is true, then T must be false. Thus, there appears to be an important asymmetry between the processes of confirmation and disconfirmation. Let us say that a series of observations *verifies* theory T if it establishes that $p_2(T) = 1$, and that it *falsifies* T if it establishes that $p_2(T) = 0$. We have seen that no finite series of observations can ever verify a universal law. But apparently a law can be falsified by even a single observation. This was emphasized by Karl Popper (1934–35), who argued that the falsification of theories is the only mechanism whereby science progresses.

There are some unexpected problems with the foregoing analysis, however. Historians of science tell us that every scientific theory ever proposed has been confronted from the start with "anomalous" data that show some of its observational consequences to be false (Kuhn 1962). Even the most precise theories of physics predict numerical values for some experiments that diverge from observed values by an amount greater than can be attributed to experimental error. The magnitude of the divergence is unimportant. If a theory predicts that an object will travel 7.0854 meters in a certain time period, and if measurement establishes that the distance traveled is 7.0855 meters, then the premises that generate the prediction of 7.0854 meters are surely false. A real-life example of exactly this situation involved the most successful scientific theory of all time: Newton's theory of gravitation. The theory's prediction of the orbit of Mercury was off by a minute amount. The anomaly was eventually explained by the general theory of relativity, but knowledge of Mercury's anomalous orbit managed to coexist with the Newtonian theory for 85 years.

The history of psychology is replete with less momentous but formally identical episodes. A case in point concerns latent learning and the law of effect. By the 1930s, the law of effect had become enshrined as the best-established theoretical principle in psychology. Yet Edward Tolman and his colleagues had provided as clear a disconfirmation of the law as can be imagined. Tolman demonstrated that response frequency could be altered in the absence of any rewards or punishments. In one of Tolman's numerous demonstrations of this "latent learning effect," two groups of rats were run (individually) in a complex, multiple-unit maze. One group found food in the end box on every daily trial. The other found nothing at all for the first ten days. For this second group, the only thing that differentiated the "end box" from any other point in the maze was the experimenters' future intentions. At the end of the first ten days, the rewarded group was making much fewer errors in navigating to the end box than the non-rewarded group. This is what the law of effect would have predicted. On the eleventh day, the previously non-rewarded group began to find food in the end box. According to the law of effect, this group should then have begun to recapitulate the history of the always-rewarded group—their errors should have gradually begun to drop at about the same rate as the rewarded group's did during the first ten days of the experiment. What happened, however, was that the previously non-rewarded group's errors plunged *immediately* to the level that had been painstakingly achieved in ten days of trial and error by the always-rewarded group (figure 5.1).

From a cognitive point of view (of which Tolman was an early champion), these results are not at all surprising. Evidently, in their unrewarded explorations of the maze during the first ten days, rats in the unrewarded group learned something—a great deal, in fact—about the layout of the maze. When, on the eleventh day, they unexpectedly found food at what the experimenters had designated as the end box, they immediately knew how to get back to the same spot. But this is not what should have happened if response frequency were a function of the number of times the response had been rewarded. This elegant disconfirmation had no perceptible effect on the history of psychology. By the early 1930s, the phenomenon of latent

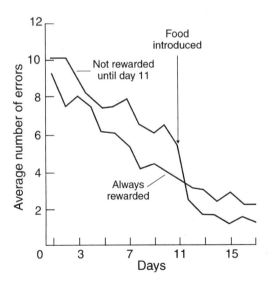

Figure 5.1
The latent-learning phenomenon (after Tolman and Honzik 1930).

learning had been replicated many times, in a variety of experimental arrangements. Yet the law of effect continued to be the centerpiece of the most influential theories of learning through the 1940s and well into the 1950s. The single most influential theory of the 1940s and the 1950s among North American experimental psychologists was undoubtedly Clark Hull's (1943, 1952) *drive theory*. Like most of its competitors, this theory adopted the law of effect as a basic postulate—despite its apparent experimental refutation decades before. Even when the popularity of drive theory began to diminish, in the late 1950s, the cause of the decline still wasn't the latent-learning phenomenon. Drive theory was done in by the disconfirmation of an altogether different hypothesis concerning the nature of reward (White 1959). In any event, the most influential theory in psychology coexisted with its apparent experimental refutation for about 20 years.

How can a theory be maintained in the face of even a single anomaly? One possible answer is that scientists are constitutionally irrational. There are a few other possibilities, however. The simplest line of defense is to point out that the data falsify the theory only if the data themselves are known to be true with absolute certainty. If the probability that the distance traveled by an object in a certain time is 7.0855 meters is less than 1, it is not yet irrational to hold out some hope for the theory that predicts the object will travel 7.0854 meters. The discussion in this book has been conducted under the idealizing assumption that what is observed to take place is known to be true with absolute certainty. But, as was noted in chapter 3, there are no incorrigible observation statements. It is always possible that an observational error has been committed. This point is well worth making. But it does not provide a complete justification for scientists' toleration of anomalies. Scientists often ignore anomalous observations when they do not have any serious doubt as to their truth. Nobody doubted the measurements of Mercury's orbit, for instance.

Another line of defense for established scientific practice alludes to the fact that, strictly speaking, universal laws per se do not have any observational consequences unless they are conjoined with a statement to the effect that certain *initial conditions* have been met. By itself, the law that water boils at 100°C does not entail any prediction about the boiling point of any particular sample of liquid. Only the conjunction of the law and the initial condition that the liquid being tested is water can yield such a prediction. But then the falsification of the prediction does not necessarily falsify the theory. Modus tollens gives us the negation of the *conjunction* of the theory T and the initial condition I:

(13) [T & I] → P.

(14) ~P.

(15) Therefore, ~[T & I].

By DeMorgan's Law, (15) is equivalent to

(16) ~T ∨ ~I.

The failure of a theoretical prediction establishes that *either* the theory is false *or* the initial conditions were not met. If our experimental substance fails to boil at 100°C, it follows *either* that water does not always boil at 100°C *or* that the substance is something other than water. Thus, it is feasible to continue to assign a nonzero probability to T after one of its predictions has failed. Once again, this analysis is correct as far as it goes, but it does not go far enough. In fact, it adds very little to the previous point: that observation statements cannot be known with absolute certainty. It is an arbitrary matter of taste whether we consider a prediction P to follow from the conjunction of a theory T and a set of initial conditions I or whether we say that the theory by itself predicts that either P will take place or I is false. That is to say, (13) is logically equivalent to

(17) T → [P ∨ ~I].

In this mode of representation, the prediction from T is the disjunctive statement P ∨ ~I. The theory that water boils at 100°C leads to the prediction that this substance before me (and indeed any other substance) either boils at 100°C or fails to be water. On this manner of describing the situation, the failure of an initial condition is one way in which the theory's prediction can turn out to be correct. But the question still remains: What do we do when the theoretical prediction is incorrect? The only change is in what we decide to count as the prediction. In the present case, establishing that the prediction is false means establishing that P is false *and* that I is true. We can always save the theory by saying that such a claim cannot be established with certainty. This is the same point that was made before our introduction of initial conditions. Once again, however, this point does not account for the fact that scientists do not automatically abandon theories even when they fully accept that some of the predictions derived from them are false.

There are two factors that do adequately account for the unfalsifiability of theories.

First, theories cannot make correct observational predictions unless they incorporate, either explicitly or implicitly, a special qualificatory statement known as a *ceteris paribus clause*. Consider a prediction from the law of gravity that an object X to be released 5 feet above the earth's surface will fall to the ground. We perform the experiment—we drop X from a height of 5 feet. But a pranksterish laboratory assistant reaches out and catches the object before it hits the ground. Our prediction has proved false. But surely we would not want to abandon the law of gravity on the basis of such a result. Perhaps we want to say that one of the initial conditions required for making our prediction is that X not be intercepted by any other object. So we do the experiment again, this time making sure that no other object intercepts X. But this time X, which happens to be metallic, *rises* because it is subjected from above to a magnetic force that is stronger than gravity. Evidently, we must add yet another initial condition: that the object is not in a magnetic field. Of course, there may be other forces that counter the gravitational force. We are going to have to specify the absence of every one of them in our initial conditions. But even if the experiment fails when none of the listed forces is present, it is still possible that the law of gravity is universally true but that it was countervailed by another force that was not on our list because we previously had no knowledge of its existence. Indeed, it was by predictive failures of this kind that new forces were discovered in the twentieth century. Obviously, the only way to cover ourselves is to say is that an object released 5 feet above the earth's surface will fall to the ground *if no other factors are currently operative that might influence its motion.* The italicized portion of the preceding sentence is the ceteris paribus ("other things being equal") clause.

The defense of the law of effect against the putative refutation of the latent-learning phenomenon followed exactly the same pattern as our contrived gravitational example. The law of effect predicts no change in response frequency in the absence of food rewards *only if there are no other sources of reward to be obtained by entering the end box.* We can be sure that none the obvious sources of reward—food, water, air, avoidance of electrical shock, rats of the opposite sex, and so on—were contingent upon a rat's entering the end box. But this is merely akin to ruling out the known forces that might counteract the predicted effect of gravity. There is always the possibility that an unknown force has the same effect. By the same token, psychologists were not logically compelled to give up the law of effect in the face of Tolman's findings because it could not be shown with deductive certainty that there weren't any exotic sources of reward associated with the end box (Hilgard and Marquis 1940).

We can, if we wish, regard the ceteris paribus clause as a special kind of initial condition that we must conjoin to the theory whenever we want to make a prediction. We must understand, however, that its invocation is mandatory in *every* case. There can be no observational predictions without it. Even "All emeralds are green" can be falsified with a brush and a bucket of red paint. Furthermore, this ubiquitous initial condition has a fundamentally different character from those we considered before. Like the law being tested, the ceteris paribus clause is a universal proposition with an infinite number of observational consequences. Consider once again the law of effect. The phenomenon of latent learning seemed to refute the prediction that there would be no change in response frequency without reward. It is even easier to seem to refute the prediction that there *will* be a change in response frequency when the response *is* rewarded. Here are some ways this prediction might go wrong: The rewarded organism might be too exhausted after its first response to emit another. It might suffer a stroke. It might be given an injection of curare. It might be tied up with rope. It might be hit by a meteor. There is no possibility of listing all the potential mitigating factors ahead of time. All we can say is that the frequency of a response increases after reinforcement *if* no other factors influencing response frequency are currently operative. It might be obvious that the rat has not been tied up with a rope or hit by meteor. But there are always other potential mitigators that could not be ruled out without further investigation—for example, that this particular organism has an as-yet-undiscovered form of brain damage that renders it incapable of learning in certain situations. We might investigate some of the more plausible of these possibilities and lay them to rest. But the claim that the ceteris paribus clause has been satisfied can never attain the status of a claim that a particular observational datum has been established. This is one reason why theories can survive after it is observed that their predictions are false. When a theoretical prediction fails to be borne out, we have the delicate task of choosing whether to reject the substantive law or to suppose that the ceteris paribus clause has not been satisfied. There may be principles that tell us what to do in such a case, but such principles could only be probabilistic. Thus, observation alone can never falsify a theory.

Second, in an analysis that was half a century ahead of its time, Pierre Duhem (1906) noted yet another factor that renders falsification as out of reach as verification. According to Duhem, every observational prediction from a theory presupposes the truth of other theories, which in this context are called *auxiliary hypotheses*. In testing an astronomical hypothesis by telescopic observation, we take for granted a theory of optics that tells us how to interpret the telescopic image, as well as a theory of sensory physiology that tells us how the telescopic images is transformed into a visual observation. Similarly, the average psychology experiment, with its tachistoscopes, automated counters, and computer-controlled stimuli, presupposes enormous amounts of physics. If the physical theories that explain the workings of these devises are in error, our experimental results would not bear the interpretations we choose to put on them. If any prediction goes wrong, it is an open question whether the theory that was explicitly being tested is to blame or whether one of the auxiliary hypotheses must be revised. This is what happened with Galileo's discovery of the moons of Jupiter. His report was so drastically at odds with the prevailing world view that some individuals preferred to attribute the observation to aberrations in the telescope. Since the telescope was a recently developed and unfamiliar research instrument, this was not a strikingly irrational reaction.

In sum, the failure of a prediction does not require us to abandon the theory, because it is always possible that the ceteris paribus clause has not been satisfied or that one of the auxiliary hypotheses is false. When a theoretical prediction fails to be borne out, all we can say is that the theory's confirmational status has been decreased.

5.5   The Cycle of Empirical Testing and Theoretical Accommodation

If a theory is repeatedly disconfirmed, there comes a time when scientists begin to seek out alternatives. There is a cyclical process involving construction and modification of theories, generation of predictions, and empirical tests of these predictions.

In the first stage, a theory T1 is constructed to explain a set of data D1. Let us call D1 the *initial domain* of T1. Note that this is a broadening of our previous definition, according to which the initial domain was the set of data against which a theory was initially checked for consistency. Henceforth we will say that the initial domain is the set of data against which a theory is initially checked for whatever relation our philosophy of science stipulates should hold between theories and data. If we are hypothetico-deductivists, we will want our theories to entail their initial domains; if we are Bayesians, we will want them to have a high prior probability relative to their initial domains. The definition of prior adequacy undergoes a corresponding change: A theory now possesses prior adequacy if it succeeds in having the right relationship (entailment, or whatever) to the data in its initial domain.

In the second stage, predictions—say P1, P2, and P3—are derived from T1 and tested. Some of these tests (say, the tests of P1 and P2) may confirm the theory; others (say, the test of P3) may disconfirm it. At this point T1's confirmational status depends on its relation to its *extended domain*, D1*, which includes both its initial domain and the results of its tested predictions. In this case, D1* = D1 $\cup$ (P1, P2, ~P3). The task now is to construct a new theory, T2, whose initial domain, D2, is D1*, the extended domain of T1. The cycle then repeats itself. Naturally, T2's explanations of P1, P2, and ~P3 do not yet count as confirmations. Also, T2 will be considered an improvement over T1 even if there is some "problem loss"—i.e., even if there are some items in its predecessor's initial domain that it can no longer explain—so long as this loss is sufficiently compensated by the capacity to explain ~P3 and other results that contradict its predecessor.

T2 may be a radical departure from T1, or it may be a relatively minor modification. Other things being equal, scientists generally prefer the least theoretical change that will accommodate contradictory data. This principle of *cognitive conservatism* dictates that we should always try to patch up an old theory before constructing a radically new one. What is the status of this principle? It is undoubtedly correct as a description of what has actually taken place in the history of science. But is it a rationally warranted prescription? It is certainly not a consequence of Bayesian confirmation theory. Perhaps it should be understood as a utilitarian strategy. Suppose we contemplate a choice between making a minimal theoretical change and constructing an entirely new theoretical edifice to account for anomalous data. If there is nothing else to suggest a preference for one course over the other, it may be more sensible to adopt the first course simply because it is easier. By making a minimal adjustment instead of starting from scratch, we leave ourselves more time for other work and so end up ahead in the end. But if someone were to ignore the advice to be conservative and devise a radically new theory anyway, our evaluation of the theory would have to be based on the classical virtues of probability and scope. If the radically new theory turned out to be superior on both counts, repudiating it on the grounds of conservatism would be irrational. Of course, one might want to argue that conservative changes tend to produce more probable or more general theories than radical changes—in brief, that conservatism is a derivative as opposed to an intrinsic theoretical virtue (see section 4.5). I have never encountered such an argument, however.

Which comes first in the cycle of empirical testing and theoretical accommodation: a theory, or a set of data? On the one hand, the first theory can take the null set of data as its initial domain (i.e., anything goes). On the other hand, the first datum need not be obtained as a result of testing a theoretical prediction. Prescriptively speaking, it is not clear that either way of starting has any great advantage over the other. Descriptively, it may very well be the case that we have no choice in the matter. By the time we are sufficiently sophisticated to reflect on our epistemic practices, we already find ourselves immersed in a sea of theories and data. Indeed, we humans may very well be born with certain theories and/or data wired into our cognitive apparatus

5.6 Prediction as a Theoretical Activity

Confirming or disconfirming a new prediction is a matter for empirical research, but *obtaining* the prediction to be tested is a theoretical task. This distinction has not usually been made in psychology, because deductions from psychological theories have generally been too easy to impress themselves as distinct acts. This is due to the fact that, until quite recently, psychological theories have had very simple logical structures. They have also employed concepts that are not very far removed from the observational level. Hence, inferences from theory to prediction have tended to be self-evident. For the same reason, psychological theories have seldom yielded hidden consequences—that is, predictions that the constructors of the theory had not foreseen. The situation is very different in physics: Deriving new consequences from existing theories is a major professional occupation for a substantial number of theoretical physicists. To be sure, this theoretical activity does not in itself affect the confirmational status of the theory. Nevertheless, it is an essential prerequisite to empirical attempts at confirmation.

The importance of deriving new consequences does not entirely depend on subsequent empirical tests. In physics, theoretical derivations are routinely considered to be major scientific advances, even if it is not feasible to test them empirically. A recent example is the derivation of the existence of black holes from the general theory of relativity. Such a derivation constitutes a scientific advance in and of itself because it enhances our understanding of the theory by exposing some of its hidden ramifications. The discovery of an unexpected consequence also has the effect of demonstrating that the theory has a larger *scope* than had previously been supposed: The theory answers more questions about the world than we first thought it would. Such an a priori discovery therefore has the effect of altering our assessment of a theory's total degree of virtue.

Of course, it might have been the case that the subject-matter of psychology did not lend itself to nontrivial theorizing. Recent developments, discussed in the next section, have laid this depressing possibility to rest.

5.7 Weak AI as a Style of Theoretical Psychology

There are several quite different enterprises that go by the name "artificial intelligence." They all involve attempts to write programs that enable computers to perform cognitive tasks, such as alphabetizing lists (which turns out to be easy to program) or writing summaries of longer texts (which turns out to be very difficult). To write a program for a task is to give a series of absolutely explicit instructions (an *algorithm*) for how to do it. Naturally, any form of instruction must presuppose that the instructee is able to perform certain *primitive operations* without being told how. It is widely believed that any set of instructions that can be followed by a computer of any design can be analyzed into the following primitive operations:

recognizing the difference between two symbols (e.g., 0 and 1); following the instruction either to leave the symbol as it is or to change it to the other symbol; and following the instruction to move on to the next symbol to the right or to the left, or to halt. This is one version (the weakest) of the *Church-Turing thesis*. A *Turing machine* is a device that is capable of performing the above primitive operations and nothing more. The Church-Turing thesis claim that a Turing machine can do anything that any computer can do, although it may take longer to do it.

There are various reasons why one might want to write programs that enable computers to perform cognitive tasks. One reason is simply to get the job done so that humans don't have to do it. This is *non-psychological AI* (Flanagan 1984). The goal here is a practical one. It has no bearing on the problems of psychology. There are (at least) two types of psychological AI, which Searle (1980) has called *weak AI* and *strong AI*. In this chapter, I will discuss only weak AI. (Strong AI will come up in chapter 8.)

Suppose we have a theory about how humans alphabetize lists or summarize texts: We hypothesize that they go through certain steps in a certain order. If the theory can be written as a program, then there are some definite benefits to doing so. By writing out the theory in the form of a program, we have a convenient way of checking its prior adequacy: Just run it and see if the computer is really able to perform the task. If the machine runs, the theory is adequate and therefore worthy of serious consideration; if it doesn't run, then it is inadequate and it must be either abandoned or changed.

In weak AI, the computer is used like a pocket calculator—to save time in deriving an initial domain from a theory. But computers save so much time that this difference in degree becomes a difference in kind. Computers enable us to check the prior adequacy of theories that are far too complex to be evaluated "by hand." This increases the range of theories that can reasonably be entertained. In principle, the theory-*cum*-program can also be used to derive new predictions. If the program leads to unexpected behavior on the part of the computer, then the corresponding theory has generated the prediction that humans will also produce the same behavior. (As Pylyshyn (1984) notes, not all features of the program are intended to have psychological realism.) In principle, we might be able to obtain predictions whose derivations would be too complex for anyone to arrive at by hand.

In practice, AI programs have not yet arrived at the stage where they can be used in this way. The struggle is still to achieve prior adequacy. This is why AI researchers are not very interested in new experimental results. The philosopher-psychologist Margaret Boden (1977, p. 37) writes:

For many [AI researchers] . . . visual, reasoning or language-understanding programs . . . quite clearly cannot do many things which people can do; no further experimentation is needed to show this. Such experiments will only be needed when the programs concerned are powerful enough to give a close approximation to human behavior, so close as to make discriminatory experimental tests appropriate.

However, the criterion for having *achieved* prior adequacy is unprecedentedly stringent in AI: The machine must run! In contrast, traditional psychological theorists have often contented themselves with loose and impressionistic derivations of the data in their theories' initial domains.

The rigors of AI have already borne fruit in revealing hidden difficulties in theories whose prior adequacy seemed intuitively self-evident. When the theory was put in program form, the machine did not run. The most notable example is the *frame problem*, which, according to Dennett (1987, p. 42), is a "new, deep epistemological problem—accessible in principle but unnoticed by generations of philosophers—brought to light by the novel methods of AI, and still far from being solved."

The frame problem arose in the course of trying to devise a program for updating one's stock of beliefs (misleadingly called a "knowledge base") upon receipt of new information. Suppose, for example, that we receive and accept the information that an Antarctic penguin has been found that speaks fluent English. As a result, there are many propositions that we might previously have endorsed but which we must now repudiate. These might include the propositions that only human beings can master a natural language, that no beings native to the Antarctic speak English, and that only featherless bipeds possess the ability to give a passable after-dinner speech. On the other hand, a great many of our beliefs will remain totally unaffected by the new discovery. These include the belief that penguins are native to the Antarctic, that Paris is the capital of France, and that $2 + 2 \neq 5$. What is the procedure followed in making such a revision?

Before AI, it had been tacitly assumed that something like the following account is more or less adequate: The new item of information P is checked for consistency against our old beliefs Q1, Q2, . . . , Qn. When a Qi is found that is inconsistent with P, it is changed to its negation ~Qi. When AI researchers actually tried to implement this idea, they ran into an immediate difficulty: Any knowledge base comparable to a human's is so large that the requisite exhaustive check is simply impractical. According to the account we are considering, the discovery that a penguin speaks English is followed by a process of ascertaining that the new information is *not* inconsistent with our arithmetical beliefs, or with our beliefs about the genealogy of the royal houses of Europe, or with the recipes of all the foods that we know how to prepare, and so on.

Evidently, we cannot assume that the consistency check of the knowledge base proceeds randomly, or in alphabetical order, or in any other order wherein the items that must be negated are distributed randomly. We need to develop an algorithm whereby the great mass of knowledge that is clearly irrelevant to the new item is bypassed altogether. But how do you specify a priori what class of beliefs may potentially be affected by the news that a penguin speaks English? Consider the suggestion that we should look at the items in our knowledge base that make reference to penguins, or to English, or to any other non-logical term that appears in the new item. On the one hand, this recommendation will cause us to overlook indefinitely many necessary changes, for the fact that a penguin speaks English has indefinitely many consequences in which neither "penguin" nor "English" appears. For example, it is incompatible with the proposition that no bird speaks a Germanic language. On the other hand, even the apparently narrow scope of a search through items relating to penguins still leaves us with too many irrelevancies to wade through—we would have to ascertain that the new item has no effect on our beliefs that penguins are not mammals, that penguins have no credit cards, that no penguin has ever been elected to the U.S. Senate, and so on.

Moreover, suppose that we *can* tell whether a particular item in the knowledge base is sufficiently relevant to the new information that it deserves to be checked for consistency. How, exactly, is this capability going to be deployed? To be sure, we now have access to the information that the existence of English-speaking penguins is irrelevant to our belief that Paris is the capital of France. But it isn't at all clear how this access helps. On the face of it, it seems that we still have to consider each and every item in the knowledge base in its turn. The only difference is that previously we assessed each item in turn for consistency with the new item. Now we assess each item for *relevance* to the new item. Only the items that are found to be relevant are sent along for evaluation of their consistency with the new item. But because this stage has to be preceded by an exhaustive differentiation of the relevant items from the irrelevant items, there is no theoretical gain.

Thus, we need even more than an algorithm for relevance. We need to come up with a procedure wherein the irrelevant items don't have to be attended to at all—or at least where the number of irrelevant items that have to be attended to is greatly thinned out. But how can we avoid the irrelevancies without first having to identify them as irrelevancies? Nobody has any idea. It had been thought that the general idea of searching through a memory store would do the explanatory job, and that it was just a matter of working out the details. But when AI researchers started to work on the details, they found that they didn't know how to proceed. The importance of this failure for psychology stems from the incontrovertible fact that we humans *are* capable of updating our knowledge base, although we are unable to describe how we go about doing it. Thus, to the extent that AI programs are regarded as models of human cognitive processes, they fail to achieve prior adequacy. The failure of AI in this regard is its most important accomplishment, for it has alerted psychologists to the existence of a major theoretical problem that everyone had previously overlooked.

It is clear that weak AI is a style of constructing theories and, at least potentially, of deriving theoretical predictions. The only differences between weak AI and traditional work in theoretical psychology are the former's more stringent standards of adequacy and the non-obviousness of some of its results. However, AI researchers themselves often talk as though they were doing empirical research. Indeed, Newell and Simon (1981) have explicitly claimed that AI research *is* empirical work. I am not certain whether this self-presentation is motivated by the prestige associated with empirical matters in some circles or whether it is due to the greater availability of funding for empirical as opposed to theoretical research. In any case, it is important to understand why Newell and Simon's claim is misleading at best. Newell and Simon offer two arguments in favor of their view. One of these applies only to strong AI; it will be taken up in chapter 8. The second argument applies to both weak and strong AI. According to the second argument, AI is empirical because we do not usually know whether a program will do the job it was designed to do until we run it and see. In principle, the adequacy of the program can be settled by purely theoretical work; in practice, the programs are too long and too complicated to be evaluated in this manner. We therefore have to rely on *observation* of what the computer does. Thus, AI is an empirical science. This second argument has the same structure as Tymoczko's (1979) claim that recent computer proofs of mathematical theorems (such as the four-color-map theorem) have turned mathematics into an empirical science. But, as Teller (1980) points out in relation to Tymoczko's claim, there is no difference in principle between relying on computers and relying on paper and pencil (without which we would have been unable to obtain many of our pre-IBM theoretical and mathematical results). It is true that there is an empirical element in all theoretical work. Even without paper and pencil, we cannot devise a deductive argument without *remembering* the preceding line in the proof. This is a point worth making. But the fact remains that AI is not any different from traditional theoretical work in its relation to the empirical. In sum, weak AI is a style of doing theoretical work in psychology. Longuet-Higgins (1981, p. 200) writes:

It is perhaps time that the title "artificial intelligence" were replaced by . . . "theoretical psychology." . . . The time has come . . . when the task of theory construction is altogether too intricate to be consigned to spare moments away from the laboratory; it is at least as much of a discipline as good experimentation.

AI is armchair psychology made respectable again by the acquisition of the symbolic prerequisite for big-time science: expensive equipment. But computers are not essential to the enterprise of weak AI. In principle, we could write programs and simply run them in our heads. In principle, we could have written and evaluated programs in the Stone Age. The computer is nothing more than a helpful tool, like the pocket calculator. Its only function is to speed up deduction.

6

Theoretical Amplification

One of the most persistent misconceptions about theoretical work is that it is coextensive with the construction of new theories. According to this view, the theoretician's role in the scientific enterprise is to devise a new theory, hand it over to the experimentalists for testing, and disappear into the woodwork. As was discussed in the previous chapter, this is a truncated vision of the scope of theoretical activity. When theories are highly formalized, as in physics or AI, deriving empirical consequences to be tested is itself a challenging theoretical task that calls for one form or another of conceptual expertise. As the reader can guess by the number of pages remaining in the book, the story does not end here.

The erroneous identification of theoretical work with theory construction fosters the illusion that theoretical work can be fruitful only when it is closely coordinated with past and future empirical research. If "theorizing" means "constructing theories," then the notion of theorizing without knowing what the data are is obviously a non-starter: You can't very well come up with a good theoretical explanation of the data unless you know the data. But there are theoretical projects other than theory construction, and it happens that most of them have a substantially greater degree of autonomy from the vicissitudes of empirical research. These include some of the commonest theoretical activities (in terms of the amount of time spent on them by full-time theoreticians). In a science with a well-developed theoretical tradition, theoretical researchers do not spend most of their working hours trying to construct new theories. The proposal of a new theory is a special event in a theoretician's professional life. Theoreticians' day-to-day work consists of various sorts of analyses and modifications of existing theoretical structures. Furthermore, many of these analyses do not require knowledge of the data relating to the theory, nor does their success or failure depend on the outcome of future empirical research. An understanding of the theory itself is enough. Here is an astronomer's description of this realm of scientific activity (Barrow 1991, p. 114):

> Despite the popular notion that the work of the scientist is discovery—the creating of new ideas and the discovery of new facts about the universe—many of the books and articles that scientists publish are devoted to a third enterprise: the refinement of existing ideas into simpler, more intuitively embraceable forms, the effacement of the complex into the trivial.
>
> When a new and deep idea is discovered for the first time, it may well appear in a cumbersome language principally designed to express some quite different set of ideas. Gradually, others will re-examine the discovery and find more succinct representations which relate it more naturally to existing ideas. This new relationship may be one of simple logical progression from known ideas or it may be marked by a clash of opposites wherein one must make a radical choice between competing alternatives. The distillation of existing knowledge, to make it simpler and clearer, to refine the true metal of deep truth from the superficial dross surrounding it, is a continuous and vital part of the scientific enterprise. Some scientists are especially good at it and may spend all their activities in furthering its aims rather than pushing forward the far frontiers of discovery.

In the case of heavily mathematical theories, theoretical scientists sometimes comport themselves like mathematicians, proving theorems and solving equations, except that their mathematical labors serve the aims of science. Entirely analogous work can be performed on non-mathematical theories, where it usually goes under the omnibus heading of "conceptual analysis." Each of the remaining chapters in this book is devoted to a different variety of conceptual analysis.

6.1   Amplification Defined

Scientific work, whether empirical or theoretical, can be seen as largely (but not entirely) a matter of performing operations that increase or decrease the plausibility of extant theories. Consider once again the testing of empirical hypotheses derived from theories. When a new empirical consequence is tested and found to be true, we say that the theory is confirmed and we grant that its probability has increased. If the empirical hypothesis turns out to be false, the theory is disconfirmed and its probability goes down. As we saw in chapter 5, scientists and philosophers disagree about various details about this process. But these disputes do not concern us here. The testing of empirical hypotheses is, for most scientists and philosophers, an *empirical* means of altering theoretical probabilities. The important point in the present context is that it is also possible to alter theoretical probabilities by means of a purely a priori theoretical analysis. This is what is meant by a theoretical *amplification*: An amplification is a *logical*, as opposed to empirical, discovery about a theory T as a result of which p(T)—the probability assigned to T before the discovery—has to be changed.

There are indefinitely many ways to amplify theories, including many that remain to be devised by clever theoreticians of the future. The following sections correspond to certain fundamental and recurring argumentative patterns that effect a change of theoretical probabilities.

6.2   Internal Inconsistency

The most extreme form of amplification is the discovery that a theory T is *internally inconsistent*. Suppose that, before this logical discovery, T is assigned the nonzero probability p(T). If T has undergone many successful empirical tests, p(T) may be very high. But suppose that it is now shown that T entails some proposition P and also that proposition's negation, ~P. By axiom P1 of the probability calculus, the probability of the conjunction P & ~P is equal to 0. P4 tells us that the probability of any proposition cannot be greater than the probability of another proposition that it entails. Thus, if T entails P & ~P, p(T) too must be 0. Our opinion to the contrary was simply mistaken. The requirement of probabilistic coherence forces us to change our mind.

The discovery that a theory is inconsistent results in a catastrophic decrease in theoretical probability. However, no empirical work is involved: The proof that T entails a contradiction requires a *deductive* argument. Furthermore, such an argument can very well be discovered by someone who is utterly ignorant of the previous empirical work bearing on T. It does not matter whether P or ~P has been empirically tested, or what the outcome of such tests might have been. Nor can the outcome of future research make a difference. Indeed, P and ~P need not be empirically testable propositions: They may themselves be theoretical statements far removed from the observational level. For any proposition P, if T entails both P and its negation then p(T) must be reset to 0 regardless of T's previous empirical track record.

The fact that T is shown to be inconsistent does not necessarily mean that the theory has to be completely discarded, however. The contradiction may be due to an inadvertent and reparable misstatement of the theory's postulates. Also, if T has a good record of empirical successes, it may be worthwhile to try to save most of its structure, altering only what must be changed in order to block the inconsistency. As it stands, however, the theory is surely false.

A contrived example that illustrates the theoretical operation to perfection is the so-called *barber paradox* (Quine 1966). Consider the hypothesis H that there is a male village barber who shaves all and only those men in a village who do not shave themselves. If we have interrogated a substantial proportion of the male population of the village and encountered nothing but corroborative results, we may grant H a high probability of being correct on the basis of the empirical data. Nevertheless, there is a purely a priori argument that shows that H cannot be true. The argument is that H entails the contradictory conclusions that the barber shaves himself and that he does not shave himself. If the barber does not shave himself, it follows (since H stipulates that the barber shaves every man who does not shave himself) that the barber does shave himself. Therefore the assumption that the barber does not shave himself is false (by indirect proof—see section 2.8). The conclusion is that the barber shaves himself. But conversely, if we suppose that the barber does shave himself, it follows from H that he does not, since H tells us that the barber shaves only the men who do not shave themselves. Therefore he does not shave himself. But the barber cannot both shave himself and desist from shaving himself. The conclusion is that H is false: There can be no such barber. Regardless of how well the data may have seemed to support it, the falsehood of H is ensured on logical grounds alone. If someone were actually to claim that H is true, however, it is likely that the inconsistency would be due to an inadvertent misstatement of the intended hypothesis. No doubt the intended claim would be that the barber shaves all and only those men in the village *other than himself* who do not shave themselves. This alteration effectively blocks the contradictory result.

A famous example of an inconsistency claim in psychology is to be found in Heinz Hartmann's (1958) influential critique of the Freudian theory of ego development. Freud claimed that newborns function entirely on the basis of the *pleasure principle*, according to which activity is always aimed at the gratification of biological needs. In this stage, infants do not seek to acquire knowledge about the world, since knowledge does not *directly* gratify a biological need—you can't eat information, or rub up against it. However, this inability to learn from experience must inevitably get us into serious trouble. Direct and unreflective acquisition of the object of one's desire is often dangerous. In the long run, it is sure to be fatal. For example, an organism functioning solely in accordance with the pleasure principle would not hesitate to try to get a piece of food out of the grasp of an ill-tempered grizzly bear. Freud says that there is an inevitable conflict between our demand for immediate and direct biological gratification and the constraints of reality. If the status quo were to be maintained, this conflict would lead to an untimely death. But instead the conflict is "resolved" by the development of the ego. For Freud, the ego is a rational calculating organ whose function is to acquire the knowledge needed for gratifying one's biological needs without breaking one's neck. Once the ego is in place, we are said to function in accordance with the *reality principle* rather than the pleasure principle. According to the reality principle, all our activities are still aimed at biological gratification, but we are now capable of taking the constraints of reality into account in our eternal quest for food and sex. In non-psychoanalytic terms, the question is: Why do we exert ourselves to acquire knowledge about the world? Freud's answer is: Because, and only because, we learn that knowledge is instrumental in gratifying our biological needs.

Hartmann's criticism of Freud's developmental theory can be easily understood if we represent the theory as follows:

(F1) All our actions are always aimed at the gratification of biological needs.

(F2) At birth, we don't know that knowledge helps to gratify our biological needs.

(F3) Therefore, by F1 and F2, we don't acquire knowledge at birth.

(F4) Eventually, however, we discover that knowledge *does* help to gratify our biological needs.

(F5) Therefore, we start to acquire knowledge—i.e., we develop an ego.

When the argument is put this way, the inconsistency is apparent: F3 entails the negation of F4, so both F4 and ~F4 are consequences of the theory. If we don't acquire knowledge about the world (F3), then we can never find out that knowledge is instrumental in gratifying our biological needs (~F4). Hartmann's claim is that if we function solely in accordance with the pleasure principle at birth then it is not possible for the reality principle to develop. The inevitable conflict with reality can lead only to death.

If Hartmann's interpretation of Freud is correct, it is superfluous to investigate the psychoanalytic theory of ego development by empirical means. The theory can be proved false on logical grounds alone. Once again, proving that a theory is inconsistent does not necessarily mean that we must throw the whole theory away. Perhaps the inconsistency can be repaired by adjustments that preserve much of the theory's structure. Hartmann himself suggested that most of psychoanalytic theory could be preserved if only we were to adopt the hypothesis that the ego is an innate endowment rather than a postnatal development. Other, more conservative psychoanalytic theorists preferred to take the view that Hartmann had misunderstood Freud's theory, and that his argument had merely demolished a straw man (White 1959). The problem here is that the principles of psychoanalysis have never been formalized to a degree that would permit an absolutely unambiguous determination of their logical consequences. In this regard, psychoanalysis is typical of most psychological theories before the advent of AI. Claims about the logical properties of traditional theories of this type are always based on a particular reading of the theory with which other may disagree. This is not a reason to minimize the importance of such logical arguments. Defenders of a traditional theory who are confronted with an inconsistency argument have at least the burden of providing an alternative reading. In any case, the same uncertainty exists with regard to an ambiguous theory's empirical entailments. To the extent that a theory is ambiguous, its proponents can always deflect the force of a purported disconfirmation by reinterpreting its tenets. You do what you can.

Here is a very brief account of another inconsistency argument: According to both the classical British empiricists and contemporary cognitive scientists, we are capable of entertaining various ideas. I may, for example, think of butterflies, whereupon the idea of butterflies appears in my mind. But what is it about this idea—this particular mental object— that makes it an idea of a butterfly and not an idea of a tree? The classical

British empiricist reply is that an idea is a mental image, and that such an image represents what it does by virtue of *resembling* its referent. What makes my idea an idea of a butterfly is that it is an image that looks like a butterfly. This view has been subjected to devastating criticisms for several centuries. One of these criticisms is that the resemblance theory is inconsistent. It claims that when I think of a butterfly I am entertaining an image that is in effect a picture of a butterfly. But a picture of a butterfly is also a picture of an *insect*, of a *living thing*, of a *creature that flies*, of a *beautiful thing*, and of indefinitely more things. Thus, if the resemblance theory is right, my idea of a butterfly is at the same time an idea of an insect, a living thing, a creature that flies, and so on. But this contradicts the fundamental principle that any particular idea in a particular person's mind at a particular time must always have a unique referent.

Just for the record, inconsistencies have been found in sciences much more advanced than psychology. The most famous twentieth-century example is the theory of quantum electrodynamics before the work of Richard Feynman in the late 1940s (Brown 1991, p. 162). It has also been claimed that some of the initial resistance to John Dalton's atomic theory was due to internal inconsistencies in its earliest formulations (Whitt 1990). In general, however, it is my impression that inconsistency claims do not loom large in the history of theoretical science. Nevertheless, it is useful to contemplate the nature of inconsistency arguments in detail, because they demonstrate the essential nature of amplification in a particularly clear and incontrovertible form.

6.3   Intertheoretical Entailment

A much commoner type of amplification is occasioned by the discovery of an unexpected logical relationship *between* two theories. The scenario runs as follows. Theories T1 and T2 are believed to be logically independent and are assigned probabilities p(T1) and p(T2) on the basis of their empirical track record. Then a logical relationship between them is discovered. The principles of the probability calculus (more generally, the requirements of rationality) impose definite constraints on the probabilities that can be ascribed to logically connected propositions. If p(T1) and p(T2) fail to meet these constraints, the demand for coherence dictates that these probabilities be changed. As a result, we are forced to adopt a new opinion about the likelihood that the theories are true. As in the case of an inconsistency proof, this change of probabilities is effected without new empirical work, and its perpetrator need not have any knowledge of the relevant data. In the next four sections, we will consider several sets of circumstances that fit the above description. What differentiates them is the nature of the logical relationship that is discovered to hold between the two theories.

In the case of *intertheoretical entailment*, one discovers that T1 logically implies T2. As we know, it is a theorem of the probability calculus that if any proposition X implies another proposition Y then $p(X)$ must be less than or equal to $p(Y)$: A hypothesis cannot entail something less probable than itself. For example, let T1 be the hypothesis that all emeralds are green and let T2 be the hypothesis, entailed by T1, that all African emeralds are green. Clearly, it is irrational to ascribe greater likelihood to T1 than to T2. Sometimes, however, the entailment of one proposition by another is not immediately obvious; its discovery comes as a surprise. In such a case, we might have assigned a greater probability to T1 than to T2 on the basis of their empirical track records. To be sure, every empirical success for T2 is also an empirical success for T1; however, we might not know that. If, prior to the discovery that T1 entails T2, we were of the opinion that $p(T1) > p(T2)$, then we were simply mistaken. Rationality requires that we change our probability assignments: $p(T1)$ must be decreased, or $p(T2)$ must be raised, or both. The axioms of probability theory do not specify which of these options is to be followed. It is an interesting and unresolved question whether there are general logical principles that dictate the nature of the change in such a case (Kukla 1995b). I suspect that the decision whether to lower the antecedent probability or raise the probability of the consequent is determined largely by how well entrenched our opinions about the two theories are. If a new and relatively untested theory is shown to be entailed by an old, well-tested, highly probable theory, we will likely opt to elevate the probability of the former rather than diminish the probability of the latter. At any rate, we must change one opinion or the other, for our opinions are incoherent as they stand.

An excellent example of an intertheoretical entailment argument occurs in the famous debate between Noam Chomsky and Hilary Putnam concerning the innateness of grammatical knowledge. (This example needs some setting up, but it will subsequently provide us with an instance of yet another type of theoretical strategy.)

The basic Chomskian argument for innateness is well known. Chomsky (1980b) notes that the linguistic data available to first-language learners fall far short of the information needed for a rational reconstruction of the grammar. Yet all neurologically intact children learn their native language anyway. Chomsky's explanation for this remarkable fact is that we are all innately endowed with additional linguistic information. We are able to learn the grammar on the basis of inadequate linguistic data because the missing data are supplied from within. Let us call this the *innateness hypothesis* (IH). Chomsky notes that IH also provides an explanation for the existence of "linguistic universals" (grammatical features that are shared by all natural languages), for if our innate grammatical knowledge is indeed correct then it must be the case that all human languages obey the rules we innately suppose them to obey.

A rival explanation for linguistic universals is the *common-origin hypothesis*, according to which language was invented only once. On this account, all human languages have common features simply by virtue of their common descent. Chomsky (1980b, p. 235) has explicitly repudiated the common-origin hypothesis:

Deep structures seem to be very similar from language to language, and the rules that manipulate them and interpret them also seem to be drawn from a very narrow class of conceivable formal operations. . . . It would be quite impossible to argue that this structure is simply an accidental consequence of 'common descent'.

However, Putnam (1980a, p. 246), in an ingenious argument, has pointed out that IH *entails* the common-origin hypothesis:

Suppose that language-using human beings evolved *independently* in two or more places. Then, if Chomsky were *right*, there should be two or more *types* of human beings descended from the two or more original populations, and normal children of each type should fail to learn the languages spoken by the other types. Since we do not observe this . . . we have to conclude (if the IH is true) that language-using is an evolutionary "leap" that occurred only *once*. But in that case, it is overwhelmingly likely that all human languages are descended from a single original language.

As Putnam reads him, Chomsky wished to ascribe a high probability to IH and a low probability to the common-origin hypothesis. Putnam's argument shows that this position is incoherent. Since IH entails the common-origin hypothesis (CO), we must either accept CO as being at least as likely as IH, or concede that IH is at least as unlikely as CO. It appears that a historical thesis about the origin of language can be established on the basis of an a priori argument that connects it to a theory of language learning. To be sure, Putnam's argument does allude to some empirical data—e.g., that any human child can learn any human language. Strictly speaking, what entails CO is not IH alone but the conjunction of IH with these empirical facts. This conjunction can be regarded in its own right as a more detailed theory, IH'. What is still true is that the perpetrator of the amplification (in this case, Putnam) need not have acquainted himself with the empirical track record of IH, or that of IH', before doing his theoretical work. Putnam need not even have *believed* that any human child can learn any language. His point was that the innateness hypothesis, in conjunction with the empirical claim that any child can learn any language (a claim Chomsky accepts), cannot be regarded as more plausible than the hypothesis of common descent. This is not the end of the Chomsky-Putnam story, however. In chapter 7, we will see that Putnam's amplification is an opening move in a broader theoretical strategy designed to unseat IH altogether.

What happens if $p(T1)$ is already less than $p(T2)$ before it is established that T1 implies T2? The requirement of probabilistic coherence does not dictate any changes in $p(T1)$ or $p(T2)$ in this case. Furthermore, it can be argued that there should not be any changes in $p(T1)$ or $p(T2)$. The fact that a less plausible T1 implies a more plausible T2 should not affect the probability of T2 because *every* theory is implied by an indefinite number of less plausible theories. The proof of the latter claim runs as follows: Consider any theory T2. For the sake of concreteness, think of T2 as Einstein's theory of relativity. Now let T3 be any extremely implausible hypothesis that is independent of T2—say, the hypothesis that every time someone says "Manitoba" somewhere an elf splits cleanly in two. Then the conjunction T2 & T3 is less plausible than T2—it is less likely that both relativity theory and the elf hypothesis are true than that relativity theory alone is true. But T2 & T3 implies T2—if the conjunction of relativity theory and the elf hypothesis is true, then relativity theory alone is true. Thus, we have constructed a theory, T2 & T3, that both implies and is less plausible than T2. Moreover, the method of construction is entirely general: We could stick the elf hypothesis onto *any* independent theory to make a less plausible conjoint hypothesis that entails the theory. It follows that being implied by a less plausible hypothesis cannot be regarded as a special liability of some theories that might warrant a lowering of their probability.

Similarly, the less plausible theory T1, which implies T2, should not be affected by the discovery that T1 implies T2, because every theory implies an indefinite number of more plausible theories. Let T3 be any theory with probability greater than 0 and independent of T1. Then the *disjunction* T1 ∨ T3 is more plausible than T1; but T1 implies T1 ∨ T3. For example, the theory that emeralds are green (T1) implies the more plausible theory that either emeralds are green or snow is white (T1 ∨ T3). Once again, the construction is entirely general: *Every* theory implies hypotheses more plausible than itself. Therefore, implying a more plausible hypothesis cannot be regarded as a special virtue of some theories that might warrant an augmentation of their probability.

In sum, a demonstration that T1 implies T2 alters the probabilities of T1 and of T2 only when $p(T1) > p(T2)$ before the discovery of the implication. However, the discovery that T1 entails T2 *always* has the effect of increasing $p(T1 \& T2)$, the probability that both theories are jointly true. Before the discovery that T1 implies T2, $p(T1 \& T2)$ must have been assigned a value *less* than $p(T1)$, since it is less likely that T1 and something else are both true than that T1 alone is true. But once it is discovered that T1 entails T2, then T1 & T2 must be assigned exactly the *same* probability as T1. (The probability that emeralds are green *and* African emeralds are green is the same as the probability that emeralds are green.) That is to say, $p(T1 \& T2)$ changes from some value less than $p(T1)$ to exactly the same value as $p(T1)$. Thus, the discovery of a new intertheoretical entailment is always an amplification of *some* theoretical claim.

6.4   Intertheoretical Inconsistency

In section 6.2 we considered the consequences of discovering that a theory is internally inconsistent, which means that it entails a contradiction of the form P & ~P. In addition, it might be discovered that *two* theories T1 and T1 are *mutually* inconsistent—i.e., that their *conjunction* entails a contradiction. These two cases should be clearly differentiated. The internal inconsistency of a theory T shows that T must be false. By the same token, the mutual inconsistency of T1 and T2 shows that their conjunction, T1 & T2, must be false. By DeMorgan's Law, it follows that either T1 or T2 is false (or both are false). But the mutual-inconsistency argument itself does not tell us which theory is the culprit. However, as was the case with intertheoretical entailment, the probabilities ascribed to mutually inconsistent theories must obey certain definite restrictions. Let us say that a theory is "plausible" if its probability is greater than 0.5—equivalently, if it is more likely to be true than to be false. Then it can easily be shown that *two mutually inconsistent theories cannot both be plausible*: If we believe that one of them is very likely to be true, we are committed to believing that the other is very *unlikely* to be true. More precisely (and more generally), *the sum of the probabilities of two mutually inconsistent theories must be less than or equal to 1*. Here is the proof: Suppose that T1 and T2 are mutually inconsistent—i.e., that either T1 or T2 must be false. This state of affairs can be represented by saying that T1 entails ~T2 (equivalently, that T2 entails ~T1). But if T1 entails ~T2, then, by the ubiquitous probabilistic principle P4, it follows that $p(T1) \leq p(\sim T2)$. Now, P5 tells us that $p(\sim T2) = 1 - p(T2)$. Thus, $p(T1) \leq 1 - p(T2)$, which is the same as $p(T1) + p(T2) \leq 1$.

Now suppose that, before the discovery that they are mutually inconsistent, it was thought that T1 and T2 were both highly plausible theories. If $p(T1)$ and $p(T2)$ had both been assigned probabilities greater than 0.5, then $p(T1) + p(T2) > 1$, which means that our probability function was incoherent. It is irrational to maintain that two mutually inconsistent theories are both plausible. At least one of them must be reassigned a probability less than or equal to 0.5. Once again, the precise nature of the change in probabilities depends on factors that are not prescribed by the probability calculus.

Laudan (1977, p. 56) has claimed that an inconsistency between two theories must always make *both* of them less credible:

The fact that a particular theory is incompatible with another accepted theory creates a conceptual problem for *both* theories. . . . Intrascientific conceptual problems inevitably raise presumptive doubts about both members of the incompatible pair.

Let us call this *Laudan's rule*. It is demonstrably too strong. Note, to begin with, that it logically implies that when an intertheoretical *entailment* is discovered the antecedent theory must always go down in probability and the consequent theory must always go up. Suppose that T1 entails T2. Then

T1 is inconsistent with ~T2; thus, by Laudan's principle, T1 and ~T2 must both go down in probability; i.e., T1 must go down and T2 must go up. There is a simple argument that shows that this rule about entailment, and hence also Laudan's rule, cannot be universally valid. Suppose we have *three* theories, T1, T2, and T3, which are believed to be logically independent, and suppose it is discovered that T1 implies T2 and that T2 implies T3. Then the principle entailed by Laudan's rule tells us that the probability of T2 must go down (because it entails T3), and that it must go up (because it is entailed by T1). Whatever we decide to do with p(T2), Laudan's rule must be falsified in at least one of its applications.

The same result can also be arrived at, albeit less definitively, by another route. It was argued in the preceding section that there are scenarios in which the discovery that T1 entails T2 should not have any effect on p(T1) or p(T2)—namely, scenarios in which p(T1) ≤ p(T2) right from the start. An entirely similar argument leads to the conclusion that there are scenarios in which the discovery of an intertheoretical inconsistency should not affect that probabilities of the theories involved—namely, scenarios in which p(T1) + p(T2) ≤ 1 right from the start. For given any theory T1, it is easy to contrive indefinitely many theories T2 such that (1) T1 and T2 are mutually inconsistent, and (2) T2 is so extremely implausible that p(T1) + p(T2) ≤ 1. (Thinking up implausible theories is easy; plausible theories tax one's capacities.) If we accept Laudan's rule, we will then have to keep diminishing the probability of every theory ad infinitum, which is absurd. Thus, there are circumstances in which the discovery of a mutual inconsistency has no effect on the theories' individual probabilities. As in the case of an entailment proof, however, the discovery of an intertheoretical inconsistency always changes the probability of *something*. If nothing else, it always diminishes the probability of T1 & T2 (the conjunction of the two theories) to 0.

Needless to say, the amplification due to the discovery of an intertheoretical inconsistency does not require any knowledge of the data. The contradiction may exist only between the *theoretical* principles of T1 and T2, without implicating any observational statements at all. Indeed, two mutually inconsistent theories may have exactly the same observational consequences, so that empirical research is powerless to affect them differentially. For example, let T1 be the usual evolutionary account of the nature of fossils, and let T2 be the theory that God created the Earth just a few thousand years ago, complete with the fossil record of a more ancient past, His purpose being to test our faith.

A famous case of intertheoretical inconsistency took place in the closing decades of the nineteenth century. The theories involved were the theory of evolution and the second law of thermodynamics, both of which were considered highly plausible by the scientific community. In order for evolutionary processes to have enough time to produce the diversity and complexity of existing species, the earth had to be very old. However, Lord Kelvin calculated that if the earth were as old as evolution required it would long ago have lost its internal heat. Thus, it appeared that either one theory or the other had to go. According to Laudan (1977, p. 57), who discusses this episode in detail, "general perplexity abounded." "Thermodynamics, Laudan continues, "had much going for it in physics, but the dominant . . . biological theories also could point to a huge reserve of solved problems. The dilemma was acute: ought one abandon thermodynamics . . . or repudiate evolutionary theory?" As it turned out, a resolution of this inconsistency was discovered. There existed a source of energy with which Lord Kelvin was not acquainted: radioactivity. When the additional heat due to the spontaneous decay of radioactive materials was added to the calculation, the laws of thermodynamics did after all allow enough time for evolutionary processes to have run their course. The important point in the present context, however, is that Lord Kelvin's theoretical analysis required the scientific community to modify its beliefs in some manner. Scientists could not continue to regard both theories as highly plausible just as they stood.

A classical issue of this type in the history of psychology concerns the incompatibility of Cartesian interactionism and the conservation laws of physics. According to Descartes, the human mind is an immaterial substance that enters into causal relations with the material world. In particular, our mental acts can cause our physical bodies to move in various ways. The doctrine of the immateriality of the mind marks Descartes as a *dualist*; the view that mind and body nevertheless enter into causal relations with each other identifies his brand of dualism as *interactionism*. Descartes knew that the assumption that an immaterial mind can cause our bodies to move might conflict with the law of conservation of energy. The latter stipulates that the total quantity of motion in the universe is constant. This effectively rules out the possibility of an increase in motion produced by any means other than a decrease in the motion of a physical object (as when one billiard ball imparts some of its motion to another). Descartes therefore specified that the immaterial mind cannot produce motion out of stillness—it can only alter the direction of pre-existing motion. However, this formulation of interactionism still runs afoul of the law of conservation of momentum, according to which the total quantity of motion in any direction is also constant. Evidently, the conservation laws of physics do not allow for any immaterial causes of material effects. Thus, one cannot ascribe a high probability both to interactionism and to the conservation laws. The choice of history was to abandon the former thesis. Post-Cartesian dualists, beginning with Descartes's disciple Geulincx, were forced to invent alternative hypotheses concerning the relation between mind and body (Russell 1945, p. 561).

6.5   Intertheoretical Complementarity

T1 is *complementary* to T2 if it is logically impossible for both of them to be false. Complementarity is the mirror image of (intertheoretical) inconsistency, which occurs when it is logically impossible for both theories to be true. In the case of inconsistency, T1 entails the negation of T2 (equivalently, T2 entails the negation of T1); in the case of complementarity, the negation of T1 entails T2 (equivalently, the negation of T2 entails T1). In the case of inconsistency, the requirement of probabilistic coherence dictates that $p(T1) + p(T2) \leq 1$; in the case of complementarity, coherence dictates that $p(T1) + p(T2) \geq 1$. (The proof of the latter claim is very similar to the proof of the former and is left as an exercise for the reader.) The main consequence of this probabilistic principle is that complementary theories cannot both be regarded as implausible (i.e., as having a probability less than 0.5).

Suppose that T1 and T2 are found to be complementary, and that both theories were previously thought to be implausible. In that case, the sum of their probabilities was less than 1, and the discovery of their complementarity shows that our probability assignments were incoherent. Once again, we have to revise our views—either one or the other (or both) of the theories must come to be regarded as plausible (i.e., to have a probability of at least 0.5). Once again, the principles of the probability calculus do not tell us how this adjustment must be made in detail. Once again, the discovery of a complementary relation between two theories and the consequent probabilistic adjustment does not require any knowledge of the data relating to the theories. Once again, if the sum of p(T1) and p(T2) was greater than 1 to begin with, then the discovery of an unsuspected complementarity need have no effect on the probabilities of T1 or T2 individually. But once again, there would still be an amplificatory effect elsewhere in the system: The probability of the *disjunction* of the two theories, p(T1 ∨ T2), would have to be raised to 1.

Jerry Fodor has used a strategy based on complementarity to argue for the representational theory of mind. The representational theory makes the claim that mental states such as beliefs have semantic content, i.e., that they represent or refer to events and processes in the world. Thus, the belief that Lima is the capital of Peru refers to a situation that obtains in a certain South American country. This seems to be nothing more than common sense. Indeed, it is clear that common-sense psychology does subscribe to the representational theory of mind. But the nature of the semantic relation between internal mental states and external states of the world turns out to be extraordinarily elusive. When one tries to state precisely how the trick of referring to external events is actually pulled off, one quickly falls into unexpected and as yet unresolved difficulties. Granted that the belief that Lima is the capital of Peru and the belief that 2 + 2 = 4 are both ideas in the head, what characteristic does one of these ideas, but not the other, possess that links it to South America? The fact that one of the beliefs is expressed with "Peru" and other words that refer to South American locations does not help us at all. In the first place, it is not obvious that beliefs must be expressed linguistically in order for us to have them. A pre-verbal infant might not have any opinions about Peru, but might it not believe that milk comes in bottles before it learns the words "milk" and "bottle"? If it can, then what is it about the infant's mental state that makes it be about milk and bottles? More important, the appeal to the semantic properties of language merely pushes the problem from one place to another. Suppose all beliefs were expressed as English sentences. Then we could say that my belief that Lima is the capital of Peru is a belief about South America because the word "Peru" represents a South American country. But the semantic relation between *words* and the world is just as mysterious as the relation between *thoughts* and the world. What is it about the word "Peru" that makes it refer to Peru and not to milk? It is hard to resist the view that what makes "Peru" mean Peru has something to do with human interpretative activity—and then we are back where we started.

Despite these perplexities, Fodor recommends that we adopt the representational theory on the ground that "there aren't any alternatives that are even *remotely* plausible" (1981b, p. 309). His view is that if you have only one theory going in a field, then you should adopt it even though it faces great conceptual or empirical difficulties, because it's the only game in town. The alternative, of course, is not to play at all. But there are circumstances where the probability calculus dictates that it is more rational to play the only game in town than to sit on the sidelines, even though the game may be seriously defective. Let T1 be the "only remotely plausible" theory in some domain (e.g., let it be the representational theory of mind), and let T2 be the disjunction of all the extremely implausible alternatives to T1. Now T1 and T2 are complementary by definition: If the representational theory is false, then one of its alternatives must be true. Fodor's claim is that p(T2) is very low. If this assessment is correct, it follows that we must ascribe a high probability to its complement (the representational theory), despite its shortcomings, because the probabilities of complementary theories must sum at least to 1. Note that, for this argument to work, Fodor needs to claim that it is extremely implausible that anyone will think of a better theory of mind in the future, for T2 will be complementary to T1 only if it represents the infinite disjunction of all logically possible theories of mind. If T2 is merely the disjunction of the alternative that have been formulated to date, it becomes possible for both T1 and T2 to be false, and the argument falls apart.

It should be noted that two hypotheses can be both complementary and mutually inconsistent. This is the case with the representational theory of mind and the disjunction of all its alternatives, and more generally with any hypothesis H and its negation ~H. H and ~H are complementary because at least one of them must be true, and they are mutually inconsistent because at least one of them must be false. P5 tells us that the sum of their probabilities is exactly 1, which satisfies both the requirement that the probabilities of complementary theories be at least 1 and the requirement that the probabilities of inconsistent theories be at most 1.

6.6   Independence Arguments

There are theoretical analyses that establish the *absence* of a logical relation between two theories. Such a result has the effect of decoupling their probabilities. For example, suppose it is thought that T1 entails T2. Given this opinion, we know that it is incoherent to ascribe a lower probability to T1 than to T2. Now, it might be the case that we are strongly committed to theory T1, but that we have reasons for wanting to repudiate T2. So long as it is believed that T1 *entails* T2, however, there is nothing we can do about it—T2 gets a free ride to acceptance on T1's coattails. But suppose that it is now discovered that the argument from T1 to T2 is fallacious—that, in fact, T1 and T2 have *no* logical relation to each other. In that case, we are no longer constrained by the coherence requirement to regard T2 as at least as likely as T1. We can therefore let p(T2) sink to as low a level as we are inclined to assign it.

The most important psychological example of such an operation is the argument of token-identity theorists like Davidson (1970) to the effect that materialism and reductionism are logically independent doctrines. Materialism is the main philosophical alternative to dualism (see section 6.4). According to materialists, physical matter is the only type of substance that exists. The materialist's view of mental states is that they are identical to physical states, presumably states of the nervous system. Until the 1970s it was widely believed that a commitment to a materialist ontology also committed one to the view that psychology can ultimately be reduced to physiology, in the strong sense that the laws of psychology would eventually be derived from neurophysiological principles. (The nature of theoretical reduction will be discussed more fully in chapter 7.) This was not a happy conclusion for most psychologists, since it meant that their science was merely a stopgap enterprise, doomed to obsolescence by the advance of neurophysiology. One sees this resistance to reductionism in even so outspoken a proponent of materialism as Skinner (1974). But if materialism entails reductionism, then the denial of the latter requires us to repudiate the former. Most psychologists, unwilling to abandon materialism, became reluctant reductionists. The arguments of token-identity theorists, however, have established the logical independence of the two doctrines.

In brief, the token-identity argument points out that materialism requires only that every *individual*, or "token," mental event be identical to a physiological event. For example, if materialism is true, then my present belief that 2 + 2 = 4 must be the same thing as my brain's being in a particular physical state. Also, both the belief I had yesterday that 2 + 2 = 4 and your present belief that 2 + 2 = 4 must be identical to brain states. Now, for psychology to be reducible to physiology, we must also be able to translate general psychological *laws* into brain-state language. But psychological laws do not refer to token mental events, such as my present belief that 2 + 2 = 4. They refer to general *classes*, or "types," of mental events such "the belief that 2 + 2 = 4," regardless of who has them or when. A contrived example of such a law might be "The belief that 2 + 2 = 4 causes the belief that 4 = 2 + 2." But the assumption of materialism—that every token mental event is identical to a physical event—is not enough to give us the result that every *type* of mental event is coextensive with a class of physiological events that can be designated by the predicates of physiology. An analogy will help to make this elusive point clear. Let us define a *b-thing* as any material object that, at some time or other in the history of the universe, is designated by an English word that starts with the letter b. Thus, bison are b-things, as are bicycles, bread sticks, and balloons. Obviously, every b-thing is a material object—indeed, its being a material object is part of the very definition of "b-thing." Nevertheless, it would be impossible to reduce the concept "b-thing" to the language of physics: The b-things simply have no physical properties in common.

In the same way, it is logically possible that all the tokens of the belief that 2 + 2 = 4 have no physiological properties in common, even though each token individually is a physiological event. What goes on in my brain when I believe that 2 + 2 = 4 may simply not be the same thing as what goes on in your brain when you believe that 2 + 2 = 4, and so on. If that were to be the case, we would not be able to reduce psychology to physiology even if materialism were true. In sum, materialism does not logically entail reductionism. This means that it is not incoherent to assign a high probability to the former and a low probability to the latter. As soon as this conceptual possibility was made available, it became the theory of choice among cognitive scientists.

6.7   Theoretical Confirmation (Postdiction)

Several important types of amplification are produced by the discovery of a logical relation between a theory and old data. The possibility for this form of amplification stems from the manner in which theories are constructed in the first place. The theoretician selects a set of data as an initial domain D and tries to construct a theory T that has the proper explanatory relationship to D. As was seen in chapter 5, different views have been expressed concerning the nature of this relationship. At the very least, the propositions of T are required to be logically *consistent* with the data in D. Hypothetico-deductivism further requires that the elements of D be *deducible* from T. Whatever the relationship to T is supposed to be, it is clearly impossible for us to check all the data at our disposal to see whether they have it. Thus, there is always a possibility of discovering, some time after the theory has been constructed and subjected to various experimental tests, that there are other old data which were not placed in the initial domain but which have a profound effect on our assessment of the theory's confirmational status.

Suppose, for example, that a theory T and an empirical fact E have both been around for a long time, but that nobody has ever noted any connection between them. Suppose now that it is discovered that T provides a good explanation for E—i.e., that E is "postdicted" from T. If postdiction provides additional confirmation for the implicated theory, then it counts as an instance of amplification. In this scenario, it is true that the theoretician has to know what the data are. But the increase in probability is still not produced by new empirical work. It is effected by a purely logical discovery—in this case, the discovery of a logical connection between T and E.

At first glance, it may appear that postdiction is just like an intertheoretical entailment proof, except that an old datum plays the role of the second, entailed theory. There are profound differences between these two types of amplification, however. To begin with, the relation between the theory and the old datum is the *confirmation* relation, whereas the relation between the two theories is that of *logical entailment*. Except for classical hypothetico-deductivists, these two relations are not the same. And even for hypothetico-deductivists, there are important differences between an amplification due to an intertheoretical entailment and an amplification due to the postdiction of old data. In the former case, the amplificatory effect is dictated by the basic requirement of probabilistic coherence. But the coherence requirement does not force us to elevate the probability of a theory on the ground that it makes a successful postdiction. The probability that the old data are true is already higher than the probability of the theory that postdicts it. Hence, the discovery that the theory entails the data does not put us in an incoherent position. So far as the axioms of probability theory are concerned, we could leave our probability assignments unchanged. If we think that the probability of the theory *should* be increased as a result of a successful postdiction, we must appeal to the principles of a *confirmation theory* that goes beyond probability theory in what it claims. Hypothetico-deductivism goes beyond probability theory when it proclaims that the correct *prediction* of a theory's logical consequences increases the probability of the theory. The question is: Does hypothetico-deductivism want to go further and allow that the correct *postdiction* of logical consequences also has a confirmatory effect?

Bayesian confirmation theory allows that a new empirical discovery can confirm a theory even if it is not a logical consequence of the theory. But what about postdiction? It has often been noted that the apparatus of Bayesian confirmation theory seems to force us to the conclusion that postdiction cannot have a confirmatory effect. According to the Bayesian conditionalization rule, the new probability $p'(T)$ of T can be expressed in terms of the prior probabilities of T and E:

$$p'(T) = \frac{p(T)p(E \mid T)}{p(E)}.$$

Now, if E is an old, known datum, then $p(E) = 1$. Thus, the conditionalization rule gives $p'(T) = p(T)p(E|T)$. But $p(T)p(E|T) = p(T \& E)$ by definition. Thus, we have

$$p'(T) = p(T \& E).$$

Furthermore, if $p(E) = 1$, then $p(T \& E) = p(T)$, for the conjunction of any proposition and a sure thing is just as likely as the proposition itself. Substituting $p(T)$ for $p(T \& E)$ in the last displayed expression for $p'(T)$, we get

$$p'(T) = p(T).$$

That is to say, the new probability of T is just the same as the old! The conditionalization rule seems to tell us that the postdiction of old data should count for nothing.

To recapitulate: The confirmatory effect of a successful postdiction cannot be justified on the basis of probability theory, and it seems actually to be contradicted by the Bayesian conditionalization rule. Should we conclude that postdiction doesn't count? Quite a few psychologists and social scientists have come to this opinion, albeit on quite different grounds. Their view is that postdiction is too easy to count. Their suspicion is that if theoreticians are clever enough, they can always postdict any data from any theory. Significantly, this repudiation of postdiction is not shared by the vast majority of physical scientists, statisticians, and philosophers of science. The fact that Bayesian confirmation theory seems to deny the efficacy of postdiction has overwhelmingly been regarded as a shortcoming of the Bayesian analysis rather than a refutation of postdiction. Some have tried to modify Bayesianism in relatively minor ways so that it allows for the confirmational effect of postdiction (e.g., Garber 1983); others have used the same result as an argument against the whole Bayesian approach (e.g., Glymour 1980). But hardly anyone (among statisticians and philosophers of science) has concluded that correct postdiction doesn't do a theory any good. The historical record in the physical sciences is simply too clear to deny: Postdicted results have again and again been decisive in determining the fate of scientific theories. If we were to deny the potency of postdiction, we would have to revise enormous portions of the history of science, and go against the theoretical judgments of some of the best scientists in history.

One famous example of an important postdiction is Einstein's demonstration that the kinetic-molecular theory of heat could account for the familiar phenomenon of Brownian motion. In 1828, Robert Brown noted that small particles of pollen suspended in water displayed continuous and apparently random movement when viewed through a microscope. Various theories were offered to explain this phenomenon over the years, including that the particles were living beings, that the motion was due to a chemical reaction, and that the phenomenon was an illusion produced by making observations through a microscope. Soon after Brown's discovery, and entirely independent of it, the kinetic-molecular theory of heat was formulated, according to which phenomena relating to heat and temperature were explained in terms of the motions of molecules: The greater the temperature of a substance, the faster the average speed of the molecules composing it. This theory rose steadily in scientific status, but it did not achieve universal acceptance until 1905, when Einstein showed that it provided a detailed account of what was known about Brownian motion. The latter phenomenon, according to Einstein's analysis, is due to the multitude of collisions between the suspended particles and the molecules of the fluid in which they were suspended. The well-known increase in Brownian motion that followed the heating of the fluid was explained by the increased speed of the colliding molecules, and so on. This explanatory success was the last and most decisive step in the kinetic-molecular theory's march toward universal acceptance (Laudan 1977, pp. 19–20). Yet the data on Brownian motion preceded their theoretical explanation by some 80 years. The same time interval separates Einstein's theory of general relativity from the postdicted observational data that are regarded as the best evidence for the theory: the anomalous features of the orbit of Mercury (Lakatos 1978). In sum, there can be no doubt that actual scientific practice allows that a theory can be rendered more credible by a successful postdiction.

I will now discuss two psychological examples of the use of old data. The first does not qualify as an instance of postdiction; but its failure to qualify is instructive.

Elliot Aronson (1958) discovered that the doodles of individuals who were high in the need for achievement were characteristically different from the doodles produced by those who were low in the need for achievement. The phenomenon was so reliable that Aronson was able to develop a scoring system for measuring achievement needs based on the doodling style of the subject. He then found that he could apply the same scoring system with minimal modification to the designs on ancient Greek vases. He selected a standard collection of Greek vases for study, and discovered that the signs of high need for achievement were most frequent on the vases produced during periods of economic growth. Since the relation between the need for achievement and economic activity was already well established, this finding was interpreted as providing additional confirmation for the doodle measure of achievement motivation. Now, there is a sense in which this confirmation comes from "old data": The data concerned events that took place long before Aronson undertook his investigation. But this is not the sense of "old data" that is relevant to the phenomenon of postdiction. What makes a datum postdicted is not that it refers to events that *took place* before the formulation of the relevant hypothesis but that it refers to events that were *known* before the formulation of the hypothesis. In the case of Aronson's study, no one had yet observed that differences in the doodles on Greek vases were related to economic activity. Aronson's hypothesis was that such a relation would be found when the appropriate measurements were made. This is not postdiction but ordinary prediction. It doesn't pose the problem for Bayesian confirmation theory that postdiction does, since the prior probability of the relation between vase designs and economic activity must surely have been less than 1. It may seem odd to speak of predicting events in the past, but this is a superficial conceptual difficulty. What is predicted is not the past event but the future observation of its historical traces.

Now for an example of bona fide postdiction in psychology. According to Festinger's (1957) theory of cognitive dissonance, any perceived incongruity among a person's beliefs, feelings, or actions produces an aversive internal state—cognitive dissonance—which people try to reduce whenever possible. When an expected event fails to materialize, one method of reducing dissonance might be to give up the beliefs that produced the expectation. Sometimes, however, this straightforward means of dissonance reduction produces more dissonance than it eliminates. Consider end-of-the-world cults. These groups have always (so far) had their expectations disconfirmed by the persistence of the world. From the viewpoint of dissonance reduction, however, it can never be a simple matter for cult members to abandon the belief system that led to their apocalyptic expectation. True believers are apt to have made numerous decisions that must appear to be very ill-advised without the sanction of the underlying belief system. Professionals may have quit their job, farmers may have neglected to plant next year's crop, large sums of money may have been squandered or merely given away, and so on. But to recognize one's own actions as foolish is itself dissonance-inducing. A more effective strategy of dissonance reduction would be to hold onto the core of the underlying belief system and to explain the failure of the world to end by an ad hoc hypothesis—e.g., that the original date was based on a technical miscalculation. Moreover, Festinger also claimed that the disagreement of others with one's own opinion is a potent source of dissonance. Thus, trying to persuade others to come over to your side is an effective means of dissonance reduction. As a consequence, when dissonance is increased (as when the world fails to end), the impulse to proselytize would be strengthened—particularly when other avenues of dissonance reduction (e.g., giving up the belief system) are blocked. On the basis of this reasoning, Festinger predicted that the failure of the world to end on the appointed date would *not* result in mass defections from the apocalyptic cult. On the contrary, it should produce a frenzy of proselytizing.

Festinger and his colleagues actually studied a contemporary end-of-the-world cult and correctly predicted that the failure of the world to end would result in increased proselytizing activity (Festinger, Riecken, and Schachter 1956—although the publication date of this study is one year earlier than the 1957 publication of Festinger's theoretical statement, the theoretical ideas contained in the latter were widely circulated before the 1956 study and are referred to in that study). But in addition to the observation of the contemporary cult, Festinger et al. also cite historical accounts of earlier apocalyptic cults who evinced increased proselytizing when their expectation was disconfirmed. One of the best-documented of these concerns the Millerite movement of the nineteenth century. William Miller, a New England farmer, amassed a considerable following for his conclusion that the "Second Advent" of Christ would occur in 1843. The historian of the movement describes what occurred as the target year came to a close (Sears 1924, pp. 140–142):

> Then a fluttering of doubt and hesitation became apparent in certain communities, but soon these were dispelled when it was recalled that as far back as 1839 Prophet Miller had stated on some occasion, which had been forgotten in the general excitement, that he was not *positive* that the event would take place during the *Christian* year from 1843 to 1844, and that he would claim the whole *Jewish* year which would carry the prophecy over to the 21st of March, 1844.
>
> Having accepted this lengthening of the allotted time, the brethren who had assumed the responsibility of sounding the alarm entered into their work with renewed energy and outdid themselves in their efforts to terrify the army of unbelievers into a realization of the horrors that awaited them and to strengthen the faith of those already in the ranks.

When March 21, 1844 came and went, Sears notes (p. 147), attempts to obtain social support increased again:

> . . . in spite of the failure of the prophecy the fires of fanaticism increased. . . . Instead of decreasing, the failure seemed to excite even greater exhibitions of loyalty to the expectation of the impending Judgment Day.

Evidently, the hypothesis derived from dissonance theory is confirmed by this historical account, written a full generation before dissonance theory was conceived. The postdictive effect must be considered rather small, however. For one thing, the historical episodes cited were not independently selected, as they were in Aronson's doodle study. For all that Festinger et al. tell us, there might be as many instances of *decreased* proselytizing among disappointed apocalyptic cults. On the other hand, if the historical episodes had been independently selected, the confirming data would, as in Aronson's study, no longer have been postdicted. It may have been old data that *these particular disappointed cults* increased their level of proselytizing; but it was not an old datum that an independent selection of disappointed cults would show more instances of increased proselytizing than of decreased proselytizing.

Thus, one of my examples of the use of old data fails to qualify as a postdiction, and the other is a very feeble postdiction. Why did I not discuss a better example? Because I couldn't think of one. I expect that I will be flooded with e-mails regaling me with examples of significant postdictions in psychology as soon as these words are published. But even if my lack of a good psychological example were due to their paucity (rather than to a lack of imagination), this state of affairs would in no way cast doubt on the importance of postdiction as a theoretical activity. Rather, it would suggest that psychologists have been under-utilizing a potent theoretical resource.

6.8   Consistency Arguments

There is a type of amplification based on the argument that a datum E is *consistent* with a theory T—i.e., that T does not entail the negation of E. Such a conclusion would raise T's confirmational status if it had been incorrectly believed that E disconfirmed T. The difference between consistency arguments and postdictions is one of degree. In both cases, one has to specify a set of initial conditions and auxiliary hypotheses relative to which the theory entails the datum. The argument is considered to be a postdiction if we are confident that the additional specifications were in fact met. The same argument merely establishes consistency if it is plausible (but not overwhelmingly probable) that the additional specifications might have been met.

A famous example of a consistency argument in psychology can be found in the monumental theoretical battles between Hullian drive theorists (Hull 1943) and Gestalt psychologists in the 1930s and the 1940s. Data showed that when animals were trained to respond to the larger stimulus S2 of two stimuli S1 and S2 and then presented with a choice between S2 and a still larger S3, they chose S3. This "transposition effect" seemed to be a direct disconfirmation of drive theory: Since S2 had previously been reinforced but S3 hadn't, the choice should have been S2 (Wertheimer 1959). However, Kenneth Spence (1936, 1937) showed that a scenario could be constructed that both satisfied the principles of drive theory and led to a transposition effect. Drive theory postulated that, just as reinforcement increases the tendency to perform the reinforced response R, non-reinforcement of R increases an *inhibitory* tendency *against* performing R. This inhibitory tendency manifests itself by subtracting from the positive, or "excitatory," tendency to do R. That is, the *net* tendency to do R was assumed to be proportional to the difference between the excitatory and inhibitory tendencies relative to R. For example, suppose that an organism O performed R1 ten times and was reinforced for it each time, and suppose also that O performed R2 twelve times and was reinforced for it ten times. Then, even though R1 and R2 had been equally reinforced, O would have a greater net tendency to perform R1, since the occasional non-reinforcement of R2 would have produced a certain amount of inhibition against that response. Drive theory also assumed that both the excitatory and inhibitory tendencies *generalize* to similar stimulus situations—the more similar a stimulus S' is to the stimulus S that was displayed when R was previously emitted and reinforced, the stronger the excitatory tendency to emit R when presented with S'. Also, the more similar S' is to the stimulus S under which R was emitted and *failed* to be reinforced, the stronger the inhibitory tendency *not* to do R in the presence of S'.

Spence showed that these assumptions provide drive theory with a way of explaining the transposition effect. Suppose that O is reinforced for responding to S2 and not reinforced for responding to the smaller S1. According to drive theory, the result will be an excitatory gradient, centered on S2, that drops off as one considers both smaller and larger stimuli than S2. There will also be an inhibitory gradient, centered on S1, that drops off as one considers both larger and smaller stimuli than S1. The net tendency to respond to a stimulus of a certain size will be a function of the difference between the excitatory and inhibitory tendencies for that size. There is nothing in the theory that tells us precisely how the excitatory and inhibitory tendencies drop off. But there is also nothing that rules out the possibility illustrated in figure 6.1. Suppose the gradients do have the form shown in this figure. Then, when O is given a choice between S2 (for which it has previously been reinforced) and S3 (for which it has never been reinforced), it will choose the larger S3, because the *difference* between the excitatory and inhibitory gradients happens to be larger for S3 than for S2. That is, O will exhibit the transposition effect.

Spence's analysis is not yet a postdiction of the transposition effect, since no independent reason has been given for supposing that the generalization gradients that obtained in the transposition experiments were of the required form. But Spence's argument does establish that the occurrence of transposition should not *diminish* the plausibility of drive theory. So far as the principles of drive theory are concerned, there is no reason why the transposition effect should not take place.

6.9   Theoretical Disconfirmation

Old data can also be used to disconfirm a theory. Suppose once again that T and E have both been around for a while; but now suppose that an argument is discovered that leads from T to the *negation* of E. In that case, if the theory is sufficiently unambiguous and the initial conditions and auxiliary

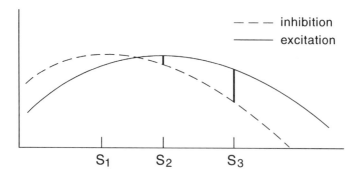

Figure 6.1
The transposition effect.

hypotheses appealed to in the argument are sufficiently plausible, T would have to be regarded as disconfirmed and its probability adjusted accordingly. As in the case of postdiction, the disconfirming effect of old data does not follow from the principles of probability theory or from the Bayesian conditionalization rule. It might seem to be only a matter of applying the logical rule of modus tollens: If T is found to entail E, but E is known to be false, then T is false. But theories entail observational consequences only when they are conjoined with initial conditions and auxiliary hypotheses (see chapter 5). Thus, it is not logically necessary to conclude that the theory is to blame when one of its consequences turns out to be false. The decision to diminish its probability to any degree at all can only be based on confirmation-theoretic principles that go beyond propositional logic, probability theory, and Bayesian conditionalization. Nevertheless, as was the case with postdiction, it is a decision that is almost universally made.

A famous case of theoretical disconfirmation in psychology is to be found in one of several arguments mounted by Fodor (1981b) against Locke's tabula rasa theory of mind. The tabula rasa theory is essentially that all our concepts are learned on the basis of sensory experience. According to this theory, the mind of the newborn infant is a blank slate. Fodor's argument is based on the principle, discussed in chapter 5 above, that there are always infinitely many theories that account for any finite set of data. As applied to the concept-learning situation, this principle tells us that there are infinitely many different concepts that will fit any finite set of instances and non-instances. For example, having ten cats pointed out to us as instances of the concept "cat" doesn't rule out the possibility that the concept being learned refers to both cats and furniture. Having a few tables pointed out to us as non-cats rules out that particular possibility. But the data at our disposal are still consistent with the hypothesis that the concept to be learned is "cats or furniture other than tables." It should be clear that any finite collection of instances and non-instances is going to be compatible with indefinitely many concepts. Naturally, concept learners never have more than a finite number of instances and non-instances upon which to base their choice of concept. Thus, if they have no innate predispositions to choose one concept over another, their choice from the set of infinitely many concepts that fit the data must be random. But if we all choose a concept at random from an infinite set, the chance that two of us end up choosing the same concept, or even a closely similar concept, is effectively 0. This means that a child could never learn the conceptual scheme of the older generation, no matter how many instances and non-instances of the concepts he or she had to work with. Thus, the tabula rasa theory is disconfirmed by the obvious fact that children do learn the concepts of their elders.

The "old data" appealed to in the foregoing argument are worthy of note. No one has ever done an experiment designed to show that children learn the concepts of their elders. But there is no reason why theoretical confirmations or disconfirmations should be restricted to experimental data. "Anecdotal" evidence can also lead to far-reaching theoretical conclusions. Even entirely casual and unconstrained observation may be enough to establish certain kinds of *existential* propositions. For instance, we can taken it as given that there are pencils, that automobiles have license plates, and that people sometimes wear coats, even though we would search in vain through the annals of experimental science to find such results. Existential claims of this type are so obvious that no one has ever bothered to write them down, much less to establish them systematically. But this does not disqualify them for use in scientific arguments. If a theory is shown to entail that there is no such thing as pencils, or that coats do no exist, then its confirmational status must be drastically reduced: "It is often quite familiar facts which, in the first instance, constrain one's models of the mental life." (Fodor 1975, p. 28)

We are in possession of innumerable data that as yet have no place in any systematic and explicit theory. In principle, it is possible for a theory to obtain an enormously high confirmational status simply by postdicting a large and diverse array of "familiar facts." In principle, we could do productive scientific work forever without ever having to do any empirical research. The passage by Boden quoted in chapter 5 shows that many AI researchers think that we already have data enough to keep us busy for quite a while. Substitute "theories" for "programs" and "explain" for "do" in this passage and the result is a general call for a hiatus in empirical research. This argument against doing any more empirical research is inconclusive, for a choice between two theories may very well require us to settle an unresolved question of fact upon which the theories disagree. The vast collection of data already at our disposal may simply not be relevant here. The history of science would be incomprehensible if this were not so, for humanity has always possessed empirical information that systematic science could not yet explain. Nevertheless, it is undoubtedly the case that a pro-*experimental* bias, as distinct from a more general pro-*empirical* bias, has hindered psychology from fully exploiting the theoretical value of famil- iar facts—as though a fact were tainted by not issuing from an official lab. It is true that we should not *routinely* try to publish our laundry bills and grocery lists, but the day may come when someone's grocery list will settle a momentous theoretical dispute.

7

Theoretical Simplification

Considerations of simplicity have played an enormously important role in the history of science. The switch from Ptolemaic to Copernican astronomy was initially based almost entirely on the argument that the latter system provided a simpler account of observational data. In psychology, simplicity accounts for the attraction of S-R theory, which tried to explain all behavior in terms of two concepts (stimulus and response) and two laws (classical and instrumental conditioning). Simplicity is also the basis for the standard argument against dualism: Materialism makes do with one kind of substance in the universe, whereas dualism posits the existence of two kinds of substance.

We will soon see that the term "simplicity" has been used in a number of disparate senses. However, all the varieties of simplicity share the following negative characteristic: The simplicity of a theory T is unaffected by the properties of T^*, the set of T's observational consequences. The empirical import of a theory is one thing; its simplicity is another. Indeed, in elucidating the several types of simplicity, it will generally be convenient to assume that the theories under discussion have identical observational consequences. Let us define the *simplification* of a theory T1 as the construction of a theory T2 that is simpler than T1 but has the same observational consequences ($T2^* = T1^*$). Naturally, there are as many types of simplification as there are varieties of simplicity.

The principle that we should prefer the simpler of two theories (ceteris paribus) commands almost universal assent among scientists in all disciplines and all historical eras. Here is a representative statement by a psychologist (Wertheimer 1962, p. 156):

The principle of parsimony asserts that an explanation or method should be as simple as possible. The smaller the number of concepts and principles in a theory, the more parsimonious it is, and the more satisfactory is it generally considered to be; if two theories account equally well for some set of phenomena, the one which does so with fewer assumptions, that is, the one which is more parsimonious, is generally considered the preferable one.

In this passage, the author tries to define what simplicity is: "The smaller the number of concepts and principles in a theory, the more parsimonious it is." We shall scrutinize this definition shortly. But first there is another issue to grapple with. Wertheimer tells us that the more parsimonious a theory is the "more satisfactory" it is, and that more parsimonious theories are "generally considered to be preferable." Now, the rationality of a preference can only be assessed relative to a *purpose*. Which is preferable, a banana or a stone? The banana is preferable if you are looking for something to eat, but not if you are looking for a doorstop. Whether simple theories are preferable to complex theories must also depend on what we are looking for in the way of theories. This point was made in chapter 4 in regard to theory evaluation. If we are looking for something to *believe*, then we must ask whether simple theories are likelier to be true. But there are other things that can be done with theories besides believing them. For one thing, we can use a theory to calculate empirical predictions without necessarily believing that the theory is true. All we must believe is that the result of such a calculation will be the same as the one given by the true theory. For example, the principles of Newtonian mechanics are believed to be false by contemporary physicists. Yet, because the calculations are easier, Newtonian physics continues to be used for making predictions in circumstances where it gives the same answer as the theories currently believed to be true. If we are looking for a theory that enables us to make calculations as quickly and as painlessly as possible, then the question whether simple theories are preferable may require us to investigate an entirely different set of issues. We cannot assume beforehand that criteria relevant to these two types of preference must coincide.

The fact that there are various purposes for which we might select a theory, as well as several types of simplicity, means that the status of the "principle of parsimony" cannot be settled in one fell swoop. We must divide the claim into cases and consider each case separately.

7.1 Theoretical Preference

It was noted in chapter 4 that theoretical virtues may be classified as derivative or intrinsic. To say that a virtue is *derivative* is to say that our preference for that particular characteristic can or should be justified on the basis that it is conducive to another theoretical virtue. To say that the virtue is *intrinsic* is to say that we value it for its own sake. Most scientists regard truth as an intrinsic virtue. If we were to ask them why theories should be true, they would have nothing to say.

What about simplicity? Some writers regard it as a derivative virtue; others treat it as an intrinsic virtue. Roger Rosenkrantz is an example of the former category. According to Rosenkrantz (1977), simpler theories are to be preferred because they are likelier to be true. Paul Thagard (1988) and Michael Wertheimer (1962) belong to the latter category. Consider the following passage (Wertheimer 1962, p. 157):

> . . . in an overall general comparative evaluation of . . . two theories [parsimony] would . . . be only one dimension along which to compare the two formulations; many other dimensions, such as the scope of the phenomena encompassed by the theory, the efficiency with which the theory accounts for and can predict various events, its ability to generate interesting new experiments, how well the theory fits the facts, and so on, would also be taken into consideration.

Wertheimer does not state in so many words that simplicity (or "parsimony") is to be regarded as an intrinsic virtue. But there is no mention of anything that simplicity will buy for us. Rather, simplicity is "one dimension" among others that determine the overall standing of a theory. What are we to say about such an intrinsic preference? At this point, it is important to remember that the rationality of a preference can only be assessed relative to a purpose. If my purpose is to construct theories that are as simple as possible, then my subsequent theoretical activities are rational to the extent that they further this aim. To be sure, the value of my undertaking could itself be challenged on some other basis. But so might the value of knowledge itself. Perhaps we should all be working to feed the hungry and heal the sick instead of trying to discover the truth. However, frivolity is not the same sin as irrationality. There is nothing to stop me from counting simplicity as an intrinsic virtue if I so desire. But, as was mentioned in chapter 4, there is equally nothing to stop me from preferring complex theories, or funny ones, or theories that are offensive to the bourgeoisie. In the passage quoted above, Wertheimer does not explicitly tell us that simplicity is being treated as an intrinsic basis for theory selection. As a result, the reader tends to presume that the purpose of the selection is for *believing in*. But relative to *this* purpose, simplicity is no longer a value that we are free to posit.

In fact, if we were trying to decide which theory to believe, it would be *irrational* to prefer the simpler of two theories that have identical probabilities, because to say that the theories are equiprobable *is* to say that they have the same rational claims to being believed.

As long as we are clear about what we are doing, it seems a perfectly acceptable employment of theoretical talent to try to simplify theories for the sake of simplification. The impulse to do so would presumably be aesthetic. I see no reason why our aesthetic impulses ought not to be exercised in the matter of theory construction, as in all other departments of life. Indeed, many scientists—particularly twentieth-century physicists—have suggested that their theoretical simplifications were motivated largely by the desire to beautify existing theories (Dirac 1963). But it is curious that the aesthetic tastes of theorists so often run to simplicity. After all, delight in simplicity is not an aesthetic universal in other domains of life. It is a feature of the classical sensibility, along with the taste for Doric architecture and Haydn quartets. One cannot help wondering why there are no rococo theorists, who would prefer the intricacies of epicycles within epicycles to the stark austerity of the circle. And where are the romantic theorists who revel in the rich tapestry of a scientific theory riddled with exceptions? Perhaps they couldn't get tenure in a system captured by fanatical classicists. I suspect, however, that the overwhelming emphasis on the aesthetics of simplicity is due to the belief that simplicity is an indication of other theoretical virtues. There are two major candidates for such a virtue: utility, and truth.

By "utility" I mean the ease with which a theory can be used to make predictions. We will see below that certain types of simplicity make for greater utility in this sense. In such a case, it is certainly a sensible policy to *use* the simplest available theory in our calculations. But, as the philosopher Bas van Fraassen (1980) has pointed out, the decision to use a theory is not the same as the decision to believe that it is true. Indeed, we often use theories that are believed to be false (e.g., Newtonian physics) because we know that, in a given context, they will supply us with the same answer as the true (but more complex) theory. The main focus of this chapter, however, will be on the question whether the simplicity of a theory gives us grounds for believing it to be true. This is not to claim that truth is more important than beauty, or utility, or funniness, or offensiveness to the bourgeoisie. These are all commendable goals. But truth is what the historical game of science happens to be about.

Let us now turn to a consideration of the several varieties of simplicity. In each case, the task is to describe what is meant by this type of simplicity and to figure out what (if any) theoretical purposes it may serve.

7.2 Syntactic Simplicity

In trying to clarify what we mean by "simplicity," our first impulse is probably to try to formulate a *syntactic* criterion. According to such a criterion, the Copernican theory is simpler than the Ptolemaic because of the *forms of expression* that are used in stating the theories: Copernican circular orbits can be described very succinctly, whereas Ptolemaic epicycles require a much longer and more intricate description. It seems obvious that syntactic simplicity makes a theory more beautiful (in the classical sense). It also seems plausible that syntactically simpler theories are easier to use. And it has often been suggested—particularly by twentieth-century physicists— that the syntactic form of a theory can also be evidence of its truth, in the spirit of Keats: "'Beauty is truth, truth beauty'—that is all / ye know on earth, and all ye need to know" ("Ode on a Grecian Urn").

Before assessing such claims, one must state the criterion whereby one theory is judged to be syntactically simpler than another. Wertheimer takes a stab at it in the first passage quoted above. He says that the simpler theory is the one with the smaller number of concepts and principles. But this will not do. We cannot consider the number of principles contained in a theory to be a measure of its simplicity because any finite set of principles P1, P2, . . . , Pn can always be written as a single *conjunctive* principle P1 & P2 & . . . & Pn. Conversely, it is always possible to divide a single principle into two. For example, the principle "All cats are neurotic" can be represented as the pair of principles "All male cats are neurotic" and "All female cats are neurotic." Thus, the fact that S-R theory is *conventionally* described in terms of two principles does not yet make it simpler than psychoanalysis. If there is to be any hope for a syntactic criterion, it will have to be a criterion for assessing the relative simplicity of *single sentences*.

An example of such a criterion would be sentence length: Theory T1 is simpler than T2 if the single sentence expressing T1 has fewer symbols than the single sentence expressing T2. This particular criterion is very unlikely to capture our intuitions about simplicity, since it does not take into account complexities of sentence structure. But it is an instructive example to consider, for one of the reasons it fails is so general that it applies to any and all criteria for sentential simplicity. Can we say that S-R theory is simpler than psychoanalysis because the sentence expressing the former is shorter than the sentence expressing the latter? One problem with this suggestion is that there are infinitely many sentences that are logically equivalent to any given sentence. A conjunction P & Q can also be expressed as ~[~P ∨ ~Q], or as P & Q & [R ∨ ~R], and so on. Thus, we would have to take the *shortest* expression of S-R theory as a measure of that theory's simplicity. But any expression can be shortened by the simple device of introducing a new definition into the system. For example, we could define the predicate "Freudish" as "X is Freudish just in case X has all the properties attributed to people by psychoanalytic theory." Then the whole of psychoanalytic theory can be succinctly expressed as "Everyone is Freudish." What could be simpler than that? In fact, by introducing predicates like "Freudish" for other scientific theories we can put them all in syntactically equivalent and maximally simple form (barring a few technicalities about quantifiers). Einstein's theory of relativity is just "The universe is Einsteinian," the theory of evolution becomes "Life is Darwinian," and so on.

What if we forbid the use of defined expressions and insist on measuring the simplicity of theories in primitive notation? The problem here is that there is no unique manner of selecting the primitives of a system. In classical physics, for example, the primitive concepts are traditionally taken to be length, mass, and time. Other concepts such as speed, acceleration, force, and work are then defined in terms of these concepts. But it is well known that other choices of primitives will do the job just as well. We could take mass, time, and *speed* as primitive, and define length as the product of the speed of a particle and the time during which it travels at that speed. The same point can also be illustrated by means of Goodman's "grue" construction (see chapter 4). Consider once again the following candidates for a scientific law:

(1) Emeralds are green.

(2) Emeralds are grue.

We have already seen that these two principles fit the known data equally well. Why do we prefer (1)? We are tempted to say that (1) is a better theory because it is a *simpler* way to account for the data. We are not yet ready to assess the validity of this claim. First we must understand what the claim means. Why do we suppose that (1) is simpler than (2)? Presumably because we think that (2) "really" says (3).

(3) Emeralds are green if discovered before the year 2100, and blue otherwise.

And *this* expression is undoubtedly more complex than (1)—in fact it *contains* (1) as a proper part. To think about the issue in this way is to suppose that "green" is intrinsically more suitable than "grue" as a primitive. But what basis do we have for supposing this? To be sure, "grue" can be defined in terms of "green" and "blue." But "green" can just as readily be defined in terms of "grue" and "bleen," where "bleen" is synonymous with "blue if discovered before the year 2100, and green otherwise." The definition would look like (4).

(4) X is *green* if and only if X is discovered before the year 2100 and found to be grue, or X is discovered in 2100 or later and found to be bleen.

The concept "blue" can be defined in the same manner:

(5) X is *blue* if and only if X is discovered before the year 2100 and found to be bleen, or X is discovered in 2100 or later and found to be grue.

In term of *these* definitions, the deceptively simple law (1) actually proves to be an abbreviation for the much longer and more complex principle (6).

(6) Emeralds are grue if discovered before the year 2100, and bleen otherwise.

The claim that (1) is simpler than (2) cannot be based on the syntactic properties of these sentences, for all syntactically based arguments in favor of (1) have symmetric counterparts that favor (2).

In sum, syntactic simplicity is an incoherent notion. There is therefore no point inquiring whether syntactically simpler theories are more likely to be true. If we equate the beauty of a theory with any of its formal properties, then we must recognize that one and the same theory can be expressed either beautifully or hideously. Therefore, Keats was mistaken: ~(Beauty = Truth). But there are other notions of simplicity to consider.

7.3   Rc-Simplicity

By *R-simplicity* I mean syntactic simplicity *relative to a specified language*. It is stipulated that different choices for the primitives and different sequences of definitions constitute different languages, even if the total sets of concepts are the same. Thus, the language in which "green" and "blue" are defined in terms of "grue" and "bleen" is not the same as the language in which "grue" and "bleen" are defined in terms of "green" and "blue." Undoubtedly, "grue" and "bleen" are defined in terms of "green" and "blue" in all the dialects and idiolects of English that have ever existed. Thus, it is safe to say that "Emeralds are green" is R-simpler than "Emeralds are grue" *in English*. It must be understood, however, that even this relativized judgment is not being deduced from any general algorithmic specification of R-simplicity. There is no known rule that enables us to determine which of two expressions is syntactically simpler, even if the question is relativized to a particular language. It is possible, however, to give partial rules for R-simplicity that will command universal assent. For example, sentence S1 will be R-simpler than S2 if S1 is literally a proper *piece* of S2, as when S2 is the conjunction of S1 and another sentence.

Is R-simplicity a desirable feature for theories to have? Put this way, the question is meaningless, like the question whether standing 10 feet from the origin is a good place to be. In the latter case, we must specify which coordinate system we are using; in the former, we must specify a language. If there is some language L that is uniquely suited for doing science, then of course we will be primarily interested in the properties of R-simplicity relative to L. We will consider the possibility of singling out such a language in the next two sections. But first let us briefly look at the properties of *Rc-simplicity*, which is defined as R-simplicity relative to the *current* language of science. This notion is, of course, an idealization, for we employ many different languages at once in the conduct of science. But it will serve for present purposes.

What is there to be said about the desirability of Rc-simplicity? We could, of course, treat Rc-simplicity as an intrinsic desideratum: When shopping for theories, some look for a high probability of truth, but we look for Rc-simplicity. Once again, I see no reason to gainsay such an artistic enterprise, so long as it is understood that the quest for Rc-*complexity* is on the same footing (except, of course, for the fact that Rc-simplifying a theory can be a challenge, whereas its Rc-complexification is always trivial). Does Rc-simplicity buy us anything else? It is a reasonable empirical hypothesis that Rc-simpler theories have greater utility. We will return to this point in the next section. The most important question for us is whether there is a connection between Rc-simplicity and truth. If there is such a connection, it can only be because there is something special about the primitive concepts and definitions that constitute the current language. Thus, we are returned once again to the question whether some languages are more special than others.

7.4   Rm-Simplicity

Are some concepts more suited to being taken as primitives than others? One way to make sense of such a notion is to relate it to the "language-of-thought" hypothesis of contemporary cognitive science (Fodor 1975). According to this view, we are born with a number of innate concepts that enable us to think even before we learn our first public language. Indeed, learning our first language is a matter of learning to associate various verbal expressions with our prelinguistic "Mentalese" concepts. If this hypothesis is correct, then we would expect that concepts that map directly into Mentalese would strike us as simpler than those that require a long definition in Mentalese. This type of simplicity is essentially R-simplicity relative to the language of Mentalese. Let us call it *Rm-simplicity*. If we make the reasonable assumption that our public languages are similar in structure to Mentalese, it follows that Rm-simplicity is roughly coextensive with Rc-simplicity.

Generally speaking, one would expect that Rm-simpler theories—hence also Rc-simpler theories—are going to be easier to learn and to deploy. The question whether one formulation or another *is* Rm-simpler, however, can only be settled by empirical research into the structure of Mentalese. For example, empirical evidence shows that preverbal infants, like the rest of us, find it more difficult to learn disjunctive contingencies of reinforcement than conjunctive contingencies (Fodor, Garrett, and Brill 1975). This finding suggests that P & Q may be directly represented in Mentalese, whereas P $\vee$ Q has to be represented by something like ~(~P & ~Q). If this inference is correct, it follows that P & Q is Rm-simpler than P ∨ Q. If two theories have identical empirical consequences in a certain domain, it is clearly a sensible policy to use the Rm-simpler one for calculating predictions. But we have already seen that the decision to use a theory in this way does not necessarily commit us to believing that it is true.

Is there any reason to believe that Rm-simpler theories are likelier to be true? An evolutionary argument to that effect derives its inspiration from C. S. Peirce (1901). According to Quine and Ullian (1970, p. 211), for instance, natural selection

offers a causal connection between subjective simplicity and objective truth. . . . Innate subjective standards of simplicity that make people prefer some hypotheses to others will have survival value insofar as they favor successful prediction. Those who predict best are likeliest to survive and reproduce their kind . . . and so their innate standards of simplicity are handed down.

Now, one problem with this argument, at least in its fully general form, is that it is simply not borne out by the history of science. It is not the case that the theories of physics that we currently believe to be true are the ones an uninstructed person would tend to think of first. On the contrary, Newtonian physics seems much more "natural" to our way of thinking than quantum mechanics, and Aristotelian physics is Rm-simpler still. Nozick (1993) has described another problem with Quine and Ullian's argument: Subjective standards of simplicity suited to making theoretical choices in cosmology, subatomic physics, and molecular biology would have conferred no evolutionary advantage to our ancestors. (Nowadays, of course, they would lead to an increased probability of obtaining a university degree.) The most we could possibly claim is that our judgments of simplicity are a good bet when it comes to selecting hypotheses about medium-size phenomena that have to be dealt with in the pursuit of food, safety, and sex.

Now, it happens that psychology is a science that deals with one of the most important types of medium-size objects about which it is evolutionarily advantageous to have a correct theory: people. Thus, other things being equal, it seem like a good bet that the closer a psychological theory is to the "folk psychology" of common sense, the likelier it is to be true. Fodor (1988) has developed this point into an argument for the prima facie plausibility of cognitive psychology as compared to, say, S-R theory. The former is very similar to folk psychology; the latter is extremely dissimilar to folk psychology. But, by the evolutionary argument, folk psychology is quite likely innate and often correct. Therefore, cognitive psychology is often correct. This is, of course, a rather weak and indirect form of support at best. But there are a number of problems with even this vestige of the evolutionary argument. To begin with, the evolutionary argument cannot be regarded as lending support to cognitive psychology, because that argument *presupposes* the truth of cognitive psychology. By claiming that there are evolutionary pressures inclining us toward the adoption of certain hypotheses, we already buy into the view that people adopt hypotheses—that is we already buy into the paradigm of cognitive psychology. More generally, the mechanism of natural selection could only incline us toward *empirically adequate* theories. So long as the theory made correct empirical predictions, there would be no evolutionary advantage to getting the *theoretical* principles right too. In fact, it might turn out to be more advantageous to believe in a *false* theory that yielded correct empirical consequences but also provided us with a comforting, anxiety-reducing myth.

None of these criticisms of the evolutionary argument get to the heart of the matter, however. The real problem is one that we have encountered before in our discussions of theory selection (chapter 4). To begin with, there are always infinitely many hypotheses that are fully supported by any finite assemblage of data. Now, at any moment in evolutionary history, the collective experience of humankind can be thought of as an enormous but finite assemblage of data. Thus, there are infinitely many theories that fit those collective data to perfection. For example, if the collective experience of humanity supports the hypotheses that green berries are poisonous, then it also supports the hypothesis that *grue* berries are poisonous. At a specific moment, any member of this infinitude of theories will have been equally advantageous for survival in the past. Yet the adoption of infinitely many of them would lead to death in the future—perhaps even in the very next moment. For example, individuals who are wired up to believe that grue berries are poisonous will have done all right so far; but they will start to get in serious trouble in the year 2100. The point is that there is nothing in the evolutionary argument that would account for why hypotheses about green things might be "subjectively simpler" than hypotheses about grue things. Both concepts would have served us equally well in the struggle for survival, and will continue to do so until the year 2100. In sum, there is a huge gap in the evolutionary argument: It fails to show how natural selection can actually forge the postulated connection between simplicity and truth, even in the case of medium-size objects.

Whatever its shortcomings may be as a guide to the truth, it is almost certainly the case that Rm-simplicity is a guide to utility. It would be a feasible and worthwhile theoretical project to devise "calculating" versions of theories whose sole virtue is that they give us the same answers as the most probable theories in a less tedious way. Such a project would require the cooperative efforts of experimentalists and theorists. The experimentalists would discover what properties of theories make them easy to use by organisms such as we happen to be. The theorists would then formulate theories that have those properties.

7.5 Metaphysical Simplicity

We have established that syntactic simplicity can only be assessed relative to a language. Thus, "green" is syntactically simpler than "grue" in English—indeed, in every natural human language that has ever existed. But it is easy to devise artificial languages wherein "grue" is simpler than "green." For all we know, Martians may actually speak such a language. Having granted this much, however, it is still open to us to maintain that the property of greenness is *objectively* simpler than the property of grueness, regardless of the syntactic forms used to express these properties. Let us call this notion *metaphysical simplicity*.

Metaphysical simplicity is conceived to be an independent characteristic of entities, properties, and processes in the universe. If greenness is metaphysically simpler than grueness, then it would be simpler even if there were no minds to pass such a judgment. Consider again hypotheses (1) (Emeralds are green) and (2) (Emeralds are grue.) Why might we be tempted to say that (1) is a simpler preposition than (2) regardless of how it may be expressed? Well, at first blush it appears that (2) posits a *change* in the universe: As of January 1, 2100, emeralds will be found to have a different color than they had previously been found to have. Principle (1), however, posits an unbroken continuation of the status quo. Thus, a universe that follows law (2) is an objectively more complex place than one that follows (1). There are a number of difficulties with this view. For one thing, it is not clear why the *persistence* of a quality should be considered a simpler state of affairs than a change. Furthermore, by parity of reasoning, we could as well say that it is law (1) that posits a change in the year 2100. According to (1), emeralds will change from grue to bleen on January 1, 2100! Our problem is to justify the claim that greenness is metaphysically simpler than grueness. The attempted solution in terms of change fails because it begs the question.

At this point, one might make the observation that the eternal grueness of emeralds would entail a change in the way they look *to us*, whereas their eternal greenness would entail that they continue to look the same. But such an observation cannot establish the greater *metaphysical* simplicity of greenness, because it refers to the operating characteristics of the human mind. For another creature, it may be eternal grueness that is perceived as changeless. For instance, suppose that intelligent creatures evolve on a planet that circles two suns, one green and one blue. Suppose also that, as a result of the planet's orbit about its suns, many of the objects important to these creatures' survival are periodically green and then blue. In that case, it might prove evolutionarily advantageous for their sensory transducers to output a "no change" message when (according to us) objects change from green to blue at a certain time, and to signal the presence of a change if they remain green when they should have become blue. In sum, perceived change cannot be a criterion for metaphysical simplicity.

So far as I know, there are no other candidates for criteria of metaphysical simplicity. At this juncture, one could concede that there are no explicit criteria but maintain that our intuitions of simplicity are sufficient to get us by. After all, we have already seen that the game of science involves a number of judgments that (so far) can only be made on an intuitive basis. Even if we accept this appeal to intuition, however, there still remains the problem of justifying our preference for theories that are metaphysically simpler. Assume that principle (1) is metaphysically simpler than principle (2). Does this assertion justify our assigning a higher probability to (1)? Salmon (1966, p. 126) has suggested that such a preference may be warranted on inductive grounds: "We judge the simple hypothesis more likely to be true. We have learned by experience that this works. . . ." The next phrase in this passage, however, is "and at the same time we have learned by experience to avoid oversimplification." Unfortunately, this proviso undermines the inductive argument completely: If some theories are too complicated to be true and some are too simple to be true, then we do not have an inductive basis for preferring the simpler of two theories.

In fact nobody knows how to justify a preference for the metaphysically simpler of two theories, just as nobody knows how to discern which of two theories is metaphysically simpler in the first place. The situation looks grim. But it must be recalled that we face precisely the same state of affairs in regard to induction itself. Hume's argument showed that we cannot justify our preference for inductively supported hypotheses, and Goodman's "grue" argument showed that we do not even know how we *decide* which hypothesis is inductively supported by a given body of evidence. In the case of induction, we "resolve" Goodman's problem by relying on our intuition, and we "resolve" Hume's problem by giving uncritical assent to the Principle of Uniformity. Thus, we would not be committing any new types of epistemic sins if we (1) relied on our intuition to decide which of two theories is metaphysically simpler, and (2) gave uncritical assent to a *Principle of Simplicity*, according to which metaphysically simpler theories are likelier to be correct. This is how many scientists have in fact operated.

There is a close conceptual connection between the problems of simplicity and the problems of induction. Indeed, if we could solve the problems of simplicity, then we would automatically have solutions to the corresponding problems of induction. Suppose that we have an objective manner of deciding which of two hypotheses is (metaphysically) simpler, and that we are permitted to infer that the simpler one is likelier to be true. Now, what are we to make of the observed fact that all previously observed emeralds have been green? There are infinitely many hypotheses that can account for this finding, including "All emeralds are green," "All emeralds are grue," and "All previously observed emeralds have been green, but the others come in different colors." With an effective Principle of Simplicity in hand, however, we can quickly pick out a favored hypothesis. First, given that two hypotheses have the same structure, the one referring to metaphysically simpler properties is more likely to be true. Hence, if greenness really is metaphysically simpler than grueness, the Principle of Simplicity directs us to assign a higher probability to "All emeralds are green" than to "All emeralds are grue." This resolves Goodman's problem. Second, the Principle of Simplicity tells us that, of two hypotheses that refer to equally simple properties, the one with the simpler structure is likelier to be true.

Hence, "All emeralds are green" is more probable than "All previously observed emeralds have been green, but the others come in different colors." This polishes off Hume's problem.

Is it also true that a solution to the problems of induction provides us with a solution to the problems of simplicity? If it were, then the two problems would have turned out to be equivalent. I do not think they are equivalent, however, for there are judgments that can be made on the basis of the Principle of Simplicity and which seem to elude the grasp of the Principle of Uniformity. For example, consider the hypothesis that the laws of nature (expressed in metaphysically simple terms) will undergo a single discontinuous change at time t. The Principle of Simplicity would lead us to favor this hypothesis over the hypothesis that the laws of nature will undergo *twelve* discontinuous changes at t1, t2, . . . , t12. But both hypotheses fall outside the scope of the Principle of Uniformity, which claims that the unobserved portions of the universe follow the same laws as the observed portions. In sum, the Principle of Simplicity is a *generalization* of the Principle of Uniformity.

Let me summarize this section with reference to a concrete question of psychological theory: Is S-R theory metaphysically simpler than psychoanalysis? Intuition tells us that it is. Furthermore, most psychologists would agree that if the two theories had identical empirical consequences (which, of course, they do not) we should ascribe a higher probability to S-R theory on the basis of its greater simplicity alone. But our judgment that S-R theory is simpler is not based on any explicit criterion of simplicity, and there are no non-question-begging arguments that support the ascription of a higher probability to the metaphysically simpler theory. Shall we therefore repudiate this assessment of the relative status of S-R theory and psychoanalysis? The problem with taking the purist's course here is that it makes our tolerance for inductive arguments, which are equally based on a combination of intuition and faith, look very arbitrary. I will have more to say about this in the last chapter.

7.6   Epistemic Simplicity

I have proceeded thus far by delineating various conceptions of simplicity and asking what each one is good for. There is a great deal to be said for reversing this procedure and asking what properties we *want* our theories to have and then discovering what sorts of theoretical changes will produce the desired effect. For instance, we could set out to construct theories that are empirically equivalent to our current theories but are easier to calculate with. Or we could try to produce empirically equivalent theories that have a higher probability of being true. Since we are particularly interested in the latter type of theoretical task, we will need a name for it. Let us call it *epistemic simplification.*

Epistemic simplification is a very different affair from Rc-simplification, Rm-simplification, or metaphysical simplification. For one thing, the question of justifying our greater credence in epistemically simpler theories does not even arise. Epistemically simpler theories are more credible *by definition.* The reason for introducing such a concept is as follows: If what we want is high probability (or whatever), then why bother to expend time and effort in formulating a concept of simplicity and then inquiring into whether this variety of simplicity gives us what we want? Why not eliminate the middle step? If a particular theoretical change can be shown to produce the desired effect, we need not know whether it also qualifies as simple on the basis of some independent criterion. Indeed, why don't we just call any such change a simplification and be done with it?

Perhaps it will turn out that the class of epistemic simplifications includes all members of another type of simplification. To establish such a result, we would have to show that every instance of the second type produces an increase in probability without altering the original theory's empirical consequences. For instance, the Principle of Simplicity discussed in the preceding section asserts that every metaphysical simplification is an epistemic simplification. It may turn out, however, that the class of epistemic simplifications cuts across the other types of simplifications, including some members of each and excluding others. The important point is that we need not settle such issues before engaging in epistemic simplification. So long as we can show that a particular theoretical change increases probability without altering empirical consequences, we know that an improvement has been made, regardless of what the relation may be between this change and the classical varieties of simplicity. Unless otherwise indicated, the terms "simplicity" and "simplification," used without any qualifiers, should from now on be understood to refer to epistemic simplicity and epistemic simplification.

In sum, to *simplify* a theory T is to construct a modified theory T' such that (1) $p(T') > p(T)$ and (2) $(T')^* = T^*$. That is to say, the simplification of

T is more probable than T, even though it has all the same empirical consequences. Because the empirical consequences of the new theory are the same as those of the old, empirical research is once again irrelevant to the process: Our preference for one theory over the other cannot hinge on the outcome of empirical research, since any empirical result would have the same confirmatory or disconfirmatory effect on both theories. Furthermore, it is not necessary for the theoretician to know what the data relating to T are, for it can be established that T and T' have the same empirical consequences without knowing which of these consequences have been tested, a fortiori which of them have been confirmed.

A straightforward case of simplification is the strategy of *conjunct deletion*. Suppose that the basic principles of theory T are P1, P2, . . . , Pn, and that these principles are all probabilistically independent. Suppose now that it is discovered that P1, P2, . . . , Pn – 1 alone entail all of T*—i.e., that the empirical consequences of the full theory T can all be derived from the weaker theory T', which is obtained from T by deleting Pn. In effect, the discovery is that the postulate Pn is not doing any empirical work. Now the probability that T is true is given by

$$p(T) = p(P1)p(P2) \cdots p(Pn).$$

The probability of T' is

$$p(T') = p(P1)p(P2) \cdots p(Pn{-}1) = \frac{p(T)}{p(Pn)}.$$

Since Pn is a contingent scientific hypothesis, it must have a probability less than 1. Therefore $p(T') > p(T)$. Since both theories have the same empirical consequences, a switch from T to T' is clearly desirable: T' explains just as much as T, but it is more likely to be true.

Strictly speaking, simplification may be regarded as a variety of new-theory construction, since the process results in a theory T' which is not identical to the theory T that we started with. However, when we think of "new theories," we generally have in mind theories that have different (and, we hope, more correct) empirical consequences than their predecessors. The arbiter between new and old theory in this case is, largely, empirical research. But there are also theoretical innovations that aim at providing a better theoretical account of the *same* empirical consequences as the old theory. Such a case is different enough from the ordinary sort of theory construction to warrant a special name. Why call it simplification? Well, conjunct deletion looks to be a sort of syntactic simplification. But this is an accidental feature of a particular case. In fact, any conjunct deletion can as well be represented as a *disjunct addition*. Consider, for example, the theoretical move from a theory that asserts the conjunction P1 & P2 to one that asserts only P1. This change can be described as a deletion of P2 from P1 & P2, which makes it appear to be a syntactic simplification. But the same change can also be described as an addition of the disjunct P1 & ~P2 to P1 & P2, for (P1 & P2) ∨ (P1 & ~P2) is logically equivalent to P1. Thus, both syntactic shortenings and syntactic lengthenings may qualify as (epistemic) simplifications. The term "simplification" seems suitable for this type of theoretical analysis because it connotes a change in the structure of a theory that does not affect its empirical consequences.

A psychological example of conjunct deletion is to be found in the argument for materialism alluded to at the beginning of this chapter: Dualism posits both the existence of matter and the existence of mind, whereas materialism deletes the second of these two conjuncts. Therefore materialism is more likely to be true. There is a catch to this argument, however: We must distinguish two varieties of materialism. The thesis that states only that matter exists will be called *weak* materialism. This thesis is indeed obtained from the dualist thesis by deleting a conjunct, and it is therefore more probably true than dualism. But as we have defined it, weak materialism is not a thesis that is in *conflict* with dualism. In fact, dualists *are* weak materialists: They believe that matter exists, which is all that is required for being a weak materialist. The thesis that conflicts with dualism is the *strong* materialist thesis: that matter exists *and that mind doesn't exist*. But this strong materialist hypothesis cannot be obtained from the dualist hypothesis simply by deletion. The principles of probability theory give us no reason to suppose that strong materialism is more probable than dualism. In sum, weak materialism is not in contention between dualists and materialism, whereas strong materialism, which does contend with dualism, is not a conjunct deletion of dualism.

A comparison between simplification and amplification is instructive. Each involves a change in the probabilities of the theories we have at hand. In amplification, we change our opinion about how probable a theory T is; however, T itself remains unchanged. In simplification, we change the theory so that its probability becomes higher. Amplification is a logical *discovery* about the old theory T. Simplification is a logical *invention* of a new theory T'. In the case of amplification, we are just as interested in discoveries that force us to diminish p(T) as in those that make us augment it. In the case of simplification, however, we are interested only in augmentations. There is no point inventing a theory that is less probable than the one at hand. Even if (for some perverse reason) one were to think that such an undertaking might be of interest, its accomplishment would be trivial. Given any theory T, we can always obtain a theory that is empirically equivalent to T but less probable than T by the expedient of conjoining to it a proposition devoid of new empirical consequences.

If we were to accept the Principle of Simplicity, we would immediately obtain the result that every metaphysical simplification is also an epistemic simplification. But the claim that conjunct deletion is a simplification does not depend on the prior acceptance of any obscure or debatable principles. It follows directly from the axioms of probability theory. Of course conjunct deletion is a narrower principle than the Simplicity of Nature—it does not even warrant capitalization. But it provides a justification for many important theoretical moves in the history of science. For example, the S-R theorist Edwin Guthrie (1952) devoted most of his professional life to trying to effect a single conjunct deletion. Traditional S-R theory posits two principles for explaining behavioral change: the laws of classical and instrumental conditioning. Guthrie argued that the behavioral phenomena for which instrumental conditioning was invoked could as well be explained on the basis of classical conditioning, and hence that the former law was superfluous. Unfortunately, Guthrie's claim could not be sustained. But if he had been right, then the substitution of a one-law S-R theory for the traditional two-law theory would not have been a merely cosmetic improvement. The one-law theory would have been *more probable*, since the two-law theory requires us to assume everything that the one-law theory assumes and more.

7.7 Two Types of Simplification

The strategy of conjunct deletion is a special case of a broader category that involves the substitution of a logically weaker theory for its empirically equivalent predecessor. To say that T2 is logically weaker than T1 is to say

(1) that T1 logically implies T2 and (2) that T2 does not imply T1. The principles of probability theory stipulate that in such a case p(T2) must be strictly greater than p(T1).

The debate between Chomsky and Putnam discussed in chapter 6 provides us with a clear example of this strategy. Recall that Putnam had argued that Chomsky's innateness hypothesis (IH) entails the common-origin hypothesis (CO). Therefore one cannot ascribe a high probability to the former without granting that the latter is at least as probable. In fact, since CO does not reciprocally entail IH, it must be the case that CO is *more* probable than IH. This much is an amplification. But Putnam (1980a, p. 247) continues the argument by noting that CO alone is sufficient to explain the existence of linguistic universals: ". . . this hypothesis—a single origin for human language—is certainly *required* by the IH, but much weaker than the IH. But just this *consequence* of the IH is, in fact, enough to account for 'linguistic universals'!" Putnam concludes that CO ought to be preferred to IH, since it is more probable than IH yet it explains the same empirical facts (the existence of linguistic universals). In other words, Putnam argues that CO is a simplification of IH. This analysis serves admirably as an example of a putative simplification. In the end, however, it does not succeed. Chomsky (1981b, p. 302) writes:

Let me then turn to Putnam's . . . argument, that even if there were surprising linguistic universals, they could be accounted for on a simpler hypothesis than that of an innate universal grammar, namely, the hypothesis of common origin of languages. This proposal misrepresents the problem at issue. . . . The empirical problem we face is to devise a hypothesis about initial structure rich enough to account for the fact that a specific grammar is acquired, under given conditions of access to data. To this problem, the matter of common origin of language is quite irrelevant. The grammar has to be discovered by the child on the basis of data available to him, through the use of the innate capacities with which he is endowed. . . . [The child] knows nothing about the origin of language and could not make use of such information if he had it.

Recast in terms of the major themes of this book, Chomsky's theoretical defense of IH goes as follows: To be sure, both IH and CO provide explanations for the existence of linguistic universals. But IH also explains how children manage to learn their first language on the basis of inadequate linguistic data. The common-origin hypothesis is of no help in this regard. It is undeniably true, as Putnam claims, that CO must be ascribed a higher probability than IH. But the latter theory has a much broader explanatory scope. This may be a reason to adopt IH even though CO is more probably true.

Scientific arguments that appeal to Ockham's Razor seem often to be instances of the same type of probabilistically justifiable simplification. Ockham's Razor (named after the medieval philosopher William of Ockham) is a frequently cited principle in scientific debates. It tells us not to multiply theoretical entities beyond necessity: If a scientific theory T posits the existence of nine kinds of entities and an empirically equivalent theory T' posits the existence of only eight of these types, then we should adopt T' and make do without the ninth. Why should we accept Ockham's Razor? Here is a probabilistic justification. Suppose that theory T posits the existence of a theoretical entity E, and that we can obtain all the empirical consequences of T without invoking the assumption that E exists. In that case, we can rewrite T as the conjunction

E exists and T',

where T' is the theory that asserts everything that T does *except* that E exists. By hypothesis, T' has exactly the same empirical consequences as T. Yet it is more probable than T, since it is obtained from T by deleting a conjunct. Therefore T' is a simplification of T. It is commonly believed that applications of Ockham's Razor depend on an appeal to the Principle of Simplicity whose problematic status we have already noted. The probabilistic argument given here is designed to show that one may judiciously wield the Razor without getting entangled in metaphysical hypotheses about the simplicity of the universe. All one needs is probability theory.

A second unproblematic type of simplification is the invention of a theory that has the same empirical consequences as its predecessor but that simply strikes the scientific community as more plausible than its predecessor. If Bayesian confirmation theory is correct, subjective assessments of prior probabilities are in any case unavoidable in the scientific enterprise. Whether or not one is a Bayesian, one can hardly deny that coming up with a theory that is prima facie more plausible is a progressive theoretical step, even if the new theory does not generate any new empirical consequences. If we did try to deny this, then we would have no grounds for dismissing the infinitude of utterly implausible theories that can be invented to explain any set of empirical consequences. Of course, rational individuals may disagree about prior probabilities; that is the essence of the Bayesian analysis.

It follows that rational individuals may disagree as to whether a putative simplification really does succeed in simplifying. But the existence of problematic cases does not affect the status of central cases: The construction of a new theory T' that has the same empirical consequences as an old theory T but which the vast majority of researchers agree is more plausible than T must be regarded as a scientific advance.

7.8   The Structure of Theoretical Reduction

The above catalog of amplifications and simplifications is by no means exhaustive. I expect that a careful historical analysis of theoretical controversies would reveal that theoreticians deploy extremely intricate and variegated argumentative strategies in promoting their views and attacking those of their rivals. In principle, there is no upper bound to the complexity of the logical considerations that can be brought to bear on a theoretical issue. The historically important strategy of *theoretical reduction* provides an example of a maneuver that has a more convoluted structure than any we have yet discussed.

A number of quite different relations between theories have been described as reductions. The prototypical example is the reduction of the theory of heat to the kinetic-molecular theory of matter. In this classical type of reduction, the theoretical concepts of one theory (e.g., "temperature") are equated with certain concepts of the other theory (e.g., "mean kinetic energy"). These equations are known as *bridge laws* (Nagel 1961). The principles of the first theory are then derived from the principles of the second together with the bridge laws. In psychology, the most famous reductive claim is the *central-state identity theory*, according to which the laws of psychology can be derived from the laws of physiology together with bridge laws connecting each psychological event type to a physiological event type (Smart 1959). Consider any would-be law of psychology, say (7):

(7) If X wants S and X believes he can succeed in obtaining S, then X tries to obtain S.

According to the central-state identity hypothesis, we can render this law superfluous by deriving it from a physiological principle like (8).

(8) If X is in physiological state P1 and also in physiological state P2, then X enters into physiological state P3.

Of course it is inconceivable that the psychological law (7) can be derived from a physiological principle like (8) without any further ado, since psychological concepts like "wants," "believes," and "tries" simply do not make an appearance in pure laws of physiology. One could try the gambit of claiming that "wants" can be *defined* in physiological terms. This move would be akin to the logical behaviorists' attempts to define psychological concepts in behavioral terms. But such a semantic claim is even more implausible in relation to the language of neural events than it is in relation to behavioral language. The fact is that we do not *know* what the physiological equivalent of a desire or a belief may be. Thus, the thesis of semantic identity in this case leads to the absurd conclusion that we do not know whether we have a particular desire or belief. In fact, it leads to the even more preposterous consequence that we don't even know what it *means* to say that we have a belief. However, it is open for the neurally inclined to maintain that there is a *contingent* identity between mental states and brain states (Place 1956; Smart 1959). A desire is not a particular physiological state by *definition*, but it is some particular physiological state *as a matter of fact*. One has to discover which mental states are identical to which brain states, just as it has been discovered that lightning is identical to an electrical discharge, or that water is identical to H_2O. Thus, the reduction of (7) to (8) is effected by adding the following contingent identities to the physiological theory:

(9)
wanting S = being in physiological state P1
believing one can obtain S = being in physiological state P2
trying to obtain S = being in physiological state P3.

The identities listed in (9) are the bridge laws involved in the reduction of (7) to (8).

There is an enormous difference between the thesis of central-state identity and some of the more famous reductive claims in the physical sciences, such as the reduction of the theory of heat. The difference is that the latter reduction was actually carried out, whereas the former is sheer conjecture. Central-state theorists are betting that the psychological laws of the future will prove to be reducible to the physiology of the future. Since we do not yet know what the future laws of psychology and of physiology will be, one wonders where this conjecture comes from. The only basis for it seems to be the belief that a successful reduction is ensured by the tenets of materialism. But we have seen that this belief is itself unwarranted.

Successful reductions are routinely regarded as major theoretical accomplishments. It is not immediately obvious why this should be so, however. The attempt to reduce T2 to T1 is not primarily motivated by the desire to explain more empirical data. What, then, is reduction for? Why do scientists get excited about reductive claims? Reduction seems to be undertaken in a spirit of simplification: If we can reduce T2 to T1, then we can get as much explanatory mileage out of T1 alone as we could out of the conjunction of T1 and T2. At first glance, this seems to be a straightforward case of conjunct deletion. However, what is substituted for T1 & T2 is not T1 tout court but the conjunction T1 & B, where B represents the bridge laws that coordinate the theoretical concepts of the two theories. Now, there can be no blanket assurance that T1 & B is more probable than T1 & T2. Indeed, we might be able to reduce one theory to another—say, classical economics to auto mechanics—by means of an utterly implausible set of bridge laws that equate money with gasoline, banks with fuel tanks, and so forth. It thus appears that, in order for a theoretical reduction of T2 to T1 to constitute a scientific advance, the conjunction T1 & B must be more plausible than T1 & T2. But in a successful reduction, T1 & B *entails* T1 & T2. Recall that if a proposition X entails another proposition Y then $p(X)$ can be at most as great as $p(Y)$. Thus, the condition that T1 & B be more plausible than T1 & T2 is a requirement that our probability function be incoherent! I think this is exactly right. Reduction is a two-stage theoretical strategy. First one finds a set of bridge laws B such that (1) T1 & B has a greater prior probability than T1 & T2 and (2) T1 & B entails T1 & T2. Therefore, T1 & B is a *simplification* of T1 & T2. The simplification is short-lived, however, for as soon as an appropriate B is found our probability function becomes incoherent: If T1 & B entails T1 & T2, we cannot allow that T1 & B is more plausible than T1 & T2. Thus, if our high opinion of B is relatively fixed, the only way to restore coherence is to elevate the probability of T1 & T2 until it is at least as large as the probability of T1 & B. That is to say, the simplification is immediately followed by an amplification. As a result of this second step, T1 & B is no longer a simplification of T1 & T2, because it is no longer more probable than T1 & T2. But the reduction has had the net effect of boosting the probability of the conjunction T1 & T2. This is, I think, the bottom line in theoretical reduction: The reduction of T2 to T1 makes the theories involved jointly more plausible. The fact that the theory of heat could be reduced to the kinetic-molecular theory gave us reason to be more confident of the truth of *both* theories. And if the fantasies of central-state theorists should ever come to pass, the same would be true of the laws of psychology and the laws of physiology that were involved in the reduction.

7.9   Theoretical Unification

Theoretical unification is a process whereby two disparate theories, T2 and T3, are replaced by a single theory, T1. A famous case in the recent history of science is the unification of the theory of electromagnetism (which was itself a unification of two previously disparate theories) and the theory of the weak nuclear force into a single "electroweak" theory. The topics of unification and reduction have engendered different literatures in the history and philosophy of science. However, they are merely two different ways of looking at the same phenomenon. The unification of T2 and T3 by T1 is nothing more or less than a reduction of T2 and T3 to T1. Whether we regard the process as a reduction or as a unification seems to depend on how well entrenched the theories are in the science of the day. When T1 is a brand-new theory (as it is when it is specifically devised for the purpose of generating T2 and T3), we say that T1 unifies T2 and T3. When T1 is already well established, however, we say that T2 and T3 are reduced to T1. Just as in the case of reduction, we cannot assume that every unifying theory is automatically an improvement over the conjunction of the theories that are unified.

Psychologists have often decried the absence of unifying theories in their science. The following laments are characteristic of a persistent malaise that cuts across diverse theoretical orientations:

The present scene in psychology is . . . one of fragmentation and chaotic diversity. (Maher 1985, p. 17)

Certainly, the continued fragmentation of the field can only support the view of our field as pre-scientific. (MacIntyre 1985, p. 20)

Arthur Staats has expanded on this theme in a series of articles and books (the most important of which are Staats 1983 and 1991). His remedy for

the ailment of disunity is "unified positivism," which is (at least in part) the
enterprise of trying to construct a unified theory that brings the radically
disparate principles of psychology under a single explanatory scheme. As
noted above, it is far from obvious that any and all theoretical unifications
are epistemically desirable. But I will not prosecute this point against Staats.
For the sake of the argument, I assume that theoretical unification is a major
scientific desideratum. However, I wish to express some reservations about
the strategy for achieving unification that Staats calls "unified positivism."
Staats seems to assume that the acceptance of unification as a scientific goal
automatically entails the acceptance of unified positivism. In any case, he
devotes most of his discursive efforts to extolling the merits of unification,
and he has very little to say in defense of unified positivism per se. But the
latter is one theoretical strategy among many for achieving unified theories. My main criticism of Staats's position is that he does not give us good
reasons for supposing that the indicated strategy has any special merit.

The strategy of unified positivism, as Staats describes it, stipulates that we
begin with an existing body of information, such as the heterogeneous principles of psychology, and that we try to find unifying principles that sub-
sume the entire body. Some passages in Staats's writings suggest that the
existence of such unifying principles is logically ensured, like the existence
of a solution to a quadratic equation, the only question being one of difficulty. Consider the following (Staats 1991, p. 901):

> . . . the number of knowledge elements in psychology is astronomically greater than
> the knowledge elements that existed for Newton; and that means that the diffi-
> culty of solving the "puzzle" of unification, of putting the pieces together, is much,
> much greater.

At other times, Staats comes close to acknowledging that there is no a priori guarantee that a solution to the "puzzle" exists. So is there or is there
not a guarantee that a unified theory exists? The answer depends on the
constraints we place on what counts as a unifying theory. Let K1, K2, . . . ,
Kn be any set of disparate "knowledge elements." If the only constraint on
the unifying theory is that it be a proposition that entails all the Ki, then
unification of all the Ki is ensured. In fact, there are demonstrably infinitely
many unifications available. Consider any proposition of the form K1 & K2
& . . . & Kn & X, where X is any other hypothesis that is consistent with
K1 & K2 & . . . & Kn. This proposition entails each of the Ki and there-

fore satisfies the one and only constraint on unifying theories. The lesson to be learned is, of course, not that unification is easy; it is that unification must satisfy additional constraints before it can be counted as a scientific advance. In line with my analysis of theoretical reduction, I suggest that a unification T1 of two theories T2 and T3 is scientifically progressive if (1) T1 entails T2 & T3 *and* (2) T1 is initially more plausible than T2 & T3. The rest of my remarks about unified positivism do not depend on the adoption of this constraint, however. They presume only that Staats and I would generally agree about whether a given unification is progressive. I assume, for example, that Staats would not consider theories of the form K1 & K2 & . . . & Kn & X to be progressive unifications of the Ki.

When we restrict our attention to progressive unifications, there is no guarantee that any particular body of information can be unified. In an arbitrary collection of "knowledge elements," there may or may not exist a unified set of plausible theoretical principles that subsumes the entire collection. It depends on how the world is. For example, consider the empirical lore belonging to the ill-advised science of *bology*, which studies the properties of things that begin with the letter "b." There is no shortage of empirical work for bologists. They can ascertain whether bison are benevolent, whether barium is denser than barley water, and so on. But no one would seriously propose that we apply the philosophy of unified positivism to this domain. The theoretically progressive step in this instance would be to dissolve the discipline of bology and to reapportion its empirical results to other sciences. This theoretical step could very well be taken by scientists who are committed to the goal of unification. Indeed, it could be the right step to take even if it is true that all the data in the world can be subsumed by a nested set of interrelated and unified theories. The problem may simply be that the particular body of data being dealt with is a gerrymandered collection of items that are more at home in other intellectual districts.

The example of bology shows us that an arbitrary assemblage of data need not be amenable to (progressive) unification, *even if the unification of science as a whole is an achievable goal.* Thus, Staats must convince us of more than the desirability of unification. He also must tell us why we should try to unify the data of psychology in particular. After all, Staats himself tells us that these data were collected haphazardly, without concern for how they bear on any theoretical issues. Might it not then be the case that this assemblage turns out to be akin to the data of bology? This was, in fact, the opinion expressed by Sigmund Koch (1981), whom Staats cites. However, beyond stating that it makes strange bedfellows, Staats does not tell us why Koch's view should be repudiated.

The only part of Staats's analysis that sounds like an argument in favor of unified positivism (as opposed to the goal of unification) is the historical part. According to Staats, sciences are characteristically disunified in their early stages, and they characteristically progress by the discovery of unifying principles. Therefore, by a kind of induction, it is reasonable to suppose that the same thing will happen to psychology if only we devote sufficient resources to the task. And therefore we should become unified positivists. This argument makes the mistake of looking only at the currently unified sciences and noting that all of them were once disunified. It is true that 100 percent of *these* sciences were successfully unified (as compared to the extreme fragmentation of psychology). But the sample we are looking at excludes the sciences that underwent a different theoretical development right from the start. If bology had existed, for instance, its data would have been dispersed rather than unified. I cannot think of any real scientific field that was so completely heterogeneous as bology. But there have been countless fields that underwent a beneficial theoretical development other than that stipulated by unified positivism. Astrology is one example. Astrology included data on the positions of the planets and on human behavior. The aim was to find deep principles that unified this domain. Most scientists came to believe that such principles do not exist. The traditional subject matter of astrology was never unified. Rather, its data were divided neatly in two and reapportioned to the two separate sciences of observational astronomy and psychology.

The unification of a predetermined body of data, its dispersion (as in the case of bology), and its bifurcation (as in astrology) are only three of indefinitely many theoretical strategies that may profitably be pursued by scientists who are committed to the unification of science. Let us look at one additional strategy. Consider once again the kinetic-molecular theory. This was one of the great unifying theories in the history of science. It brought under a single explanatory scheme such diverse items as Brownian motion (section 6.7) and the phenomena of heat (section 7.8). But this unification did not follow the recipe of unified positivism. In fact, a unified-positivistic enterprise had to be abandoned before it could take place. The body of data that went under the heading of "heat" included many items that were eventually explained by the kinetic-molecular theory, such as the ideal-gas laws and the phenomenon of thermal equilibrium. However, it also included items about which the kinetic-molecular theory had nothing to say, such as the distinction between hot and cold. Before the kinetic-molecular theory, many scientists believed, like good unified positivists, that an adequate theory of heat should explain both the ideal-gas laws and the distinction between hot and cold. Progress came only with the abandonment of that goal. In this case, the strategy that was conducive to unification was to delimit a subset of phenomena and to unify them with other phenomena that were originally not even in the same domain of discourse (e.g., Brownian motion). Theoretical progress could not have come until one was willing to ignore a substantial amount of the data in the original collection. A doctrinaire unified positivist who was bent on "examining all of the phenomena" in the original set (Staats 1991, p. 905), insisting that "unified positivism does not accept unconsidered exclusions" (p. 908), would only have obstructed the proceedings.

In sum, the lesson of history is not that we should try to find unifying principles for predetermined bodies of data. The lesson is that theoretical improvement, including improvement in the dimension of unification, is achieved by diverse theoretical strategies. The strategy Staats recommends is certainly one of them. But there is no reason to suppose that it is a particularly promising approach to the problems of psychology. Rather than pre-committing ourselves to the unification of psychology, we should simply do the best theoretical work we can and let the chips fall where they may. My guess is that what currently passes for psychology will prove to be quite a bit like bology, except that it may contain two or three coherent clumps that have scientific value.

8

Necessary Propositions

There are portions of every theory whose truth can be established by non-empirical means because they deal with logical necessities. The classic textbook example of a logically necessary truth is "Bachelors are unmarried." An example with a more psychological flavor is "The reinforcer of a response R does not terminate before the onset of R." Such *necessary* propositions are to be distinguished from *contingent* prepositions such as "The average bachelor weighs 160 pounds" or "Extinction takes longer after partial reinforcement than after continuous reinforcement." Recall that contingent propositions are true in some possible worlds and false in some possible worlds. This is why we must look at the actual world to see whether a particular contingency is satisfied therein. But necessary propositions are either true in all possible worlds or false in all possible worlds. Thus, it is generally unnecessary to observe the actual world in determining their truth value. In cases where their truth or falsehood is not evident from inspection, the issue can often be settled by the a priori methods of proof and refutation.

There are two theoretical tasks relating to necessary prepositions. The first is to distinguish necessary from contingent prepositions in scientific discourse. To do this is to establish the *modal status* of our claims. The second is to discover brand-new necessary truths.

8.1 Distinguishing Necessary from Contingent Prepositions

To be mistaken about the modal status of a statement is not yet to have any incorrect beliefs about the (actual) world. But it is a mistake nonetheless. Furthermore, there are other problems that characteristically ensue from such an error: One is led to the use of inappropriate methods of investigation, and in some instances to the adoption of false beliefs about the world.

There are three ways of making a mistake about modal status.

First, one may employ the same sentence ambiguously to express both a necessary proposition and a contingent proposition. Bradley and Swartz (1979) call these "Janus-faced sentences." Consider, for instance, the sentence "Everyone acts selfishly all the time." If "selfish behavior" is defined so that it includes behavior performed for any motive whatsoever (it is "selfish" because it's *our* motive that actuates the behavior—we are always doing what, all things considered, *we* want to do), then the sentence expresses a necessarily true but uninteresting proposition. But it is easy to fall into the error of supposing that the trivial proof of the uninteresting necessary proposition establishes the truth of an interesting contingent one: that some logically possible motives (the "unselfish ones") never actually occur among humans (though they may occur among Martians). In this case, failing to clarify the modal status of our claims results in a false belief about the world. The remedy for such a confusion is an analytic procedure that Bradley and Swartz (ibid., p. 114) call *possible-world testing*: "We confront the utterer of a given ambiguous sentence with the descriptions of various sets of possible worlds and ask the utterer to say in which sets, if any, the proposition he or she is asserting is true and in which sets, if any it is false." Thus, if someone claims that everyone acts selfishly all the time and we are unsure of the modal status of the claim, we can ask the claimant to describe what it would be like for someone to act unselfishly. If there is no possible form of behavior that would qualify, the conclusion is that "Everyone acts selfishly all the time" is true in all possible worlds. It is a confusion of the first order to suppose that such a result makes our hypothesis about the world all the more secure. Rather, it shows that our claim was not a hypothesis about the world in the first place.

The second type of error relating to modal status is to mistake a necessary proposition for a contingent one. In rationalistic eras, ignorance of the distinction led some to treat every claim in a manner suitable only to necessary propositions. In our empiricist era, however, the same ignorance manifests itself in the treatment of every claim as though it were contingent:

It is supposed that every proposition must be confirmed by empirical means. This particular mistake does not of itself lead to the formation of false beliefs about the world. If we try to confirm a necessarily true proposition by empirical means, we may very well succeed. If we test the hypothesis that bachelors are unmarried by doing a survey, the data will undoubtedly yield a gratifyingly high level of statistical significance. Things work out nicely like this because a proposition that is true in every possible world is also true in the actual world, and a proposition that is false in every possible world is also false in the actual world. Indeed there are circumstances where it is legitimate and useful to try to establish the truth value of a necessary proposition by empirical means. This happens when the a priori proof of the truth or falsehood of the necessary proposition eludes us. The problem of the seven bridges of Königsberg (discussed in chapter 1) provides an example. The townspeople of Königsberg knew by empirical trial and error that there was no way to cross all seven of their bridges without crossing any bridge twice. But it is certainly a mistake to suppose that necessary prepositions should *routinely* be confirmed by empirical means. Such a supposition, it is true, may not cause us to adopt any false beliefs about the world. But, in addition to being a misapprehension in its own right, it will cause us to waste time and effort in useless empirical investigations.

Does this problem ever arise in psychology? Jan Smedslund (1984) claimed that *all* psychological laws are logically necessary, and that all attempts to confirm them are superfluous. No doubt Smedslund overstates his case (Vollmer 1984). But it is certainly true that *some* necessary propositions have been put forward in the guise of contingent claims about the world. For instance, consider the law of effect, which may be expressed as follows: When a response is followed by reinforcement, the probability of its recurrence increases. "Reinforcement" in turn has sometimes been defined (see e.g. Skinner 1953) as an event that produces an increment in the probability of a preceding response. But if that is what we mean by reinforcement, then the law of effect merely states the following logically necessary (and trivial) truth: When a response is followed by an event that produces an increment in the probability of a preceding response, the probability of its recurrence increases. To be sure, this isn't the whole story about the law of effect. It is a simplified version of a complex theoretical issue, devised to make a pedagogic point. Paul Meehl's (1950) famous discussion of the problem, in which he strives to disentangle the necessary from the contingent elements in the law of effect, is a paradigm of the first of our two type of theoretical tasks relating to necessary prepositions: distinguishing them from contingent propositions. Meehl concludes that the contingent claim implicit in the law of effect is the proposition that there *are* events that increase the probability of any preceding response of which the organism is capable—in brief, that reinforcers exist.

Along the same lines, Jochen Brandtstädter (1987) has presented an illuminating collection of redundant empirical investigations of necessary truths in social psychology. Representative of these is a study of the determinants of pity, anger, and guilt by Weiner, Graham, and Chandler (1982). Weiner et al. related these three emotional states to a three-dimensional taxonomy of perceived causality, according to which the cause of an event is seen as residing within or outside of the agent (locus), as temporary or relatively enduring (stability), and as subject or not subject to volitional influence (controllability). Their hypotheses were the following (ibid., p. 227):

One feels pity for others who are in need of aid or in a negative state due to uncontrollable conditions.

Anger is experienced given an attribution for a personally relevant negative outcome to factors controllable by others. . . .

Guilt is suffered when one has brought about a negative consequence for a personally controllable cause.

In one study, subjects recalled and recorded situations in which they experienced each of the target emotions, then indicated the perceived causes of the emotion-arousing situations. The results confirmed the hypotheses. For example, 94 percent of the instances of anger and 94 percent of the instances of guilt were reported to be due to controllable events, as compared to 24 percent for pity.

Brandtstädter claims that this and many other social-psychological studies provide us with no information at all about the contingencies of the psychological world. Surely it is a part of the *meaning* of "guilt" that its cause is perceived to be a negative event produced by one's own controllable behavior. Is it really conceivable that the experimenters might have discovered, to their surprise, that the cause of guilt is perceived to be a *positive* event *outside* one's own control?—that one might feel guilty about the fact that the weather was delightfully warm and sunny on May 5, 1805, in the

Canary Islands? Brandtstädter (1987, p. 75) asks another rhetorical question: "Would such strange findings suggest eventually a revision of our hypotheses, or would they rather be indicative of conceptual or methodological flaws (be it on the part of the researcher or on the part of the subject reporting in such ways on his or her emotional experience)?" In sum, Brandtstädter's thesis is that the experimental hypotheses of Weiner et al. are logically necessary truths.

But what about that residual 6 percent of anger episodes that were attributed to uncontrollable events? If one were to ascertain empirically whether there are any square circles, one would expect more than a statistically significant trend. One would, in fact, expect to find that *not a single circle* is square. By the same token, if being caused by someone's controllable behavior is a part of the *definition* of anger, then surely there cannot be a single case of anger that is caused by uncontrollable events. If Brandtstädter's thesis is correct, then the occurrence of exceptions to the hypotheses of Weiner et al. must be due to the presence of "conceptual or methodological flaws" in their study. And indeed, such flaws are not hard to find. Weiner et al. asked their subjects to report whether the cause of their anger was controllable or uncontrollable. Thus, their data do not speak directly to the issue whether anger *is* produced by controllable causes. The data tell us that, when asked, *people will say* that anger is due to controllable causes. This is akin to the proposition that, when asked, people will say that there are no square circles. Unlike the proposition that there are no square circles, the propositions about what people will say are clearly not logically necessary. Whether the issue is square circles or anger produced by uncontrollable causes, what people will say is only in part determined by the truth value of the proposition they are being asked to judge. Other factors influencing what people will say include the idiolect of the subject (he or she may define "anger" in an eccentric manner) and how carefully the subject attends to the experimenter's instructions. Thus, it is no wonder that the data are not unexceptional. If we asked a million randomly chosen Americans whether there are any square circles, we would almost surely get some affirmative replies.

Thus, the experimental hypotheses actually tested in the study of Weiner et al. are contingent after all: They tell us what people tend to say about anger, guilt, and pity. But the contemplation of this study still provides an object lesson in the importance of being clear about the modal status of one's claims. In this case, the modal confusion resulted in the testing of a set of hypotheses altogether different from those the investigators set out to test. (Weiner et al. did not intend to investigate their subjects' linguistic practices!)

The third type of error about modal status is to mistake a contingent proposition for a necessary one. An error in this direction may very well result in a false belief about the world. If we believe that P has the same truth value in all possible worlds, we may decide that it is true (in the actual world) on the basis of a demonstration that it is true in other possible worlds. If P is really contingent, however, such a demonstration is entirely compatible with its being false (in the actual world). Even if we do not make any mistakes about truth values, the erroneous belief that certain propositions are noncontingent will result in our failing to engage in needed empirical research. As will be seen immediately below, entire fields of research have been paralyzed by this kind of confusion.

The remedy for mistaking a contingent proposition for a necessary one is to construct a *possible-world parable* (Bradley and Swartz 1979)—a description of a possible world, however outrageous it may be, wherein the proposition has the opposite truth value from the one it has in the actual world. An early paper by Putnam (1965) contains a spectacular series of increasingly bizarre possible-world parables. His topic was *logical behaviorism*, which at the time of this article was still the received view of the relationship between mind and body. Indeed, logical behaviorism had become so deeply entrenched in North American psychology departments that research into mental processes had virtually disappeared. Putnam's parables played a major role in the demise of this doctrine. As was noted in chapter 3, logical behaviorism is the view that sentences describing mental states can invariably be translated into sentences about actual or possible behavior. Presumably, "John is in pain" is synonymous with a behavioral statement like "John grits his teeth and says 'ouch'." Now, this particular translation is patently inadequate: It is obvious that John can be in pain without saying "ouch." One way in which logical behaviorism was attacked was by arguing that all behavioral translations that have ever been offered were demonstrably inadequate. This left it open that some future translation might still do the job. Putnam's argument, however, demonstrates the inadequacy of any translation that anyone might ever come up with.

Suppose that "X is in pain" is claimed to be translatable into some behavioral description of X—call it B(X). This is tantamount to saying that "X is in pain if and only if B(X)" is a necessary truth. Let us call this proposition P. If P is indeed necessarily true, then there is no possible world in which X is in pain but B(X) is false. Putnam (1965) invites us to engage in "a little science fiction." He asks us to imagine a community of "super-spartans" who have developed the ability to suppress all involuntary pain behavior. Moreover, their culture greatly values the control of any involuntary expression of pain. In conversation, the super-spartans admit that they sometimes feel pain, but they never grit their teeth, or say "ouch," or exhibit any of the other manifestations of pain. Thus, whatever form of behavior we try to substitute for B(X), the super-spartans live in a possible world in which P is false. Therefore P cannot be *necessarily* true. Therefore logical behaviorism is false.

It may be objected that there must have been a time in the life of every super-spartan *before* he or she had been socialized to suppress the behavioral indications of pain—that the very young children of the culture must still exhibit the usual behavioral correlates of pain. It is not at all clear that this state of affairs saves the thesis of logical behaviorism from refutation, but Putnam charitably allows us to suppose that it does. He now asks us to imagine a world wherein the super-spartans, after millions of years of selective breeding, begin to have children who are born fully acculturated. These children would have both the innate ability and the innate desire to suppress all behavioral indications of pain. In this possible world, there would be no time at all in the super-spartans' life during which pain was correlated with any candidate for B(X).

The weakness in the case that Putnam has constructed so far is that the super-spartans *report* that they have pains (albeit in "pleasant well-modulated voices"). This leaves it open for the logical behaviorists to claim that the verbal report itself is the sought-after behavioral correlate of pain—that "X is in pain" can be translated into a statement describing X's disposition to *say* that he or she is in pain. Once again Putnam proposes to overlook several problems with this suggestion. Charitably granting that the equation of pain with its verbal report is a feasible hypothesis, he asks us now to imagine a world of "super-super-spartans," who are like the super-spartans except that they also suppress all *talk* of pain. The inhabitants of this world do not even admit to having pains. They pretend not to know either the word or the phenomenon to which the word refers. Here then is a possible world wherein being in pain is not correlated with any combination of words or deeds.

Logical behaviorists might complain that Putnam's hypothesis about the super-super-spartans is "untestable in principle": By hypothesis, we have no basis for distinguishing super-super-spartans from beings who really never experienced pain. As was noted in chapter 3, logical behaviorism derived its inspiration from the broader philosophical stance of logical positivism, the main tenet of which was that all meaningful statements could be translated into observation language. From this point of view, the non-equivalence of "X is in pain" with any statement describing X's overtly observable behavior leads to the conclusion that "X is in pain" has no meaning. This, in turn, entails that the world of super-super-spartans is not a logically possible world at all, for it is clear that the description of logical possibilities cannot contain parts that are meaningless.

Putnam's reply to this defense is that the logical positivist criterion of meaning is false. He grants for the sake of the argument that meaningful hypotheses about the world have to make a difference to what we may potentially observe. But this is not yet to say that hypotheses must all have observational implications when taken in isolation. It is enough for them to be part of a *theory* that has observational implications when taken as a whole. Putnam then proceeds to construct just such a theory. He supposes that we begin to detect a new kind of wave emanating from human brains— V-waves—that can be decoded so as to reveal individuals' unspoken thoughts. It is then found that the super-super-spartans also emit V-waves. When their V-waves are decoded, however, it is discovered that the super-spartans have pain-induced thoughts just as we do. The V-wave readings indicate that they complain to themselves about their toothaches and headaches, though they never reveal any distress in word or deed. To be sure, it is possible to devise other theories that account for the same imaginary data. For example, it is possible that the super-super-spartans are able to produce misleading V-waves at will, and that they are having "a bit of fun" at our expense by pretending to have thoughts about pain. But this state of affairs is universal in science: There are *always* alternative theories available to explain a given set of data. The hypothesis that super-super-spartans have pain which they never reveal in word or deed can be embedded in a testable theory. That is enough to put this hypothesis on the same footing with numerous run-of-the-mill scientific hypotheses whose meaningfulness is never questioned.

It is easy to misunderstand the import of parable construction. Its force doesn't depend at all on how plausible the parable is. Putnam was not suggesting that there is a reasonable probability that creatures like the super-super-spartans actually exist. The claim was only that their existence is logically possible. A probability of one in a trillion trillion trillion is enough to make the point that mental processes aren't equivalent to behavioral responses by definition. Putnam (1965, p. 11) writes: "If this fantasy is not, in some disguised way, self-contradictory, then logical behaviorism is simply a mistake." Putnam's argument leaves it open that the proposition "X is in pain if and only if B(X)" might be *contingently* true—that there is, in fact, an invariable relation between pain and behavior (although other arguments make even this contingent relation extremely implausible). But such a contingent relation would be insufficient to underwrite the logical behaviorists' claim that "B(X)" is an adequate *translation* of "X is in pain."

There are theoretical debates in which one group claims that another group is mistaking a contingent preposition for a necessary one and the second group accuses the first of the opposite error. One issue of this type concerns Piaget's theory of cognitive development. According to Piaget (1929, 1952), cognitive development proceeds through four qualitatively different stages. In the earliest, the *sensory-motor* stage, an infant doesn't yet differentiate between external objects and its own sensory impressions. The achievement of the notion of object permanence ushers in the *pre-operational* stage, in which a child is capable of representing objects in thought and amassing information about them but still incapable of forming generalizations or otherwise manipulating ideas internally by the application of rules. In the *concrete operational* and *formal operational* stages, a child is capable of symbolic manipulation. The difference between these two stages is that in the formal operational stage children become capable of manipulating their concepts on the basis of entirely abstract and formal rules. Very roughly, and in reverse order, these stages can be identified with

(4) the capacity to formulate theoretical laws like "$F = ma$" (formal operational stage), (3) the capacity to formulate empirical laws like "All emeralds are green" (concrete operational stage), (2) the capacity to formulate data like "This emerald is green" (pre-operational stage), and (1) the absence of all the aforementioned capacities (sensory-motor stage).

Piaget's theory has been subjected to a great deal of empirical and theoretical scrutiny. I will discuss only a single criticism having to do with the modal status of Piaget's account. John Flavell and Joachim Wohlwill have claimed that any sequence other than the one posited by Piaget is logically impossible, and hence that Piaget's theory makes no contingent claims. They defend this modal hypothesis by the following assertion: "Providing one accepts Piaget's characterization of what these [concrete and formal] operations consist of, it is logically possible for the child to be capable of the former and incapable of the latter, but not conversely." (Flavell and Wohlwill 1969, p. 86) That claim can hardly be denied: The capacity to formulate theoretical laws requires all the abilities that are necessary for formulating empirical laws, and then some. Similarly, the concrete operational child's capacity to formulate general rules requires the pre-operational child's ability to represent the objects of those rules; but one can very well represent objects without being capable of rule-governed manipulations of those objects. There is, however, a missing step between these observations and the conclusion that Piaget's theory is logically necessary. Flavell and Wohlwill are undoubtedly correct in claiming that the capacity for concrete operations is *logically* prior to the capacity for formal operations: You can't have the latter without possessing the former, but you can have the former without the latter. But Piaget's developmental theory does not merely stipulate these logical relationships. Piaget hypothesizes that the several stages follow an invariable sequence *in real time*—for example, that the concrete operational stage is *temporally* prior to the formal operational stage. But temporal priority is not a logical consequence of logical priority. Owen Flanagan (1984, p. 132) makes this point forcefully with the following possible-world parable:

It is possible . . . that we might have burst forth from our mother's womb . . . with a full-blown (Lamarckian) memory of the things in the universe (with names attached), and a fully operative system of abstract logical abilities. And it is conceivable that these exotic inborn cognitive abilities might . . . come undone in an orderly manner so that our inborn cognitive sophistication yielded to a complete inability to abstract and only a vague sense of things by the time we were twelve!

A more complete account of cognitive development over the full life span might in fact stipulate that there eventually comes a time when cognitive abilities start to be subtracted in the manner described by Flanagan. At the very least, Piaget's theory makes the contingent claim that life begins with a period during which the child acquires cognitive abilities rather than losing them. Moreover, by dividing the stages as he does, Piaget puts forward the additional contingent hypothesis that human cognitive capacities are acquired in four clumps rather than either continuously or all at once.

Another issue in which both the necessity and the contingency of a psychological hypothesis is defended by different camps is to be found in the debate about rationality between Daniel Kahneman and Amos Tversky (on one side) and L. Jonathan Cohen. Kahneman and Tversky (1972) claim to have empirical evidence for the contingent hypothesis that people are systematically irrational in their judgment and their decision making. Cohen (1981) maintains that the rationality of human judgment is a logically necessary truth—that there is a connection of meaning between the concept of rationality and actual human judgments. Cohen does not question the truth of Kahneman and Tversky's empirical findings. The central issue is whether the several "heuristics" discovered by Kahneman and Tversky are actually irrational. Clearly this issue cannot be settled by doing more empirical research. What it calls for is a deeper theoretical analysis of rationality.

8.2   The Too-Strong Argument for Innateness: A Detailed Case Study

This section is devoted to a more detailed look at a single dispute over the modal status of a psychological claim. The issue (innateness) and the cast of characters (Chomsky, Fodor, and Putnam) will be familiar. In addition to presenting another example of a modal dispute, my aim in this section is to provide a more detailed account of the vicissitudes of a real-life theoretical debate in psychology.

I have already discussed an argument made by Chomsky for the innateness of grammatical knowledge (section 6.3) and an argument made by Fodor for the innateness of at least some of our concepts (section 6.9). Chomsky's argument is that the data available to language learners are not sufficient to enable them to figure out the syntactic rules of the language. No being, however intelligent, could parlay the linguistic data available to language learners into knowledge of syntax by a process of rational inference. Now, I have intentionally sustained an equivocation in my account of Chomsky's argument. The claim that children lack adequate linguistic data for learning their language by rational means can be interpreted in either of two ways. The *weak* sense of the claim is that children *as a matter of fact* don't receive enough linguistic data for a rational reconstruction of the grammar. The *strong* sense is that children *can't even in principle* obtain enough data to reconstruct the grammar. Chomsky almost always relies on the weaker claim. For example, consider the following passage (Chomsky 1986, p. 55):

. . . the basic problem is that our knowledge is richly articulated and shared with others from the same speech community, whereas the data available are much too impoverished to determine it by any general procedure of induction.

This talk of "impoverished data," which occurs frequently in Chomsky's work, suggests that the story might have been different if the data were sufficiently enriched. Similarly, after discussing certain intricate transformations in English, Chomsky remarks (1980c, p. 4):

In this case, too, it can hardly be maintained that children learning English receive specific instruction about these matters, or even that they are provided with relevant experience that informs them that they should not make the obvious inductive generalizations. . . .

Placing the emphasis on the lack of specific instructions once again suggests that the instructions *might* have been provided. Chomsky also often talks of the *facility* with which children learn language as evidence for the innateness hypothesis. (See, e.g., Chomsky 1962.) Here again, the reference to facility presupposes the weak argument. If the argument were that it is *impossible* to learn a language by purely rational means, it would be pointless to inquire into whether children learn it easily or with great difficulty. That they learn it at all would be the only theoretically relevant consideration. In relation to the weak argument, however, the facility of language learning is yet another manifestation of the general phenomenon of children's linguistic accomplishments' outstripping the resources made available to them. In these and countless other places, Chomsky relies on the argument that children just happen to receive inadequate data. On that view, children need innate constraints to make up for the deficiencies in the information presented to them by harried parents and teachers.

It should not be supposed that the weak argument is deficient in some way. That is not the import of calling it "weak." The argument is weak only in the sense that it presumes less. To say that language cannot rationally be reconstructed on the basis of the available data is to say less than that language cannot rationally be reconstructed on the basis of any data that *might* be made available. In fact, arguments that are weak in this sense are better at securing their conclusions than strong arguments: Since they presume less, there is less that can go wrong with them. If its premise holds, the weak argument does everything for the innateness hypothesis that the strong argument could do.

Let me make the discussion more concrete by considering a particular deficiency in the linguistic data. Chomsky (1989, p. 55) notes that children learn many aspects of language without going through a prior process of trial and error—they seem to get it right on the very first trial:

There is good reason to believe that children learn language from positive evidence only (corrections not being required or relevant), and they appear to know the facts without relevant experience in a wide array of complex cases. . . .

One of Chomsky's (1981a) favorite examples concerns the formation of interrogatives in English. He asks us to imagine a "neutral scientist" observing a child learning English. The scientist might very well observe that the child has learned to form such questions as those of (A), corresponding to the associated declaratives:

(A) the man is tall—is the man tall? the book is on the table—is the book on the table?

On the basis of these facts, the scientist might very well arrive at the tentative hypothesis that the child is following a simple word-transposition rule (ibid., p. 319):

Hypothesis 1 The child processes the declarative sentence from its first word (i.e., from "left to right"), continuing until he reaches the first occurrence of the word "is" (or others like it: "may," "will," etc.); he then preposes this occurrence of "is," producing the corresponding question. . . .

Further observation, however, would reveal that this hypothesis is false. Consider the following pair of examples:

(B) the man who is tall is in the room—is the man who is tall in the room?

(C) the man who is tall is in the room—is the man who tall is in the room?

Faced for the first time with the task of forming an interrogative out of "the man who is tall is in the room," what will the child say? Hypothesis 1 predicts (C). But this is not what the child will say—not even upon first exposure to declaratives containing subordinate clauses: "Children make many mistakes in language learning, but never mistakes such as exemplified in (C)." (ibid., p. 319) According to Chomsky (ibid.), the correct hypothesis is far more complex:

Hypothesis 2 The child analyzes the declarative sentence into abstract phrases; he then locates the first occurrence of "is" (etc.) that follows the first noun phrase; he then preposes this occurrence of "is," forming the corresponding question.

But if (as we agree all around) hypothesis 1 was a reasonable hypothesis for a neutral scientist to make on the basis of the data contained in (A), the same hypothesis should also have been a reasonable one for the *child* to make at that stage in its language learning when its only linguistic information was of the type contained in (A). But if a child ever *did* adopt hypothesis 1, it would guess that (C) is right. Presumably, it would then receive correction, whereupon it would recognize that hypothesis 1 is inadequate and begin to look for alternative rules. But this never happens. Children never make mistakes of type (C). This means that they never entertain hypothesis 1—not even when all the data available to them are of type (A). But no matter how smart you are, there is no way that you can know on the basis of (A)-type data alone that hypothesis 2 is better than hypothesis (1). "The only reasonable conclusion," according to Chomsky, is that we possess innate information on the basis of which hypothesis 1 can be ruled out a priori.

Thus, the logic of the weak argument runs as follows: Children learn their language on the basis of linguistic data that are demonstrably inadequate for the task. Therefore they must bring innate information to the task. For *my* purpose—not Chomsky's—it is important to note that this argument is entirely compatible with the view that language *can also* be learned without appealing to innate information. If the problem is inadequate data, one solution is to supply the missing data. No doubt the appeal to innate information makes the task of language learning easier, but there is nothing in the weak argument to suggest that we couldn't do without innate constraints if we had to. Of course, there is no way of knowing beforehand just how difficult it would be to reconstruct a language by a "general procedure of induction." Maybe imparting the necessary data would take hundreds of years of regimented instruction. To have an informed opinion on this issue, one would have to look in detail at what the deficiencies in the data are. Whatever they are, however, these deficiencies are in principle *remediable*.

In the hands of Fodor (1975), the problem that Chomsky has grappled with in linguistics becomes a special case of a more general difficulty. In fact, the problem is none other than the most famous conundrum of twentieth-century analytic philosophy: Nelson Goodman's (1954) New Riddle of Induction. The riddle is that there are infinitely many hypotheses, making infinitely many divergent predictions, that are compatible with any finite set of data. The point merits reviewing. Consider the data that all the emeralds that have been observed to date have been green. One hypothesis that is compatible with these data is the theory that all emeralds are green. Another is the theory that all emeralds are grue. Still another theory is that all emeralds are gred (green if observed before 2100, red otherwise). And so on. The first theory leads to the prediction that the first emerald to be observed after December 31, 2099 will be green, the second theory that the selfsame emerald will be blue, the third that it will be red, and so on. Obviously, no amount of additional data would make a difference. Nor will the overabundance of available hypotheses be diminished by the expedient of waiting until January 1, 2100. When the twenty-second century dawns, our descendants will be able to ascertain whether emeralds are green, grue, or gred—more accurate, they will be able to eliminate at least two of these three hypotheses. But there will still be infinitely many hypotheses compatible with all the data. Suppose that it turns out that all the emeralds observed in the twenty-second century are green. One theory that is compatible with these observations is that all emeralds are green. Another is that all emeralds are grue-22, defined as "green if observed before the year 2200, and blue otherwise." And so on. In sum, so long as the data in our possession are finite—and we may be sure that they always will be finite—there will always be infinitely many mutually incompatible hypotheses consistent with the data.

The difficulty is entirely general: One can construct gruish alternatives to any hypothesis about anything. In fact, we can gruify all our scientific beliefs in one fell swoop: Let S be all the laws and generalizations we currently believe to be true about the world, and let T be any alternative set of laws and generalizations (no matter how bizarre and implausible). T might entail that quasars are made of peanut butter, and that every time someone utters the word "Manitoba" somewhere an elf splits cleanly in two, and so on. The only requirement is internal consistency. Then consider the following theory of the universe: Until tomorrow, the empirical consequences of S will have been true, but from tomorrow on, the empirical consequences of T will be true. This theory of the universe has exactly the same relation to the data at hand as our current theory S does. Thus, if we prefer S, there has to be some reason other than conformity to the data.

The fact remains that we perform inductive inferences—we choose to believe that all emeralds are green rather than grue. Conformity to the data can't explain this choice. Fodor offers "innate prejudices"—hard-wired predispositions to prefer some classes of hypotheses over others—as an explanation for our preferences. When I sketched Fodor's argument in section 6.9, I restricted my discussion to the topic of concept learning. Formally, the relation between the available instances and non-instances of a concept and its actual denotation is the same as the relation between evidence and theory. Thus, it goes without saying that there are infinitely many competing concepts that can account for any finite set of instances and non-instances. The fact that we all learn approximately the same concepts requires an explanation, and innate prejudices seem to fit the bill. (Fodor subsequently developed additional arguments for conceptual innatism, from which the putative conclusion wasn't merely that *some* concepts are innate but that *nearly all* concepts are innate—see Fodor 1981b.) It should be clear, however, that the same argument applies to grammatical knowledge: The relation between linguistic data and the syntax of the language is the same as the relation between evidence and theory. Thus, it also goes without saying that there are infinitely many competing grammars that can account for any finite set of linguistic data. Suppose, then, that language learners select randomly from the set of grammars that are compatible with the data in their possession. In that case, the probability of their hitting on the *correct* grammar is $1/\infty = 0$. The fact that children do learn their language is conclusive evidence that they do *not* search at random through the solution space of possible grammars. But what could be the basis for a nonrandom selection of hypothetical grammars? As before, the innateness hypothesis provides the needed explanation for the successful performance of language learners. To be sure, the innate information can't simply have the form of additional data, for no finite amount of data is sufficient to pick out a single grammar. But there are undoubtedly packages of information that would do the job. For example, our innate endowment might specify a finite number of possible grammars for the languages we will be called upon to learn. With only a finite number of alternatives to choose from, we may indeed hope that the finite amount of linguistic data available to us will be adequate for making a selection. This is the strong argument for Chomsky's innateness hypothesis.

Now let us turn to the question of Chomsky's personal relation to the strong argument. For the most part, Chomsky has relied explicitly on the weak argument. This by itself tells us nothing about how he views the strong argument, for the two are not incompatible. In fact, the soundness of the strong argument entails the soundness of the weak one: If children *can't* get enough linguistic data in principle to reconstruct the language, then they certainly *won't* get it in fact. In such a case, one might very well choose to make one's case on the basis of the weaker argument simply for the sake of elegance—there is no point to swatting a fly with a sledgehammer. Superficially, Chomsky's manner of putting the weak argument is suggestive of an author who doesn't endorse the strong argument. Look at the first two passages quoted at the beginning of this section. In both cases Chomsky makes the point that the data would have been insufficient for the grammar to have been inferred by means of induction. This might suggest that the alternative to doing it by innate constraints is to do it rationally: If there *were* enough data for an induction, then the child would not require the assistance of its innate endowment. But the strong argument is that there can never be enough data for an inductive solution—that we need innate constraints to tell us which of infinitely many inductive generalizations to make. Once again, if Chomsky endorsed this Fodorean argument, induction would be neither here nor there.

However, in at least one place Chomsky endorses the strong argument outright (Chomsky and Fodor 1980, p. 259):

In the history of modern philosophy there is a vast literature dealing with a few very simple points about the impossibility of induction, like the whole debate about Goodman's paradox. Once you understand the paradox, it is obvious that *you have to have a set of prejudices in advance for induction to take place.* . . .

It is perhaps significant that this passage comes from a joint symposium presentation with Fodor. Nevertheless, this sketch of the strong argument appears under Chomsky's name. So does he or doesn't he endorse the strong argument? I think he does. His references to induction are not intended to contrast innate constraints with rationally warrantable principles. Chomsky is drawing a contrast between innate constraints on language that are highly specific and would have no bearing on issues of physics or psychology and the more general innate constraints on induction on which we presumably rely when we do science. It is not that we can do science without constraints; it is that the constraints are different. In other words, when Chomsky emphasizes the inadequacy of the linguistic data for reconstructing the grammar by following a procedure of general induction, he is giving an argument for the *modularity* of the language faculty. In any case, it is clear from the passage quoted above that Chomsky knows the strong argument and accepts it. However, because of personal differences in the relative frequencies of their deployment, I call the weak argument Chomsky's argument and the strong argument Fodor's.

Let me review the difference between the weaker, quintessentially Chomskian argument for innateness and the stronger Fodorean version. The former employs the highly contingent premise that the linguistic data that are *in fact* available to language learners are insufficient for the task of discovering the grammar of the language. This argument leaves open whether it might be possible to learn a language without the aid of innate propensities if only the linguistic data were greatly enriched. The Fodorean argument, on the other hand, does not depend on a contingent premise about the nature of the linguistic evidence that happens to be remediably available to language learners. It is based on the idea that all non-demonstrative inferences ultimately must rely on built-in presuppositions (a.k.a. "innate prejudices").

At last we come to the promised example of a dispute over the modal status of a proposition. The contemporary literature on innatism touches upon a third and even stronger (although short-lived) argument for innateness: the *too-strong* argument. In a symposium in which Chomsky and Fodor both participated, both men consistently referred to the innateness hypothesis as a "tautology." The implication was that it is *logically* impossible to perform induction without "prejudices"—equivalently, that the principle that induction requires innate predispositions is a logically necessary truth. The claim in the *strong* argument is that innate constraints provide a psychological solution to the problem of induction. This claim leaves it open that there may be other ways to account for our inductive practices. If innate constraints were demonstrably the only logically possible way to account for inductive learning, there would be no point in even trying to think of other accounts. The issue would be definitively settled. In the same symposium, Putnam (1980b, p. 301) disposed of this idea with another outlandish possible-world parable:

> Fodor and Chomsky are simply wrong when they say that it is a "tautology" that we can't learn anything unless some innate "prejudices" are "built in." . . . It is not *logically* impossible that our heads should be as empty as the Tin Woodman's and we should still talk, love, and so on; it would just be an extreme example of a *causal anomaly* if it ever happened that a creature with no internal structure did these things. I don't doubt for one moment that our dispositions do have a causal explanation, and of course the functional organization of our brain is where one might look for a causal explanation. . . . But this is still not a tautology.

In the face of this incontrovertible point, Chomsky and Fodor immediately backpedaled. Chomsky (1980a, p. 323):

> . . . the term ["tautology"] did not appear in any presented paper, but was introduced in the informal discussion (by whom, I do not recall) and was then used by all participants not in the technical sense of "logical truth" but in the informal sense of "obvious truth."

Fodor (1980b, p. 325):

> Professor Putnam thoughtfully reminds me (and Chomsky) that it is "not *logically* impossible that ours heads should be as empty as the Tin Woodman's and we should still talk, love, and so on"; it was "a little careless" of me to suggest the contrary. It would have been if I had. In fact "tautology" is not a term that appears in my formal presentation, nor did I introduce it into the discussion. . . . The sense of tautology at issue in the discussion was, of course, *not* "truth of logic," but rather "obvious truth, self-evident truth . . . etc."

At least in Fodor's case, this simply isn't so. It is true that "tautology" has the secondary, non-technical meaning of "obvious truth." But how does Fodor explain *this*?

> . . . *you can't carry out an induction, it is a logical impossibility to make a nondemonstrative inference without having an a priori ordering of hypotheses.* This general point about nativism is so self-evident that it is superfluous to discuss it; the only question is, how specific are the innate constraints? (Chomsky and Fodor 1980, p. 260—this passage is specifically attributed to Fodor in the text)

In any case, the issue is dead. Nobody supports this particular too-strong argument. It simply isn't true that innateness is the only logically possible way to account for induction. But the episode illustrates how easy it is for even the most conceptually sophisticated researchers to get confused about the modal status of a proposition.

Just for the record, it is worth noting that the position to which Fodor and Chomsky ultimately retreat in the face of the Tin Woodman still makes a stronger claim than does the strong argument. They admit that the innateness hypothesis isn't provable on the basis of logic alone. But they still maintain that it can be proved on the basis of "obvious truths." If this were so, it would be almost as powerful a result. But is it so? It is easy to see what some of the implicated obvious truths must be. One of them is that people don't have the infinite amount of time they would need to check out all the possible grammars. Another is that knowledge doesn't pop into people's heads as if by magic. But no one has ever been able to provide a list of self-evident assumptions that are sufficient to deduce that induction requires innate constraints. Thus, what Chomsky and Fodor claim is still more than they can deliver. Their ultimate position requires them to show more than that the hypothesis explains our inductive practices, or even that it is the best explanation for induction that we possess. The latter claim allows that a better explanation for induction might be formulated in the future, but that could never happen if the innateness hypothesis were a deductive consequence of obvious truths.

8.3   Discovering New Necessary Truths

The second theoretical task relating to necessary propositions is the discovery of new ones. We do not differentiate the necessary from the contingent merely to consign the former to oblivion. Necessary truth is after all a species of truth and is thus worth knowing for its own sake. The discovery of a new necessary truth represents an increment of knowledge just as surely as the discovery of a new contingent fact. Here again, the simplicity of most historical psychological theories may lead to an erroneous impression that necessary truths are always trivial and obvious, like "Bachelors are unmarried." But this view is clearly untenable when applied to necessary propositions generally. After all, logic and mathematics are as difficult and as full of surprises as any field of investigation, yet logical and mathematical propositions are paradigmatically necessary. (I will discuss some instances of non-obvious necessities in psychology in the next section.)

Moreover, there are situations where necessary propositions provide us with important insights even when their truth is self-evident. Consider the following claim: "If, when you achieve the condition in life that you want, you start to worry about holding onto it, then you will never experience satisfaction." Given natural definitions of a few key terms, it would be easy to show that this claim is necessarily true. Yet it does contain a bit of wisdom that might prove insightful to some individuals in some circumstances—e.g., to someone who has begun to worry about holding onto his achievements but who is by no means reconciled to a lifetime of dissatisfaction. If the necessary truth is represented by "If P then Q," then this person is in the position of already knowing P (that he is worried about holding onto his achievements) but not having drawn from this belief the logical inference Q (that he will never be satisfied). In this situation, this person's coming upon the obvious necessity "If P then Q" immediately results in the acquisition of the new *contingent* piece of knowledge Q, which is an important item of information for him. Even tautologies may have high pragmatic value.

The essential point is that we may establish new contingent truths by constructing a priori proofs of logical necessities. In the previous example, the necessary proposition was self-evidently true—it was the timeliness of the observation that made it useful. In other cases, we may have to struggle to arrive at a non-obvious proof of a necessary proposition that, when added to our other contingent beliefs, provides us with new and important contingent information. In fact, there are circumstances where the *only* way to establish the truth value of a contingent proposition is to try to prove or disprove a necessary proposition. I will give a contrived example of what I mean, followed by a real example drawn from certain contemporary research problems.

Pierre de Fermat was a seventeenth-century mathematician who is most often remembered for his "Last Theorem"—a scribbled note in the margin of a book, in which he claimed to have the discovered the proof of a certain mathematical proposition. The proposition is very easy even for the nonspecialist to understand. It is that the equation $x^n + y^n = z^n$ has no nonzero integer solutions for n > 2. For more than 300 years mathematicians tried and failed to rediscover this proof, or to show that Fermat had made a mistake and that the proposition cannot in fact be proved. Fermat's Last Theorem was finally proved in 1994 by Andrew Wiles. For the purpose of this example, suppose that it is 1993 and that the proof has not yet been discovered. Now consider the claim "Fermat's mathematical pronouncements were never wrong." This proposition (call it F) makes a certain claim about the history of Fermat's mental processes. This claim is undeniably contingent: Maybe Fermat never made a mistake, but maybe he did. Suppose that we are already in possession of all the empirical data that are relevant to the truth or falsehood of F—i.e., that we know exactly what all Fermat's mathematical pronouncements were. The other thing we must establish, of course, is that these pronouncements were all correct. But we cannot know this until Fermat's Last Theorem is either proved or disproved. Thus, a piece of mathematical work stands between us and the acquisition of a contingent fact. In this case, the only way to establish the truth of a contingent proposition is to prove a necessary one. (There is nothing about this situation that creates any new problems for an empiricist theory of knowledge. It is not as though the truth of a contingent proposition were being established without recourse to *any* data; it is just that in this hypothetical case the relevant data are already in. However, we are still stuck on a difficulty in reasoning from the data to the desired conclusion. It is important to keep in mind that such a situation may arise—that the obstacle keeping us from acquiring a piece of contingent knowledge about the world may be removable only by a priori analysis.)

8.4   Strong AI

Strong AI provides us with a real example of the situation we encountered with proposition F. Strong AI is an attempt to substantiate what Newell and Simon (1981) call the *Physical Symbol System Hypothesis* (henceforth PSSH)—the hypothesis that purely physical systems are capable of every sort of human intelligence. Strong AI proceeds, just like weak AI, by constructing programs that can perform various intelligent tasks. The new twist is that the discovery of such a program is taken to be inductive evidence for the validity of PSSH. The idea is that if we can get a computer to do it then we know for sure that a purely physical system can do it, since no one ever supposed that computers have souls. And if we can get a computer to do *anything* that we can do, then PSSH must be true.

Now, PSSH is clearly a contingent proposition. According to Newell and Simon, the fact that strong AI seeks to establish the truth of a contingent hypothesis indicates that it is an empirical science—this is their second argument for the empirical status of AI. (See chapter 5 for the first argument.) This conclusion is evidently based on the hidden premise that the truth of a contingent preposition can be settled only by empirical work. But we saw in the preceding section that this premise is false. Indeed, the enterprise of strong AI is very much like the attempt to discover the truth value of proposition F by trying to prove Fermat's Last Theorem. The empirical data relating to PSSH are already in: We know from experience that computers of arbitrarily great computing power can be realized by physical systems—at least, no one seem to be interested in disputing this empirical claim. The live question is whether every aspect of human intelligence can be programmed on a computer. This question calls for the investigation of a series of propositions: that there exists a program that can alphabetize lists, that there exists a program that can write summaries of longer texts, and so on. But each of these propositions is either *necessarily* true or *necessarily* false, and the construction of a successful program is an a priori proof of the corresponding existential claim. Such claims are in fact the examples of nonobvious necessities in psychology that were promised earlier on.

In sum, it is true that strong AI researchers are interested in establishing a contingent hypothesis. But this interest is not accompanied by any sort of empirical *work*. Strong AI research is a priori despite its bearing on PSSH, just as a person who tries to prove Fermat's Last Theorem is doing mathematics even though the result of this work may have a bearing on the psychohistorical hypothesis that Fermat never made any mathematical mistakes.

9

Conceptual Issues

9.1 The Construction of Conceptual Schemes

Still another type of theoretical activity is the *construction and evaluation of conceptual schemes*. This activity is usually run together with the construction and evaluation of substantive theories. However, one may construct a new theory out of old concepts, and one may also construct new concepts without promulgating a theory about them.

A contrived example will help to make the point. Suppose no one had ever thought to classify matter into solids, liquids, and gases. Now suppose that someone came along who made these distinctions. One would have to consider this move a scientific advance. After all, many important scientific laws are applicable only to one of these categories of matter and so presumably could not be formulated until the appropriate category system was in place. But the proposer of the solid-liquid-gas conceptual scheme need not have made any new empirical discoveries or even any substantial empirical *claims*. Indeed, the proposer need not have said anything that can be construed as true or false, because concepts per se are neither true nor false (see chapter 2). It makes no sense to ask for empirical confirmation of new conceptual schemes. Their construction and their evaluation are non-empirical activities.

There is a sense in which we are free to invent any concepts that we like, with utter disregard for the contingent properties of the world. For example, I hereby invent the concept of a "bulcar," which I define as any entity that is either a Bulgarian immigrant to Venezuela or a four-wheel vehicle registered in Idaho between 1955 and 1957. Now, there are various grounds upon which this particular construction might be criticized. These will be discussed later in the chapter. But the introduction of the concept "bulcar" is certainly not a factual or a logical *error*. In fact, now that the concept has been introduced, it is quite feasible to engage in various empirical investigations into the properties of bulcars. For example, we might very well be able to ascertain their average weight—I suspect it is only slightly less than the average weight of a car.

It is important to distinguish two very different types of intellectual issues: the *propositional* and the *conceptual*. Propositional issues arise when two individuals might have different opinions about the truth value of a proposition: Person A might believe that dogs are more intelligent than cats and person B might believe that cats are more intelligent than dogs, or A might believe that P is a logical consequence of T and B that it is not. The first of these examples is a disagreement over the truth value of a contingent preposition; the second is a disagreement over the truth value of a necessary proposition. Both, however, are propositional issues. Note that a propositional issue could not even arise unless both parties to the dispute agreed to employ the same concepts (e.g., "cat," "dog," and "intelligence") in talking about the world. Another person, C, might respond to the propositional disagreement between A and B by repudiating the terms in which the issue is cast. C might regard the concept of intelligence to be akin to the concept of a bulcar—an uninteresting amalgamation of properties that are better treated separately. Indeed, many psychologists have regarded intelligence in just this way (see, e.g., Gardner 1983). Be that as it may, it is still true that cats are either more or less intelligent than dogs (or that they are equally intelligent). But C's position may be that it is not worth her while to investigate the matter, or even to formulate a considered opinion on the subject. After all, there simply isn't enough time to formulate considered opinions on every possible subject. One has to budget one's thinking time. If asked for an opinion, C would recommend that the concept of intelligence be eliminated from our vocabulary altogether. C's disagreement with A and B is over a conceptual issue.

The distinction between propositional and conceptual issues is implicated in a discussion of "unmasking" by the sociologist Karl Mannheim (1925). To unmask an idea is not to take sides in the debate about its truth or falsehood, but to criticize its deployment from a political perspective—for example, to display the function that it serves in preserving the interests of a particular class. The "unmasking turn of mind," according to Mannheim (ibid., p. 140), is

a turn of mind which does not seek to refute, negate, or call in doubt certain ideas, but rather to *disintegrate* them, and that in such a way that the whole world outlook of a social stratum becomes disintegrated at the same time. We must pay attention, at this point, to the phenomenological distinction between "denying the truth" of an idea, and "determining the function" it exercises. In denying the truth of an idea, I still presuppose it as "thesis" and thus put myself upon the same theoretical (and nothing but theoretical) basis as the one on which the idea is constituted. In casting doubt upon the "idea," I still think within the same categorical pattern as the one in which it has its being. But when I do not even raise the question (or at least when I do not make this question the burden of my argument) whether what the idea asserts is true, but consider it merely in terms of the *extra-theoretical function* it serves, then, and only then, do I achieve an "unmasking" which in fact represents no theoretical refutation but the destruction of the practical effectiveness of these ideas.

Mannheimian unmasking is one way of prosecuting a conceptual issue: The unmasked concept stands accused of surreptitiously serving class interests. The implication is that we would be well advised for political reasons to alter or eliminate the concept at issue, regardless of the truth values of our beliefs about those concepts. But there are many other reasons for calling to question the use of a particular concept. In this chapter, I will talk mostly about the evaluation of concepts as tools for furthering the epistemic aims of science.

Once again, conceptual issues are not resolved by trying to discover whether the concept at issue is true or false. The very idea is incoherent. It often happens, however, that a conceptual issue is mistaken for a propositional issue. For example, consider the claim "There are two types of people in the world: the talkers and the doers." Someone making such a claim is almost certainly erecting a taxonomy—i.e., informing us of his or her intention to divide people up into these two categories for the purpose of discourse. As in the case of "bulcar" or "intelligence," one might very well criticize such a move on various grounds. But it would not be appropriate to claim that the proposer is *mistaken*—that in fact there are three or seven kinds of people. In psychology, similar confusions have arisen in the attempts of Henry Murray, Raymond Cattell, Hans Eysenck, and others to evaluate the numerous schemes that specify the varieties of human motives or psychological traits. Some investigators—particularly factor analysts, such as Cattell (1950)—have written as though they were on the trail of the true human traits. This is a misconceived enterprise. In *any* of these conceptual schemes it is possible to make true empirical and theoretical claims (as well as false ones) about the posited traits, just as it is possible to establish various facts about bulcars. For example, I hereby define the behavioral trait B as follows: People have B-ness to the extent that they either select blue pens over black pens to write with or have a fear of bugs. As in the case of bulcars, there are various grounds upon which this construction might be criticized. But falsehood is not one of them. In fact, now that the concept has been introduced, it is entirely feasible to engage in various empirical investigations into the properties of B-ness. For example, my guess is that empirical research would show that there is no significant correlation between B-ness and intelligence.

9.2   Russell's Paradox

There is one important limitation on our freedom to invent concepts ad libitum. Interestingly, it has nothing to do with any empirical questions about the world. At the turn of the twentieth century, Bertrand Russell announced the highly paradoxical result that merely defining concepts in certain ways leads directly to contradiction. I will follow a later presentation of the paradox by Grelling and Nelson (1908). The problem is not due to definitions that overtly refer to contradictory properties. These cause no problem at all. For example, we could define a nog as anything that both is a dog and is not a dog. It follows from this definition that there are no nogs. The concept of a nog is not of much use; but it is an acceptable concept nonetheless. The problem that Russell discovered is subtler. Let us define the terms *autological* and *heterological* as follows. An adjective is autological if the property it refers to is true of itself. Thus, "English" is autological because "English" is English. So is "polysyllabic." A word is heterological if it fails to be autological. "French" and "monosyllabic" are obviously heterological words. Now the paradox: What is the status of the adjective "heterological"? If we suppose that it is autological, then it describes itself, since that is what is meant by "autological." But if "heterological" describes itself, it must be heterological, which contradicts the assumption that it is autological. If instead we assume that "heterological" is heterological, then, since that is exactly what it says of itself, it must be autological. Either possibility leads to a contradiction. Yet every adjective must be either one or the other, since "heterological" simply means "not autological."

The dilemma has a structure similar to that of the barber paradox discussed in chapter 6. The resolution to the barber paradox was obtained by concluding that there could not be a barber who possessed the contradictory properties we tried to ascribe to him. By the same token, Russell's paradox compels us to say that the concept "heterological" is illegitimate in some way. The problem, of course, is to give some grounds for ruling it out which are not entirely ad hoc. Russell and many others used to think that the problem had to do with the fact that concepts were being made to apply to themselves. This view led to proposals to disallow self-referential language entirely. The trouble with this heroic course is that a great deal of self-reference seems to be logically unexceptionable and even downright useful. Who wants to deny that "word" is a word? This approach has been largely abandoned as a result of Quine's (1966) demonstration that we can get analogues to Russell's paradox even without self-reference.

This is not the place to try to settle this difficult issue in the foundations of rationality. The lesson to be learned here is simply that we cannot, after all, introduce any concepts we like. But the restrictions are not in any way dictated by empirical facts.

9.3   Conceptual Innovation

New conceptual schemes are usually presented in conjunction with new substantive theories. It often happens, however, that the theory comes to be repudiated and the conceptual innovation lives on. The most famous case of this in the history of science is probably Copernicus's heliocentric theory. The *conceptual* component of the Copernican revolution was a switch to describing the motions of the heavenly bodies relative to the sun rather than relative to the earth. Like all conceptual proposals, there is no question of truth or falsehood involved in this move. It is not a mistake to describe planetary motions relative to the earth, or to Venus, or to my nose, or to any other body. The *empirical* component of Copernicanism was the assertion that, in terms of the new conceptual scheme, the planetary orbits are circular. This empirical thesis was false—the orbits are elliptical. In fact, the geocentric scheme of Ptolemy, according to which the planets revolve about the earth in epicycles, provided about as good a fit with observational data as the Copernican system (Kuhn 1962, p. 156). Nevertheless, the work of Copernicus is rightly considered an enormously important scientific advance. The advance, however, was conceptual, not empirical. Copernicus introduced a manner of talking about planetary motion that made Kepler's theory of elliptical orbits and the subsequent Newtonian synthesis feasible. Empirically, Ptolemaic astronomy was as close to the truth as Copernican astronomy. But its conceptual scheme was less fruitful: The correct description of planetary motion relative to the earth is so complex that not even a Newton could have extracted the Law of Universal Gravity from it.

It is arguable that Freud's contribution plays the same role in psychology that Copernicus's plays in the physical sciences. Even if all Freud's empirical claims turn out to be false, his place in the history of psychology is secure on the basis of his conceptual innovations alone. Foremost among these, of course, is the concept of unconscious mental processes, without which contemporary cognitive psychology would go out of business. Freud himself was quite aware of the conceptual side of his work and of the importance of conceptual innovation generally. He describes his major contribution as a move "to extend the concept of 'psychical'" (1917, p. 363). In discussing his "conception of . . . the basic instincts of mental life," he writes (1933, p. 113):

I have a particular reason for using the word "conception" here. These are the most difficult problems that are set to us, but their difficulty does not lie in any insufficiency of observations; what present us with these riddles are actually the commonest and most familiar of phenomena. Nor does the difficulty lie in the recondite nature of the speculations to which they give rise; speculative consideration plays little part in this sphere. But it is truly a matter of conceptions—that is to say, of introducing the right abstract ideas, whose application to the raw material of observation will produce order and clarity in it.

The examples of Copernicus and Freud show that, even after the contingent hypotheses of new theories are completely repudiated, the conceptual schemes devised to *express* these hypotheses may live on. It is a small step from here to the realization that one may legitimately offer a new conceptual scheme to the scientific world without putting forward any new hypotheses in the first place. One may propose a manner of conceptualizing phenomena in which certain new and interesting theoretical options can be delineated without necessarily having to take sides with respect to these options. In such a case, the empirically oriented psychologist's reflex request to "see the data" is clearly misplaced. Conceptual proposals may be suggested by certain observations, but their scientific value does not always depend on the data coming out any particular way. Mendeleev's periodic table and Linnaeus's biological taxonomies are examples of conceptual proposals that were relatively unencumbered by new empirical commitments. Yet both of them proved to be indispensable for the later development of important scientific theories.

There is an argument to the effect that it is impossible to make a purely conceptual proposal. According to this argument, a concept's meaning is determined by its role in a theoretical structure; therefore, it is impossible to introduce a new concept without simultaneously introducing a theoretical structure for it to play its role in. The premise of this argument comes directly from Putnam's (1970) views on semantics, which were in turn strongly influenced by Quine's (1951). As far as I can ascertain, Putnam himself never drew this particular conclusion. Indeed, I have not seen this argument in print. But it surfaces frequently in informal discussion and in the remarks of anonymous journal referees, where it is sometimes used to question the legitimacy of a dataless and theoryless conceptual contribution. This subterranean argument is a non sequitur. Granted that concepts derive their meaning from their place in a theoretical structure, it does not follow that we must devise a new theory every time we want to introduce a new concept. We can simply introduce the new concept by means of an existing theoretical structure. To say that this move is a purely conceptual proposal is to say that the truth values assigned by the preexisting theory to its various propositions (i.e., the propositions that do not involve the new concepts) all remain unchanged. Indeed, we can avail ourselves of the resources of an existing theory for this purpose without necessarily having to believe that the theory is true. Putnam (1970, pp. 196–197) seems to agree:

I can refer to a natural kind by a term which is "loaded" with a theory which is known not to be any longer true of that natural kind, just because it is clear to everyone that what I intend is to refer to that kind, and not to assert the theory.

How else would we describe the invention of the solid-liquid-gas scheme than as a purely conceptual innovation?

9.4   How Not to Evaluate Conceptual Schemes

The fact that conceptual schemes are neither true nor false does not mean that they are all equally good. There are vast differences between Copernicus's conceptual innovation and the introduction of the concept "bulcar." In the next few sections, I will discuss several types of benefits that may accrue from the adoption of a new conceptual scheme. These benefits may be regarded as criteria for conceptual evaluation: The more beneficial the conceptual system, the more reason there is to adopt it. But first we must clear away a number of irrelevant criteria that have sometimes been applied to the evaluation of conceptual proposals.

To begin with, it might be supposed that the use of a conceptual scheme is illegitimate unless it is known that there exist phenomena that fall under the posited concepts. This is simply a mistake. The set of all unicorns is presumably empty, but this fact does not invalidate the concept of a unicorn (whatever it might mean to invalidate a concept). Indeed, the term "unicorn" plays a crucial role in expressing a zoological fact that was established only after centuries of field research: that there are no unicorns. The unfounded view that scientific concepts must be non-empty is a special case of the more general idea that the theoretical importance of a concept is a function of its numerosity. This idea might well be called the *fallacy of numerosity*. In fact, the discovery that a particular category has no members can have enormous theoretical significance. Suppose, for example, that after the construction of the periodic table of the elements it had been found that there were no elements in nature with prime atomic numbers. Without a doubt, physical theory would have immediately become preoccupied with the task of accounting for these curious gaps in the periodic table. Less fancifully, consider the current interest in the question whether cognitive functions are "modular" (Fodor 1983)—that is, whether the mind is a collection of relatively independent subsystems. Certainly the concept of a module was invented and refined because it was thought that many cognitive functions would turn out to be modular. But even if continued research were to persuade us that cognitive functions are never modular, it will still not have been a waste of time to devise the concept of a module. The concept will still have been a vehicle for the discovery of an important and non-obvious fact about cognitive architecture, namely that it is non-modular. Indeed, Fodor devotes a large part of his book on the subject to developing the thesis that central processes such as reasoning and belief fixation are non-modular.

A misapprehension closely related to the fallacy of numerosity is *Lord Kelvin's fallacy*: that "quantitative" concepts are inherently superior to "qualitative" concepts. To begin with, the quantitative-qualitative dimension is not a dichotomy. The concepts of a system may exhibit various degrees and types of order that correspond to various properties of the real numbers. A correspondence that exhausts all the properties of the real numbers is called an *absolute scale*. Absolute scales are rarely encountered in scientific work. Most correspondences relate a conceptual system to *selected* properties of the real numbers. For example, measurements of length assign a non-arbitrary meaning to the assertion that length L1 is mapped onto a number that is twice as large as the number corresponding to length L2. But the fact that the *difference* between these numbers is (say) 6 rather than 12 is the result of an arbitrary choice of unit (i.e., of which line segment corresponds to the value 1). Mappings like the one employed in measuring length are *ratio scales*. *Interval scales* (such as the temperature scale) employ even fewer properties of the reals (30°C is not "twice as warm" as 15°C except by convention). *Ordinal scales* use still fewer properties of the reals. A conceptual system of the type normally called "qualitative" can also usefully be mapped onto the real numbers. The only meaningful numerical properties in this case, however, are identity and difference: The numbers assigned to objects x and y are the same if and only if x and y fall in the same category. In such a *categorical scale*, numbers are used merely as labels for different classes. But there is no drastic discontinuity between this minimal "quantification" and the slightly less minimal use of numerical properties in an ordinal scale, or between ordinal scales and interval scales. Thus, a person who insists that scientific conceptual systems be "quantitative" has to decide where to draw the line. Clearly this cannot be a principled decision.

Even more important, a conceptual system may be characterized by complex, subtle, and *precise* relations that are not mirrored by any of the standard arithmetic functions (addition, subtraction, multiplication, division, exponentiation, etc.). These functions are, after all, only a small subset of the abstract entities whose formal properties have been rigorously investigated by mathematicians and found useful in scientific work. For example, the theory of abstract groups has been employed in the formulation of theories in atomic physics; yet group theory is not "quantitative," since it makes no reference to the traditional arithmetic functions. Such a non-quantitative theory can be as precise as we like, in any non-question-begging sense of the word. Zenon Pylyshyn (1984) has suggested that theories in cognitive psychology would profit more from the conceptual resources of symbolic logic than those of the real-number line. The paradigm here is the computer program interpreted as a theory. A computer program may be no more quantitative than a theory expressed in ordinary English. But, whatever shortcomings the program-*cum*-theory may have, lack of precision is certainly not one of them.

Another inappropriate requirement for conceptual systems is the infamous demand of logical positivists that concepts all be definable in observational terms, or that they be "operationalized." B. F. Skinner has been the foremost spokesman for this point of view in psychology. (See Skinner 1945.) As was mentioned in chapter 3, the vast majority of concepts in successful scientific theories cannot be defined operationally. A liberalized version of the positivist/operationalist thesis requires only that concepts have "partial definitions" in terms of observables. Neil Miller (1959), who has popularized this view among psychologists, concedes that, given a theoretical concept C, we are not generally able to give a definition of the form

x is C if and only if . . . ,

where the right-hand side is supplied with an observational statement. But according to Miller's liberalized positivism we should at least be able to say

If x is C, then . . . ,

where the right-hand side is again an observational statement. That is, we may not be able to define a concept exhaustively in terms of observables, but we must at least be able to state some observational implications of the concept. But even this liberalized criterion would eliminate most of what has been interesting in the history of science. The insistence that a theory have empirical import is certainly legitimate. But this requirement is met so long as there are observational consequences of the theory *taken as a whole*. This leaves it open for some theoretical concepts to derive their meaning from their relation to other theoretical concepts, so long as the system as a whole eventually makes contact with the observational level. This repudiation of logical positivism was an essential component of Putnam's critique of logical behaviorism. (See section 8.1.)

It has sometimes been claimed that we can distinguish between category systems that correspond to *natural kinds* and those that are artificial constructions. Presumably "gold" and "tiger" would be examples of the first type, whereas "bulcar" is an example of the second type. The implication is that we should prefer taxonomies that correspond to natural kinds. This advice is not so much unsound as it is inoperative, like "Buy low and sell high on the stock market." To begin with, we must distinguish between two ways of construing the doctrine of natural kinds: the *psychological* and the *metaphysical*. According to the psychological doctrine, the human mind is innately disposed to conceptualize the world along certain lines. A conceptual system that goes against the grain will at best be very difficult for us to work with. Systems that are vastly different from the natural one might simply be impossible for us to conceive. Eleanor Rosch and her colleagues have provided evidence for the existence of such natural category systems. (See Rosch and Lloyd 1978.) Though this topic is interesting and important in its own right, it has no bearing on the question at hand: What criteria should be used for selecting a conceptual system for science? If there are possible conceptual systems that are inconceivable to us, we will never face the problem of evaluating their merits. On the other hand, if we do manage to come up with a particular system, then the fact that it is not natural to us is irrelevant to its evaluation. To be sure, the fact that the artificial system is difficult to use is a good reason for preferring an easier one that is otherwise just as good. But the operative criterion here is "ease or difficulty of use" rather than "naturalness or artificiality." It is irrelevant whether the cause of the difficulty is the system's (psychological) artificiality.

One might also make the argument that innate concepts are likelier to prove fruitful in formulating good scientific theories because they have survived the test of natural selection. (Peirce seems to have held this view.) But this relation between innateness and theoretical utility can be at most a rough generalization. Certainly we have no reason to suppose that evolution has supplied us, just at this moment, with the optimal conceptual scheme for doing science. The evolutionary hypothesis may justify our trying to do science with our innate conceptual scheme first (since it is a good bet that it will turn out to be fruitful), and to explore artificial conceptual innovations only when we reach an impasse, but this is hardly advice that we need to hear. It goes without saying that we will begin with the concepts that we already have and will formulate new ones only if the need arises.

According to the *metaphysical* doctrine of natural kinds, the universe itself comes divided up into discrete entities, and our conceptual system will produce successful scientific theories only if it "carves nature at its joints." This view hearkens back to the medieval debate between *realists* and *nominalists*. The latter claimed that all conceptual distinctions were arbitrary creations of the human mind; the former believed that nature had joints at which it should be (and generally was) carved. Nominalism seemed to have scored a conclusive victory in this debate. Certainly it remained more or less unchallenged for several centuries. Very recently, however, the doctrine of (metaphysical) natural kinds has once again come into vogue. It would be inappropriate to delve into this complex issue here. Suffice it to say that theoreticians working on conceptual proposals do not have to worry about metaphysical natural kinds any more than they have to think about psychological natural kinds, for no one has ever been able to suggest any criterion whereby we can *recognize* a natural-kind concept when we encounter one except by the fact that it plays a role in a successful scientific theory. But this means that the only way to find out whether a questionable concept corresponds to a natural kind is to try to discover a good scientific theory that makes use of the concept. Theoretical success is what tells us that we are dealing with a natural kind, and persistent failure is what tells us that we are probably not dealing with a natural kind. To be sure, we have a strong intuition that there are not going to be any scientific laws involving bulcars. Presumably our intuitions in this matter are based on a rough evaluation of the kinds of concepts that have proved successful in the past. The provisional nature of such evaluations is demonstrated by the fact that they have often turned out to be wrong—for example, it was once thought that earth, air, fire, and water were the natural kinds of matter, and that astrological sun signs delineated natural kinds of persons. Thus, when we are faced with a specific conceptual proposal to evaluate, it gets us nowhere to ask whether the posited concepts correspond to natural kinds. The only operative criterion is whether the posited concepts enable us to formulate successful scientific laws. But this is a criterion to which both believers and disbelievers in natural kinds will give unquestioned assent. No doubt the best way to work up an evaluation of a conceptual proposal is to try to formulate scientific laws with them. Success or failure at this enterprise may or may not additionally be taken as evidence that the concepts are natural kinds. But this is not an issue that the conceptual innovator must address.

The question of natural kinds comes up in regard to the fascinating topic of extraterrestrial communication. It would appear that there is very little hope of managing to communicate with extraterrestrials unless nature does have joints at which it can be carved into natural kinds. If (as nominalists believe) conceptual systems are entirely arbitrary ways of carving up an essentially seamless universe, then the probability that two independent carvings are mutually translatable would be essentially 0. Conversely, the discovery that we can communicate with extraterrestrials would be a powerful argument for conceptual realism. (This issue will come up again in section 9.6.)

9.5   Minor Criteria for Conceptual Evaluation

In this section I will discuss a number of minor criteria for the evaluation of conceptual schemes. These properties are nice to have if we do not have to sacrifice anything really important for them, but they are not indispensable.

A conceptual scheme may be criticized for failing to be exhaustive and/or exclusive. A set of categories is exhaustive of a particular domain if every element in the domain belongs to one or another of the categories. If a scheme is exhaustive, then we know that no phenomenon has been left out of the account. A set of categories is exclusive if the intersection of any two categories is empty—that is, if no element in the domain appears in more than one category. The lack of exhaustiveness or exclusiveness in a system is conducive to errors of analysis. For example, we might be tempted to formulate unwarranted generalizations on the basis of a non-exhaustive set of cases. However, it is not crucial to scientific progress that a conceptual scheme be exhaustive or exclusive, so long as we don't fall into the error of making inferences that presuppose these properties.

It is also desirable to minimize vagueness. A concept C is vague if there are many borderline cases for which membership or non-membership in C is indeterminate. Most concepts in ordinary language are vague in this sense. A famous example is the concept of a *heap*. Two pebbles leaning against each other definitely do not constitute a heap of pebbles, whereas a hundred pebbles piled up definitely are a heap. But it is impossible to state the exact number n such that n pebbles constitute a heap whereas n − 1 pebbles do not. It is possible to do useful scientific work with vague concepts. Indeed, it can be argued that all concepts have an irreducible degree of vagueness about them. All other things being equal, however, a relatively determinate concept is preferable to a relatively vague one by virtue of the fact that more of the propositions involving the former will have determinable truth values.

The substitution of more exhaustive, more exclusive, and more determinate conceptual systems for their less favored counterparts is not yet the same thing as the introduction of entirely new ideas. But it is, strictly speaking, a conceptual innovation, since the new concepts are not the same as the old ones. This particular type of conceptual change is sometimes called *explication*. Quine (1960, pp. 258–259) characterizes the process as follows:

[In explication] we do not claim synonymy. We do not claim to make clear and explicit what the users of the unclear expression had unconsciously in mind all along. We do not expose hidden meanings. . . . We fix on the particular functions of the unclear expression that make it worth troubling about, and then devise a substitute, clear and couched in term to our liking, that fills those functions.

The difference between explication and wholesale conceptual change is the sense that in explication some kernel of interest pertaining to the old concept has been preserved. There can be spurious explications that pretend to preserve what interests us but are really changes of topic. For example, it does not help us to get clear about the concept of consciousness to explicate it as "being under stimulus control" (Skinner 1974, p. 242).

9.6   Expressive Power

The introduction of a concept whose meaning differs substantially from those of our previous concepts I will call a *major* conceptual change. It is useful to distinguish further between *ordinary* and *radical* varieties of major innovations. An ordinary conceptual change is the introduction of new concepts that can be defined in terms of our previous concepts. A radical conceptual innovation is the introduction of a new concept that cannot be so defined. The invention of "solid," "liquid," and "gas" is an ordinary innovation, since these concepts are definable in term of the more fundamental concepts of volume, shape, and time. Given any statement about gases, there exists an equivalent but longer statement in our old vocabulary. What, then, is the point of such an innovation? Well, it may be much simpler to describe the same phenomena in the new terms. At a minimum, this advantage saves us time and effort. But it may also have a greater significance. The increase in lucidity may make salient certain relationships and regularities that are totally obscured when we describe the same phenomena in our old scheme. The classic instance here is once again the Copernican revolution. Copernicus's conceptual innovation was of the ordinary variety, but the resultant redescription of planetary orbits revealed patterns in nature that eventually led to Newtonian mechanics. The earlier geocentric descriptions of planetary orbits were simply too complicated for anyone to have discovered the underlying regularities.

The potential benefits of radical conceptual innovation go far beyond a mere increase in facility of description. Here is one interesting possibility: Suppose that a branch of science is complete in the sense that we know the truth values of all the propositions that can be expressed in its conceptual scheme. In this situation, it would appear that there is nothing more to be done—the enterprise is finished. In fact, however, it is still possible for someone to contrive a new way of conceptualizing the phenomena of the science that proves not to be reducible to the old conceptual scheme. The result would be that the apparently completed enterprise would be thrown open again, for we would now be able to express new hypotheses that have no equivalent formulations in the old scheme. In this case, conceptual innovation would create new questions for research where none existed before.

The prevalence of radical conceptual change is a matter of some controversy. According to Thomas Kuhn (1962) and Paul Feyerabend (1975), most new scientific concepts are not definable in terms of their predecessors. If this is right, then scientists are engaged in radical conceptual innovation more or less continuously. Donald Davidson (1974), on the other hand, maintains that the idea of radically different conceptual schemes is incoherent. He asks us to contemplate whether it is possible that intelligent extraterrestrials might employ a language that is not translatable into our own. He rejects this possibility on the ground that finding a workable interpretation of a putative language is the only evidence we can have that a corpus of utterances (or tentacle waggings) *is* a language. If we cannot translate Plutonian speech into English, then we have no reason to believe that the Plutonians are communicating at all. But this is too quick. Davidson seems to presume that the ascription of a language to a society of beings can be justified only by decoding the putative language. However, it is also possible that we might encounter indirect evidence for the hypothesis that the Plutonians have a language. This point is made by Theodore Schick Jr. (1987, p. 300), who provides us with the following scenario:

There are criteria other than translatability that we could appeal to to establish the existence of an alternate conceptual scheme. If creatures from another planet flew to the earth in sophisticated spaceships and proceeded to transform the planet by building complex structures, for example, then even if we could not translate their speech, we would still have good reason for believing that they possess an alternative conceptual scheme.

The evidence to which Schick refers is not particularly strong. After all, his aliens might perform their technological feats without the benefit of a communication system, relying only on innate technological expertise (as terrestrial ants and bees do). For all that, Schick's example is good enough for the task it was designed to accomplish: The possibility of weak evidence is sufficient to block the conclusion that a hypothesis is beyond the reach of empirical confirmation.

Moreover, there are scenarios that would provide substantially more compelling (albeit still indirect) evidence for the hypothesis that the Plutonians have an untranslatable language. Suppose we encounter both Plutonians and Saturnians. We can make no sense of Plutonian communication (hence, Davidson would say, we can have no reason to suppose that they are communicating), nor is there any evidence that they can make sense of our language. The Saturnians, however, are able to learn English without difficulty. Having learned it, they seem to use it very much as we do. They agree with us on such fundamental questions as whether there is now a book on the table before us, whether 2 + 2 = 4, and so on. But they also tell us a curious thing: They claim that the Plutonians also have a language. How do they know? Because they have mastered it—they speak Plutonian and English with equal fluency. When we ask them to teach it to us, however, they protest that this would be impossible, for

English and Plutonian are not mutually translatable. Certainly these events are logically possible—it is not self-contradictory to suppose that we will encounter Saturnians who will tell us just these things. If they do tell us these things, what should we make of them? If the Saturnians have proved themselves reliable in their accounts of matters concerning which we have independent knowledge, their testimony will provide us with very strong evidence for the proposition that the Plutonians employ concepts radically different from our own.

9.7 Instant Accrual of Data

In addition to creating new hypotheses, there is a sense in which conceptual innovation can provide us with contingent information about the world without our having to do any new empirical research. Consider once again the effect of introducing the concepts "solid," "liquid," and "gas" into our talk about the physical world. As soon as this conceptual innovation is made, we can begin to recite a long list of new contingent facts without rising from our armchair: Water is a liquid, my pencil is a solid, and so on. It would be absurd to submit these "hypotheses" to empirical testing—e.g., to stick a pencil in a cup and note whether it maintains its shape. Of course, we rely here on prior observation: We have seen what happens to pencils in cups many times before. Perhaps it can be said that we "implicitly" knew that pencils are solid, but that our old conceptual scheme failed to call our attention to this implicit knowledge. Be that as it may, we have an increment in the *explicitly represented data base* of science as a result of a purely conceptual proposal. The situation is even more striking in the case of radically new concepts. Here we previously lacked the expressive power to formulate our implicit knowledge; hence there was no possibility whatever of that knowledge's entering into our data base. In this manner, a judiciously wrought taxonomy of cognitive structures or psychological traits could throw a large amount of contingent psychological information into our laps without any further empirical research. The manner in which this increment in contingent knowledge takes place does not pose any fundamental difficulties for an empiricist theory of knowledge, but it does give us some idea of the potential fruitfulness of a priori methods in furthering the aims of science.

9.8   Creation of Data

The last criterion for judging the merits of a conceptual proposal is more speculative. Unlike the previous criteria, it requires major changes in received empiricist views. So far, our discussion of conceptual change has been consistent with the assumption that our observations of the world remain the same, even though the terms we use to describe them may change. Suppose, for example, that I lack the concept of a solid. Then, when I look at a pencil, it will not occur to me to think that the pencil is solid. But I have discussed this scenario as though I could nevertheless have the same perceptual experiences as someone who does have the concept of a solid. This view has been challenged by a number of philosophers of science, notably Norwood Hanson (1961) and Thomas Kuhn (1962). These authors refer to certain empirical results of Gestalt psychology that strongly suggest that changes in one's conceptual scheme can in fact alter one's perceptual experiences. For example, consider figure 9.1, which can be seen either as a duck or as a rabbit. Imagine that society R has a concept of a rabbit but has no concept of a duck, and that society D has a concept of a duck but has no concept of a rabbit. In this circumstance, it is compelling to suppose that members of both cultures will be able to see only the aspect of the figure for which they have a concept. It goes without saying that members of culture D and culture R will make different observational reports in the same external circumstances: Members of D will say that they see a duck, and members of R will say that they see a rabbit. But beyond this, members of D and members of R *will actually have different perceptual experiences as a result of having their minds*

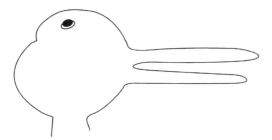

Figure 9.1
The duck-rabbit.

stocked with different concepts. In particular, members of D will have the experience that we have when we see the figure in its duck aspect, and members of R will have the experience that we have when we see the figure in its rabbit aspect.

Now, it is at least possible that adherents of two competing scientific theories—say, S-R theorists and psychoanalysts—are in the same position with respect to their subject matter that members of D and R are in with respect to the reversible duck-rabbit. Since S-R theorists and psychoanalysts employ different concepts for describing human nature, and since the use of different concepts may result in qualitatively different perceptual experiences, S-R theorists and psychoanalysts may actually see different things when they observe other people. In the provocative words of Kuhn (1962), scientists who have different conceptual schemes may "live in different worlds."

It follows that the creation of new conceptual schemes may bring a new realm of perceptual experience into being. It is not simply that these perceptions were previously indescribable, or even that they previously went unnoticed. If the possession of certain concepts is a necessary condition for *having* the perceptions, then they simply did not exist before the invention of the concepts. If no one ever invented them, then a description of the world that left the resultant perceptions out of account could still be complete. In sum, conceptual innovation may not only make data more accessible; it may *create* data. On this account, a conceptual innovation may be commended on the ground that it brings a lot of interesting new data into being.

The consequences of this line of thought are drastic and not yet fully digested in the philosophy of science. For one thing, the standard empiricist interpretation of scientific progress seems to be called into question. According to the standard view, progress means the closer and closer approximation of our theoretical predictions to the observed facts. This view presupposes that the observed facts remain the same while our theories about them change. But new theories commonly employ new conceptual schemes. Thus, if conceptual change can lead to a change in what we observe, there is no longer a guarantee that the sum of potential observations does remain constant across theoretical shifts. And then the standard view falls apart. Different theories may be *incommensurable* in the strong sense that adherents to theory A have available to them one set of observations to confirm or disconfirm their hypotheses, whereas adherents to theory B have available a different set. When theories are incommensurable in this sense, there is no possibility of deciding which of them provides a better fit to "the" data.

It would be inappropriate to pursue this profound difficulty much further here, but a tentative suggestion may help to allay the sense that abandoning the standard view of progress must inevitably lead to nihilism and despair. This suggestion is similar to (but not identical with) Feyerabend's (1975) call for "theoretical pluralism" and Bohr's (1958) principle of complementarity. Perhaps we should simply give up the idea that there is a single "best theory" of any domain. If we insist on accepting a single theory per domain, then we are committed to the employment of a single conceptual scheme—namely the one used to formulate the best theory. But if theories employing different conceptual schemes are incommensurable, then it is not obviously irrational to adopt any number of theories of the same domain—namely the best ones that can be formulated in each conceptual scheme. If it is true that there are aspects of the world that are perceptible only to S-R theorists and others that are perceptible only to psychoanalysts, we lose data if we reject either one. Conversely, the more theories we can bring to bear on the world the more we will see of what can be seen. On this account, science should not aim to eliminate either one of a competing pair of incommensurable theories. Rather, it should strive to improve them both, and indeed to supplement them with still other conceptual approaches. At least on the face of it, this approach is compatible with scientific realism. In any case, if our multiple theories each employ radically different conceptual schemes, we need not worry about contradicting ourselves by adopting them all; two theories can lead to contradictory conclusions only if they share some of the same concepts.

10

The Contingent A Priori

10.1 The Need for Presuppositions

In chapter 1 it was observed that empiricism and rationalism come in various degrees. There is, however, a natural place to draw the line between empiricists and rationalists. In locating this dividing point, Kant (1781) used two distinctions of which I have already made frequent use. First, there is the distinction between *necessary* propositions and *contingent* propositions (Kant called them "analytic" and "synthetic"). The former are either true in all possible worlds or false in all possible worlds; the latter are true in some possible worlds and false in some possible worlds. Second, there is the distinction between *empirical* knowledge (Kant called it "a posteriori knowledge"), which requires observation or experiment for its justification, and *a priori* knowledge, which does not require observation or experiment for its justification. *Empiricism* may be identified with the view that only necessary propositions can be known a priori; *rationalism* is the view that there is some contingent a priori knowledge.

There is nothing in the preceding chapters that would give us cause to doubt the correctness of empiricism in this Kantian sense. However, if rationalism were to be true, then a priori analysis would play an even more important role in science than we have demonstrated so far. Here we are dealing with philosophical matters that have been continuously controversial since the beginning of Western thought. As was mentioned in chapter 1, we are currently exiting from a severely empiricist era of intellectual history. The non-existence of contingent propositions that can be known a priori was virtually unquestioned among logical positivists in the first half of the twentieth century. Nowadays, however, there is a range of opinion on the subject. Indeed, there is a type of contingent a priori, introduced by Saul Kripke (1972), the legitimacy of which is widely acknowledged in contemporary philosophical circles. Kripke's candidate will be discussed below. We will see that it turns out to be contingent a priori on a technicality, and that it does not seriously challenge the empiricist's world view. Nevertheless, its existence has forced the philosophical community to realize that there are hidden complexities in the relation between the contingent and the a priori.

Let us begin with a brief review of the history of modern philosophy as outlined in chapters 1 and 4. First came the classical rationalists, who believed that most if not all of the features of the world could be deduced a priori. Then came the classical empiricists, who argued that all contingent knowledge comes from experience. The empiricist philosophy of knowledge led to progressive attrition in what was thought to be known. Ultimately, Hume showed that a thoroughgoing empiricism issues in absolute skepticism about all knowledge claims. In particular, Hume's analysis of induction led to the conclusion that empiricists can have no basis for any belief about the unobserved portions of the universe. This conclusion ruled out any possibility of a scientific enterprise.

Kant's work is essentially a sustained attempt to get rational discourse out of the dead end to which the classical empiricist tradition had led. He accepts the Humean argument in outline: Empiricism leads to skepticism. It follows that the only way to avoid skepticism is to give up empiricism and to accept some contingent principles on an a priori basis. Following Collingwood (1924), let us call these contingent a priori assumptions *presuppositions*. A presupposition is not merely an untested contingent hypothesis; it is a hypothesis that is at once *untestable* and *essential to the pursuit of knowledge*. The clearest examples are methodological tenets such as the principle of induction. Such principles cannot be tested without circularity, because they tell us what is to count as a test in the first place. An ordinary hypothesis may be overturned by the weight of empirical evidence. But the rules whereby hypotheses are overturned cannot themselves be overturned.

10.2   Grounded Presuppositions

Empiricists might object that establishing the *need* for presuppositions is not yet the same thing as establishing their *truth*. If a contingent principle is untestable by empirical means, what basis do we have for claiming to know it? The classical rationalists believed that such principles could be deduced a priori in the same manner in which we deduce logical theorems. By Kant's day, however, their arguments had been largely discredited. But then what reason do we have for adopting any presuppositions? There are a number of different answers to this question. The first—and the weakest—begins by conceding the point. Let us agree that we have no basis for asserting that our presuppositions are true. Let us refer to them as contingent a priori *beliefs* rather than knowledge. The point remains that we *must* adopt some contingent beliefs without empirical evidence if we are to engage in anything like a scientific enterprise. This argument does not logically force empiricists to give up their point of view. They have a choice: Either give up empiricism or give up science. Rationalism is the only game in town.

Kant himself was more sanguine about the status of the contingent a priori. He claimed to have invented a new type of a priori argument—*transcendental deduction*—that was at once valid and productive of contingent beliefs. Let us refer to contingent beliefs whose truth can be demonstrated by a priori methods as *grounded presuppositions*. How does transcendental deduction enable us to ground our presuppositions? The essence of the matter is best conveyed by a trivial (and non-Kantian) example. Consider the following proposition, denoted B:

There are beliefs.

This proposition is undoubtedly contingent, since there are possible worlds that are devoid of believing agents. Furthermore, it would be impossible to deduce it, after the fashion of classical rationalism, on the basis of the laws of logic and the definition of "belief." But proposition B has peculiar properties that set it apart from other propositions that are superficially similar, such as "There are cats." Suppose I adopt B without consulting any empirical evidence—that is to say, suppose that I *presuppose* it. Now, from the fact that I believe B it follows logically that there are beliefs—i.e., that B is true. Therefore I can come to know the truth of B on the basis of an a priori proof after all. B is an example of a grounded presupposition. It is not true in all possible worlds, but it is true in all possible worlds in which it is believed. Since we cannot believe it falsely, we are in a position to know a priori that our belief in it is true.

How do empiricists react to examples like B? According to Bradley and Swartz (1979), there is an appeal to observational evidence even in so trivial an instance as B. They argue as follows: It is unquestionably correct to say that the truth of B follows logically from our believing it. However, to know that B is true we must do two things. We must construct the deductive argument that leads from our belief in B to its truth. (This part of the enterprise is indeed a priori. In the present case, it is also trivial.) In addition, we must know that the *premise* of the argument is true—i.e., that we believe that B. And this part of the enterprise is empirical, because we cannot know what we believe without some sort of self-observation. Thus, knowledge of B involves an appeal to empirical evidence after all.

This argument points once again to the correct conclusion that grounded presuppositions do not have the properties that *classical* rationalists ascribed to our knowledge. But it does not yet show that our beliefs in such propositions as B can be completely assimilated to the category of ordinary empirical knowledge. It may be true that we *sometimes* come to know the truth of a grounded presupposition by a process of self-observation: First we note that we believe X, then we reason that belief in X implies X, and then we conclude, on the basis of both observation and reasoning, that X is surely true. This sequence of events is similar to what happens when we acquire ordinary contingent knowledge by empirical means: We see a mountain, we reason that the existence of mountains implies the disjunctive proposition that either mountains exist or rivers exist, and so we conclude that either mountains exist or rivers exist. But there is also a different sequence of events that may lead to knowledge only in the case of grounded presuppositions. We could reason that belief in X implies X *before* we come to believe X. In that case, there would be nothing for us to observe. But we would be in a position to know a priori that, *if* X is adopted, *then* it is true. And then, if we were to decide to adopt X, we could know that X is true *immediately* upon its adoption. In the case of ordinary empirical knowledge, however, the empirical evidence must precede the knowledge claim. According to classical empiricism, there is an invariable sequence of events leading to contingent knowledge. First, one gathers the evidence; second, one draws logical inferences from the evidence; third, one adopts the results. In the case of grounded presuppositions, however, one can adopt a belief with no prior evidence and yet be confident of its truth.

The reason empiricists are disinclined to accept the possibility of contingent a priori knowledge is that it seems magical to them. Kripke, himself a believer in the contingent a priori, describes the attitude this way (cited in Evans 1979, p. 171):

> I guess it is thought that . . . if something is known a priori it must be necessary, because it was known without looking at the world. If it depended upon some contingent feature of the actual world, how could you know without looking? Maybe the actual world is one of the possible worlds in which it would have been false.

Keith Donnellan poses the problem in similar terms (also cited in Evans 1979, p. 171):

> If a truth is a contingent one, then it is made true, so to speak, by some actual state of affairs in the world, that at least in the sort of example we are interested in, exists independently of our language and linguistic conventions. How can we be aware of such a truth, come to know the existence of such a state of affairs, merely by performing an act of linguistic manipulation?

Now, there is more than one answer to Kripke's and Donnellan's question. Gareth Evans (1979) has shown that there are some propositions knowable a priori, Kripke's own candidates among them, that are *not* "made true . . . by some actual state of affairs in the world," even though they turn out to be contingent on a technicality. The Kripkean example involves a stick S which, it is decided at time t, is to be used as a standard meter. That is to say, the term "meter" is stipulated to be the length that S happens to have at time t in this, the actual world. Now consider the following proposition, denoted K:

The length of stick S is one meter.

This proposition is obviously knowable a priori by anyone who knows the definition of "one meter." The novelty in Kripke's analysis is his claim that K is nevertheless contingent, because "one meter" has been defined as the length of S *in this actual world*. There are of course possible worlds where S is shorter than it is in this world. From the definition of "one meter," it would follow that S is shorter than a meter in such a world. Hence, K is a contingent proposition. As Evans points out, however, the truth of K does not *reveal* anything about the actual world to us. K is a definitional truth that we create by our own stipulations. It is just that when a term is defined in terms of a characteristic of the actual world the definition turns out to express a contingent proposition.

Evans believes that all instances of contingent a priori knowledge will turn out to be of this superficial variety—i.e., that none of them is "made true . . . by some actual state of affairs in the world." This is how he dispels the empiricist's incredulity about such knowledge. But there is another way to dispel the incredulity. Perhaps it is not so surprising that reasoning alone can lead to knowledge of some "actual state of affairs in the world" if we remember that reasoning is itself an actual state of affairs in the world. At the very least, by reasoning we establish the contingent fact that we reason, and by reasoning in a certain manner we establish that this manner of reasoning exists. Furthermore, the truth of any contingent preposition that follows logically from the fact that we reason, or that we reason in a certain manner, becomes available to us on an a priori basis. Thus, when we prove a mathematical theorem, we come to know the contingent fact that human beings are capable of proving this particular theorem (Horowitz 1985). Evidently, there are properties that describe "actual states of the world" whose epistemic status does not fit neatly into the classical empiricist's world view. In previous chapters we considered various circumstances in which theorists can arrive at new contingent knowledge without rising from their armchairs. In those cases, however, the theorist always relied on previous data obtained by empirical means somewhere along the line. For example, in establishing the contingent truth that Fermat never made mistakes by the a priori method of proving Fermat's Last Theorem, we appealed to the empirical fact that Fermat claimed to have a proof. But we need not allude to data in order to establish the contingent fact that the proof of a theorem is physically possible. Just sitting in one's armchair and constructing the proof is enough.

The remaining question, of course, is whether we can discover enough grounded presuppositions to engineer our escape from Humean skepticism. Kant believed that we could. His arguments, however, are tortuous and highly suspect. Indeed, many of the contingent a priori truths that Kant claimed to have established are now thought to be false. For example, he offered transcendental deductions of Newtonian physics, Euclidean geometry, and Christian theology. (It is no mere coincidence that these doctrines were unquestioned features of the intellectual life of Europe in Kant's time.) Newtonian mechanics has been superseded by relativistic mechanics and is now thought to be only a useful approximation to the truth. The status of Euclidean geometry depends on how we interpret the term "geometry." Regarded as a formal system, the theorems of Euclid are indeed knowable a priori, but they are also noncontingent. Regarded as a description of physical space, Euclidean principles are indeed contingent, but they are very likely false. Clarification of the status of Christian theology is left as an exercise for the reader. Of course the failure of Kant's candidates does not mean that others cannot succeed. In a later section, I will speculate about the potential of grounded beliefs as a source of a priori knowledge in psychology. But I will not try to maintain the strong Kantian thesis that the scientific enterprise can be fully justified on the basis of grounded presuppositions.

10.3   Ungrounded Presuppositions

If we cannot ground our epistemic enterprises, we must either give them up or accede to certain *ungrounded* presuppositions—beliefs in contingent propositions without any empirical or rational warrant. We must examine our scientific practices with an eye to discovering the methodological and substantive principles that would warrant these practices if only we knew them to be true. And then we must simply accept their truth.

The term "transcendental deduction" has also been used in this context. Thus, a transcendental deduction may be either the process of deriving a grounded presupposition or the process of establishing the sufficiency of a set of ungrounded presuppositions. The two processes are quite different, however. The "transcendental deduction" of grounded presuppositions is really a species of deduction, whereas the "transcendental deduction" of ungrounded presuppositions is more akin to abduction. Kant himself seem to have argued in both directions. For him, the two processes led to the same result in the end. That is, the set of grounded presuppositions turns out to be the unique set of assumptions that justify our epistemic judgments.

I do not think there is any philosopher in the world today who accepts Kant's conclusions in toto. It certainly has not been demonstrated that the set of grounded presuppositions is strong enough to warrant anything remotely like a full-fledged scientific enterprise. Furthermore, Kant was surely wrong in supposing that the set of assumptions that can sustain a process of rational inquiry is unique. For example, it is easy to think of coherent alternatives to the principle of induction. Salmon (1966, p. 12) asks us to consider the alternative of using a crystal ball:

Consider the parallel case for a radically different sort of method. A crystal gazer claims that his method is the appropriate method for making predictions. When we question his claim he says, "Wait a moment; I will find out whether the method of crystal gazing is the best method for making predictions." He looks into his crystal ball and announces that future cases of crystal gazing will yield predictive success. If we should protest that his method has not been especially successful in the past, he might well make certain remarks about parity of reasoning. "Since you have used your method to justify your method, why shouldn't I use my method to justify my method? If you insist upon judging my method by using your method, why shouldn't I use my method to evaluate your method? By the way, I note by gazing into my crystal ball that the scientific method is now in for a very bad run of luck."

I don't know whether crystal gazers really presuppose the validity of their method in this way, but there certainly are real-life instances of ungrounded presuppositions that conflict with induction. Some fundamentalists evidently presuppose that the Bible is literally true. This is what makes the controversy between creationism and evolutionary theory philosophically more interesting than most scientists are willing to admit. It is not, of course, necessary to presuppose the validity of crystal gazing or of the Bible in order to believe that they are true. A person who presupposes the validity of induction may come to believe that the Bible is literally true on the basis of inductive evidence. This kind of fundamentalism is indeed susceptible to empirical disconfirmation. But fundamentalists who presuppose the validity of the Bible do not rely on inductive evidence. If you ask them why they believe in the Bible, they are apt to cite a passage from the Bible attesting to its own veracity. This argument is circular, of course—just like the appeal to past success as evidence for induction.

Kant attributed a number of other properties to the contingent a priori. Kantian presuppositions are *inborn* rather than acquired later in life. They are *inflicted* on us, not voluntarily selected. They are *unrevisable* (we cannot voluntarily give them up). They are *universal* (everyone has the same ones), not idiosyncratic. Finally, they are *fundamental* (they are broad principles that are implicated in many sciences) rather than specific. The frequently used word "innate" seems to refer to the combination of inborn, inflicted, and unrevisable. But except for the fact that inborn presuppositions cannot be adopted, all the aforementioned dimensions are independent of one another. A presupposition might be acquired later in life as a result of a brain operation, which means that it would also be inflicted; nevertheless, this presupposition might still be revisable. In fact, we might simultaneously possess presuppositions with any and all combinations of these properties (except for the combination of inborn and adopted)—some inborn and universal, some acquired and idiosyncratic, and so on. Furthermore, any of these combinations may (as far as anybody knows) be either grounded or ungrounded.

Some combinations have received more attention than others. One particularly famous type is represented by Chomsky's (1969) notion of a universal grammar. I have already discussed Chomsky's argument to the effect that people must have certain built-in ideas about the grammar of the languages that they hear spoken about them. This belief about grammar is similar to a Kantian presupposition in that it is both inborn and universal. It is dissimilar in that it is specific (to linguistics) and ungrounded. Its ungroundedness may not be evident, since it is in fact true—everyone *does* adhere to the rules of universal grammar. But this fact cannot be deduced from the mere belief that everyone adheres to universal grammar. The truth of the belief is contingent on certain causal connections that are not themselves knowable a priori.

In what follows, I will have a great deal to say about presuppositions that (like Chomsky's) are ungrounded and are specific to particular sciences but which (unlike Chomsky's) are also adopted and idiosyncratic. The centrality to science of such presuppositions is a major theme in the writings of Pierre Duhem (1906) and Imre Lakatos (1978). Recall the argument of Duhem discussed in chapter 5. Scientific hypotheses have experimental implications only when conjoined with an indefinite number of initial conditions and auxiliary hypotheses. A negative result in an experiment shows us only that one of the conjuncts is false; it cannot tell us which one. Furthermore, since the conjunction is indefinitely long, there is no possibility of singling out the culprit by any finite string of experiments. For our ideas to progress, however, we must make some sort of decision about where to lay the blame. But since the decision cannot be dictated by empirical results, it is open to us to use any of a number of a priori rules for laying blame. One option is to take some favored theoretical hypothesis and put it beyond the reach of disconfirmation by deciding that any apparent disconfirmation will always be attributed to the failure of some auxiliary hypothesis or initial condition. According to Lakatos, such a *conventionalist stratagem* has routinely been followed in the history of science. Here is Lakatos's graphic illustration of how the process works (1978, pp. 16–17):

A physicist of the pre-Einsteinian era takes Newton's mechanics and laws of gravitation, (N), the accepted initial conditions, I, and calculates, with their help, the path of a newly discovered small planet, p. But the planet deviates from the calculated path. Does our Newtonian physicist consider that the deviation was forbidden by Newton's theory, and therefore consider that, once established, it refutes the theory N? No. He suggests that there must be a hitherto unknown planet p' which perturbs that path of p. He calculates the mass, orbit, etc., of this hypothetical planet and then asks an experimental astronomer to test his hypothesis. The planet p' is so small that even the biggest available telescopes cannot observe it: the experimental astronomer applies for a research grant to build yet a bigger one. In three years' time the new telescope is ready. Were the unknown planet p' to be discovered, it would be hailed as a new victory of Newtonian science. But it is not. Does our scientist abandon Newton's theory and his idea of the perturbing planet? No. He suggests that a cloud of cosmic dust hides the planet from us. He calculates the location and properties of this cloud and asks for a research grant to send up a satellite to test his calculations. Were the satellite's instruments (possibly new ones based on little-tested theory) to record the existence of the conjectural cloud, the result would be hailed as an outstanding victory for Newtonian science. But the cloud is not found. Does our scientist abandon Newton's theory, together with the idea of the perturbing planet and the idea of the cloud which hides it? No. He suggests that there is some magnetic field in that region of the universe which disturbs the instruments of the satellite. A new satellite is sent up. Were the magnetic fields to be found, Newtonians would celebrate a sensational victory. But it is not. Is this regarded as a refutation of Newtonian science? No. Either yet another ingenious auxiliary hypothesis is proposed or . . . the whole story is buried in the dusty volumes of periodicals and the story never mentioned again.

In this passage, Lakatos is not criticizing the scientific practice he describes. The Duhemian principle puts it beyond reproach. We have to make some decision about what to change when we get a negative experimental result, and one change is as good as another so far as the experimental evidence is concerned. So why not decide always to change something other that a favored principle? The availability of the conventionalist stratagem greatly extends the range of contingent a priori beliefs in science. Kant's arguments establish that we need some unassailable assumptions in order to overcome Humean skepticism. Duhem's arguments, as extended by Lakatos, establish that there is nothing to stop us from making unassailable assumptions, whether we need them or not. Finally, there seems to be no principled restriction on what we may take to be unassailable.

Knowing that a principle is unassailable because it is protected by a conventionalist stratagem tells us that the principle is ungrounded. But it could logically have any of the characteristics of presuppositions that were discussed above. It could be inborn, for instance: We might have an innate predisposition to shield certain principles from disconfirmation. The shielded presupposition could also be fundamental or specific, universal or idiosyncratic. But idiosyncrasy and specificity do seem to be particularly likely consequences of a conventionalist stratagem. Indeed, if a presupposition is adopted, it could only be by sheer historical accident that everyone decided to shield the same principles from being overthrown, or that these principles were always fundamental. Lakatos (1978) and Kuhn (1962) have argued persuasively that differences concerning which principles are treated as unassailable are ubiquitous in the history of science, and that they extend to hypotheses that are specific to particular sciences—even to highly specialized branches of particular sciences. The presuppositional components of specific scientific traditions are called *paradigms* by Kuhn. Lakatos calls them the *hard core* of scientific research programs.

As an example of a paradigmatic, or hard-core, difference in psychology, consider the disagreement between methodological behaviorists and phenomenologists over the status of introspective reports (Kukla 1983). According to the former, a subject S's report of an experience E yields the empirical datum "S *reported* that he had experienced E." (See, e.g., Brody and Oppenheim 1966.) According to phenomenologists, the same event yields the datum "S *experienced* E." (See, e.g., Köhler 1947.) Clearly this disagreement will not be settled by performing another experiment, since both parties to the dispute would systematically interpret the results of any experiment in accordance with their own methodological presuppositions. As Kuhn puts it (1962 pp. 109–110), "each paradigm will be shown to satisfy more or less the criteria that it dictates for itself and to fall short of a few of those dictated by its opponents."

In summary, the major historical contrast in the realm of the contingent a priori is between Kantian and Kuhnian presuppositions. The former are grounded, fundamental, universal, inborn, inflicted, and unrevisable. The latter are ungrounded, specific, idiosyncratic, acquired, adopted, and revisable.

Lakatos (1978, p. 20) draws the same distinction between "conservative activists" and "revolutionary activists":

There is an important demarcation between *"passivist"* and *"activist" theories of knowledge.* "Passivists" hold that true knowledge is Nature's imprint on a perfectly inert mind: Mental activity can only result in bias and distortion. The most influential passivist school is classical empiricism. "Activists" hold that we cannot read the book of Nature without mental activity, without interpreting it in the light of our expectations or theories. Now *conservative "activists"* hold that we are born with our basic expectations; with them we turn the world into "our world" but must then live forever in the prison of our world. The idea that we live and die in the prison of our "conceptual frameworks" was developed primarily by Kant; pessimistic Kantians thought that the real world is forever unknowable because of this prison, while optimistic Kantians thought that God created our conceptual framework to fit the world. . . . But *revolutionary activists* believe that conceptual frameworks can be developed and also replaced by new, *better* ones; it is *we* who create our "prisons," and we can also, critically, demolish them. . . .

These two types of "activism," it must be emphasized again, are neither mutually exclusive nor exhaustive of the varieties of presuppositional stances. Ironically, it is at least as much a matter for empirical research as for theoretical analysis to sort out which varieties actually exist. However, the existence of *any* type of presupposition creates special tasks for theoreticians. These are discussed below.

The next section deals with the role of ungrounded presuppositions in theoretical psychology; the section after that takes up grounded presuppositions.

10.4   Discovery and Evaluation of Ungrounded Presuppositions

Suppose that we all have an innate presupposition P. It does not necessarily follow that we *know* that we presuppose P. Even if we are fully aware that we *believe* P, it may not be obvious that P plays the special role of a presupposition in our thinking. According to Kant, it requires a special analysis to discover what our presuppositions are—a working backward from what we actually say and do to the system of presuppositions that seem to warrant these practices. This working backward is at least one type of "transcendental deduction." (Kant believed that the result of such an analysis could also be grounded, but that additional claim will play no role in the discussion that follows.)

The same kind of working backward is generally necessary to discover Kuhnian as well as Kantian presuppositions. Despite the fact that Kuhnian presuppositions are not inflicted on us, it is rare for them to be explicitly laid out at the beginning of a scientific enterprise. Individual scientists working in a field may have conflicting ideas about which conventionalist stratagem to follow. Perhaps no individual scientist deliberately chooses to engage in a conventionalist stratagem. Yet the social configuration of the scientific community may be such that a conventionalist stratagem is in fact followed by the group as a whole. As in the case of Kantian presuppositions, it is usually necessary to *figure out* what the contingent a priori assumptions of a scientific paradigm are.

Thus, another task for the theoretical psychologist is to transcendentally deduce the specific presuppositions underlying current psychological theories. A noteworthy example of this sort of work is Fodor's (1975, 1980a, 1988) elucidation of the "computational" theory of mind presupposed by most contemporary research in cognitive psychology. Fodor calls this activity *speculative psychology*. Lamenting its recent neglect, he writes (1975, p. vii):

> What speculative psychologists did was this: They thought about such data as were available about mental processes, and they thought about such first-order theories as had been proposed to account for the data. Then they tried to elucidate the general conception of the mind that was implicit in the data and the theories.

Let us call such a "general conception of the mind" a second-order theory. The Fodorean concept of a second-order theory is somewhat broader than the concept of a Kuhnian paradigm. The principles of a second-order theory can be any background assumptions that are so general and so taken for granted that first-order theorists are unaware of making them. These would include, but would not necessarily be restricted to, principles that play the role of presuppositions. The discovery of assumptions that are being implicitly invoked is an important theoretical task regardless of whether these assumptions are presuppositions.

Formally, the transcendental deduction of scientific presuppositions is similar to the task of formulating first-order theories to account for bodies of data. Here, however, the theories themselves play the role of the data. The result of a transcendental deduction is a set of principles that accounts for the *range* of theories that are considered to be viable candidates on a priori grounds.

Another task for theoreticians is to evaluate the claims of competing paradigms. How is this task accomplished? Not very easily. Certainly not by empirical research. Empirical work undertaken within, say, the computational paradigm leads only to more refined computational theories, just as S-R research leads only to more refined S-R theories. The differences between S-R theory and computational theory are too fundamental to be settled by empirical means. This is what it means to say that they are different paradigms. In a nutshell, the problem is this: What basis can there be for preferring one ungrounded presupposition over another? There is, of course, always the test of logical consistency. It may be true that a fundamentalist who presupposes the veracity of the Bible cannot be criticized on empirical grounds, but fundamentalism would be in trouble if a passage were found in the Bible that exhorted us not to believe anything simply because it was written in a book. This is the level at which adherents to different paradigm usually argue with one another, each maintaining that the other's position is internally inconsistent or that it is inconsistent with the broader presuppositions of science as a whole. I remarked in section 10.3 that the interparadigmatic debate between methodological behaviorists and phenomenologists could not be resolved by empirical means. But Wolfgang Köhler (1947), among others, has argued that methodological behaviorism is incoherent. Methodological behaviorists insist that psychology can deal only with publicly observable events, reports of merely private events being unverifiable. Behaviorism is supposed to follow from this argument because the behavior of organisms is a public affair, whereas feelings, thoughts, and images are merely private. Köhler points out, however, that we cannot establish that an event is public without persuading ourselves that other people observe it. But this, by the methodological behaviorists' own arguments, we cannot do, since observation is just as private an affair as feeling or imagery. In other words, we have no basis for the claim that behavioral events are publicly observable unless we grant that we are sometimes warranted in our beliefs about the experiences of others. But if we do grant this point, the case for methodological behaviorism falls apart. This analysis, even if it is sound, does not definitively disprove methodological behaviorism. It merely refutes an argument in its favor. But it does show that the methods of rational persuasion are not irrelevant to interparadigmatic debate.

Of course there is no guarantee that only a single system of presuppositions will pass the test of logical consistency. Whether there is a rational basis for choosing between two coherent paradigms has been the most heatedly debated issue in the philosophy of science of the past generation, with Kuhn (1962, 1977) and Feyerabend (1975) taking the irrationalist side against Lakatos (1978) and Laudan (1977, 1984, 1996). Lakatos emphasizes the importance of simplicity considerations in evaluating competing research programs. The ungrounded presuppositions of a scientific theory never get into empirical trouble because we can always explain away problematic evidence by adjusting the auxiliary hypotheses. But continued adjustments may lead to a more and more convoluted picture of the world. Observation showed that the geocentric theory could not be maintained with the hypothesis that the heavenly bodies circled about the earth in epicycles. Preserving the hard-core assumption of geocentrism, the pre-Copernican astronomers were thus forced to postulate ever more bizarre and complex planetary orbits. In psychology, Hullian drive theory went through a similar development in its attempts to accommodate problematic evidence. Hull (1943) had postulated that all behavior was directed at diminishing stimulation. Experiments in the 1950s and the 1960s showed that organisms would readily acquire new responses that led only to novel and stimulus-rich environments, in apparent contradiction to the theory. Like Lakatos's fictional Newtonian scientist, however, drive theorists did not construe these findings as disconfirmations. Rather, they took them to demonstrate the existence of a "boredom" drive—i.e., a strong internal source of stimulation that was diminished by novelty. As contrary evidence continued to pour in, drive theorists continued to postulate the existence of hypothetical sources of stimulation that were being diminished. Neither Copernican astronomy nor drive theory was ever undermined by empirical refutations. But these theoretical edifices began to crumble under the weight of "continual repairs, and many tangled up stays," because "the worm-eaten columns" could no longer support the "tottering building" (Duhem 1906). Now, this appeal to simplicity considerations is beset with all the difficulties that were discussed in chapter 7. In the first place, the notion of *absolute* syntactic simplicity is incoherent. Thus, what appears to be a "worm-eaten column" with respect to one language may be an elegant Doric structure with respect to another language. Second, even if we could make sense of the notion of absolute simplicity, there is the problem of justifying the belief that simpler theories are likelier to be true. There is little doubt that Ptolemaic astronomy and drive theory were eventually overthrown by overt appeals to simplicity considerations. But it is another matter to establish that these considerations were rationally well founded.

Lakatos suggests that it is possible to judge objectively whether theoretical repairs are *progressive* or *degenerating*. A series of theoretical repairs is progressive if and only if each theory in the series not only manages to explain away some of the negative results faced by its predecessor but also has *new empirical consequences* that could not have been obtained from its predecessor. A series of repairs is degenerating if it fails to be progressive. By this criterion, the theoretical repairs undertaken by geocentric astronomers constituted a degenerating series. The increasingly complex orbits that astronomers postulated did save the theory from empirical refutation; but they did not have any new observational consequences for astronomy. Lakatos's criterion does not succeed in objectifying the process of paradigm evaluation, however. Feyerabend (1975) notes that it is always possible to turn a degenerating theoretical change into a progressive one by tacking a low-level empirical generalization onto the theory. For example, the switch from epicycles to more complex geocentric orbits could be considered progressive if we appended "and gold is heavier than water" to the more complex theory. Evidently, we must require that theoretical additions be connected to the rest of the theory "*more intimately* than by mere conjunction" (ibid., p. 226). Lakatos was aware of this criticism and conceded that it could not be answered without some concession to the exercise of subjective taste. But *any* amount of concession here seems to destroy what he was trying to accomplish. If we postulate an objective procedure for making a certain kind of decision and then admit that subjective taste enters at one point in the procedure, then the procedure is not objective at all. It is as though we said that we should determine the relative desirability of choices A and B by performing an elaborate calculation and then adding to either one an amount of our choosing that represents the "subjective factor." Clearly, the calculations could as well be dispensed with altogether.

Furthermore, it is not clear how we are supposed to choose between two research programs that are both progressing, or between a highly successful research program that has just begun to degenerate and a brand-new program that is just beginning to progress. Indeed, as Lakatos himself notes, a research program can degenerate for a while and then start to be progressive again. Thus, it becomes a matter of personal taste whether we should drop programs as soon as they begin to degenerate or whether we should stick with them for a while and give them a chance to recover. Whether or not they do recover—indeed, whether they degenerate in the first place—is probably due above all else to the cleverness of the theoreticians who are attracted to the program. On the basis of considerations such as these, Feyerabend concludes that Lakatos's criterion for theory change is a gloss that can be made to justify any theoretical decision whatever.

What are we to do if, as seems quite possible, there are competing paradigms that pass all tests of empirical and rational adequacy? Well, theoretical analysis can lay out the alternatives. It can tell us what the presuppositions of each system are, and what their logical consequences are. In the ideal case, it can tell us whether the systems are internally consistent, and whether they are consistent with broader presuppositions that are shared by adherents to all competing paradigms. And that is all. If we wish to *choose* one theory or another to believe in, the choice will have to be made without empirical or rational justification. Perhaps this is what it means to believe something "on faith." In the discussion of conceptual schemes in section 9.8, I noted that it can be rational to accept two theories of the same domain when those theories employ radically different conceptual schemes. One is tempted to take the same line with theories that begin with different presuppositions. But there is an important difference between the two cases: Two theories with radically different concepts cannot contradict each other, but two theories that begin with different presuppositions may very well have contradictory consequences if their conceptual schemes overlap. For example, the inductivist and the Biblical fundamentalist will often make different predictions in the same circumstances. Thus, it is not open to us to say that they are both true.

10.5   Grounded Presuppositions in Psychology

Since they are demonstrably true, grounded presuppositions impose a priori constraints on all scientific theories. Thus, it would seem that their discovery is a matter for philosophers rather than for scientific specialists. What is interesting for psychologists, however, is that the most plausible examples of such constraints are largely cognitive and social in nature. At least on the face of it, there are all sorts of exotic physical environments in which we could conduct the business of science essentially as usual. In fact, it is not even clear that there must be a physical world in order for science to exist, for disembodied spirits might be able to do a kind of scientific research. But there cannot be anything like science unless there exist beings who possess a certain type of mental equipment and a certain type of social organization. The proposition that humans do in fact possess that type of mental equipment and that type of social organization must therefore be presupposed by any scientific theory. At the same time, this proposition belongs squarely to the science of psychology (and to sociology, though I will not pursue that line of inquiry here).

Grounded presuppositions of this type do not play the same role in psychology as the ungrounded presuppositions of particular theories. There is a sense in which we are free to reject the presuppositions of any particular theory and search for alternatives. But grounded presuppositions impose constraints that must be adhered to by any conceivable theory of psychology. Ungrounded presuppositions are neither confirmed nor disconfirmed by experimentation. The relation between empirical research and grounded presuppositions is more peculiar. If we were to submit a grounded presupposition to empirical test, we would not have to wait for the outcome of the experiment, because the truth of the hypothesis would follow logically from the fact that it was being tested. In sum, ungrounded presuppositions are *optional*, whereas grounded presuppositions are *mandatory*—on the understanding that we are doing science, of course.

The most fundamental—and most famous—grounded presupposition of psychology is undoubtedly the conclusion of Descartes's (1641) *cogito* argument. Descartes establishes the contingent psychological fact that there are mental processes on the ground that it is a logical consequence of his being embarked on a project of assessing the justifiability of his various beliefs. No matter how this project may turn out in detail, the very fact that it has been begun warrants the conclusion that mental processes exist. Indeed, it can be known a priori that mental processes of a very high order of intelligence exist. If we were to subject the proposition that humans are capable of performing empirical research to empirical testing, we would not have to wait for the results before deciding what its truth value should be.

How much can psychology hope to establish by this analytical route? This is a largely unexplored question. Perhaps we can get nothing more out of this kind of analysis than a few obvious existential generalizations. But it is also prima facie possible that a fairly detailed picture of our mental (and social) life can be deduced from the very existence of the scientific enterprise. Here are three speculative examples.

First, the various theories of cognitive consistency that assert that belief systems follow some dynamic rules for eliminating overt inconsistencies (see, e.g., Festinger 1957 and Heider 1958) have generated an enormous amount of empirical research. But a close analysis may show that it is incoherent to suppose that empirical research could *disconfirm* the basic postulate of consistency theory, because the concept of disconfirmation has meaning only in relation to consistent systems. Theories of cognitive consistency are contingent theories; nevertheless, some of the empirical research they have inspired may be just as redundant as research into logically necessary truths.

Second, the fact that we entertain a particular hypothesis or frame a particular concept is sufficient to establish that human beings are capable of entertaining such a hypothesis or framing such a concept. Consider then the status of psychological theories of concept formation. Such theories typically hypothesize that human minds are in fact capable of framing a certain kind of concept. A hypothesis of this type is clearly contingent. Yet, so long as we are provided with an effective description of the type of concept involved, there is no need to submit the theory to empirical testing, for *understanding what the theory says* is already enough to show that the theory is true. If we were provided with a computable algorithm for the use of, say, a Roschean prototype concept, it would immediately follow that we are capable of using Roschean prototype concepts. But then what is accomplished by the voluminous experimental literature on prototype theory? To be sure, we cannot ascertain a priori whether the use of prototype concepts is commonplace, or whether their use comes naturally to us. But these questions are of secondary theoretical importance in relation to the question whether we have the *cognitive capacity* to employ a certain kind of concept. The latter issue, however, seems to be resolvable by a priori means.

Psychologists interested in formulating a theory of conceptual capacity could proceed by simply sitting in their armchairs and dreaming up various kinds of concepts. Every type they would dream up would establish something new about our conceptual capacity.

My favorite example of a grounded presupposition in psychology is the *law of consensus*, which can be formulated as follows: Given the same data, people agree in their inductive generalizations more often than can be accounted for by chance. For example, even though all previous emeralds have been both green and grue, most of us would agree that "All emeralds are green" is a better inductive generalization than "All emeralds are grue." Now, what would we say about a proposal to submit this law to empirical test? One could, of course, object that such tests are scarcely necessary, since the truth of the law of consensus is evident everywhere in daily life: We are always agreeing with others in our inductive generalizations. This is true as far as it goes. But I wish to claim that empirical tests of the law of consensus are pointless in a much stronger sense. In fact, the law of consensus must play the role of a presupposition in *any* communal knowledge-seeking enterprise. If the law of consensus were false, the enterprise of science wouldn't make any sense. If people's inductive inferences were entirely idiosyncratic, there could be no resolution to any scientific dispute. And if there were never any resolution to any dispute, then of course there would be no science. In fact, if the law of consensus were false, there could be no public language, for each of us would generalize about the meanings of words in different ways: Some of us would conclude that the word "green" means green, and others would conclude, on the basis of the same linguistic evidence, that "green" means grue. Thus, if the law of consensus is false, there is no reason to believe that we understand one another's utterances. But science *presupposes* that we understand one another, at least to a degree. Therefore, any scientific theory has to be consistent with the law of consensus.

In AI terms, the investigation of presuppositions grounded in the existence of science is essentially equivalent to the project of building an artificial scientist. What types of structures and processes are presupposed by the capacity to gather data, formulate explanatory theories, submit these theories to empirical test, and revise them in the light of new results? Like all matters relating to AI, this calls for a priori analysis. Whatever the result of this analysis may be, we can be sure of the contingent truth that these structures and processes are realized in *us*, because we too are capable of gathering data, formulating theories, and so on. This last claim may be questioned on the ground that there may be more than one way to build an artificial scientist, in which case the question whether we are built like artificial scientist A or like artificial scientist B can be settled only by empirical research. This is true as far as it goes. But the fact that there may be more than one type of artificial scientist necessitates only a slight elaboration of the previous claim. Let $S1, S2, \ldots, Sn$ represent all the (as yet undiscovered) systems that are capable of behaving like scientists. Then the disjunctive statement "*We* are either $S1$s or $S2$s or $\ldots$ or Sns" is a grounded presupposition of psychology. The amount of detail about our mental apparatus that is supplied by this disjunction depends on the heterogeneity of the set $S = (S1, S2, \ldots, Sn)$. This set might, of course, be infinite; it might even fail to be recursively enumerable. But since the number of systems currently known to belong to S is zero, it seems premature to worry that it might be too large. At present, nobody knows how much of psychology can be derived from a purely a priori analysis of science.

References

Aristotle. De anima. In *Introduction to Aristotle*, second edition, ed. R. McKeon (University of Chicago Press, 1973).

Aronson, E. 1958. The need for achievement as measured by graphic expression. In *Motives in Fantasy, Action, and Society*, ed. J. W. Atkinson. Van Nostrand.

Bakan, D. 1966. The test of significance in psychological research. *Psychological Bulletin* 66: 423–437.

Barrow, J. D. 1991. *Theories of Everything: The Quest for Ultimate Explanation*. Vintage.

Berkeley, G. 1710. *A Treatise Concerning the Principles of Human Knowledge* (Hackett, 1982).

Boden, M. 1977. *Artificial Intelligence and Natural Man*. Harvester.

Bohm, D. 1971. Quantum theory as an indication of a new order in physics. *Foundations of Physics* 1: 359–381.

Bohr, N. 1958. *Atomic Physics and Human Knowledge*. Wiley.

Bradley, R., and N. Swartz. 1979. *Possible Worlds: An Introduction to Logic and Its Philosophy*. Hackett.

Brandtstädter, J. 1987. On certainty and universality in human development: Developmental psychology between apriorism and empiricism. In *Meaning and the Growth of Understanding*, ed. M. Chapman and R. A. Dixon. Springer-Verlag.

Brody, N., and Oppenheim, P. 1966. Tension in psychology between the methods of behaviorism and phenomenology. *Psychological Review* 73: 295–305.

Brown, J. R. 1991. *The Laboratory of the Mind: Thought Experiments in the Natural Sciences*. Routledge.

Cattell, R. B. 1950. *Personality: A Systematic, Theoretical, and Factual Study*. McGraw-Hill.

Chomsky, N. 1962. Explanatory models in linguistics. In *Logic, Methodology and Philosophy of Science*, ed. E. Nagel, P. Suppes, and A. Tarski. Stanford University Press

Chomsky, N. 1969. Linguistics and philosophy. In *Language and Philosophy*, ed. S. Hook. New York University Press.

Chomsky, N. 1980a. Discussion of Putnam's comments. In *Language and Learning*, ed. M. Piattelli-Palmarini. Harvard University Press.

Chomsky, N. 1980b. Recent contributions to the theory of innate ideas. In *Challenges to Empiricism*, ed. H. Morick. Hackett.

Chomsky, N. 1980c. Rules and representations. *Behavioral and Brain Sciences* 3: 1–15.

Chomsky, N. 1981a. On cognitive capacity. In *Readings in Philosophy of Psychology*, volume 2, ed. N. Block. Harvard University Press.

Chomsky, N. 1981b. Reply to Putnam. In *Readings in Philosophy of Psychology*, volume 2, ed. N. Block. Harvard University Press.

Chomsky, N. 1986. *Knowledge of Language: Its Nature, Origin, and Use*. Praeger.

Chomsky, N., and Fodor, J. 1980. The inductivist fallacy. In *Language and Learning*, ed. M. Piattelli-Palmarini. Harvard University Press.

Christensen-Szalanki, J. J. J., and Beach, L. R. 1983. Publishing opinions: A note on the usefulness of commentaries. *American Psychologist* 38: 1400–1401.

Christie, A. 1984. *Hercule Poirot's Casebook*. Dodd Mead.

Churchland, P. M. 1981. Eliminative materialism and the propositional attitudes. *Journal of Philosophy* 78: 67–90.

Cohen, L. J. 1981. Can human irrationality be experimentally demonstrated? *Behavioral and Brain Sciences* 4: 317–331.

Collingwood, R. G. 1924. *Speculum Mentis*. Clarendon.

Davidson, D. 1970. Mental events. In *Experience and Theory*, ed. L. Foster and J. W. Swanson. University of Massachusetts Press.

Davidson, D. 1974. On the very idea of a conceptual scheme. *Proceedings and Addresses of the American Philosophical Association* 47: 5–20.

Dennett, D. C. 1971. Intentional systems. *Journal of Philosophy* 68: 87–106.

Dennett, D. C. 1987. Cognitive wheels: The frame problem of AI. In *The Robot's Dilemma*, ed. Z. Pylyshyn. Ablex.

Descartes, R. 1641. Meditations. In *The Philosophical Works of Descartes*, ed. E. Haldane and G. Ross (Cambridge University Press, 1968).

Dirac, P. A. M. 1963. The evolution of the physicist's picture of nature. *Scientific American* 208: 45–53.

Duhem, P. 1906. *La théorie physique: Son object, sa structure*. Marcel Rivière.

Einstein, A. 1951. Autobiographical note. In *Albert Einstein*, volume 1, ed. P. Schilpp. Harper & Row.

Evans, G. 1979. Reference and contingency. *Monist* 62: 161–189.

Festinger, L. 1957. *A Theory of Cognitive Dissonance*. Stanford University Press.

Festinger, L., Riecken, H., and Schachter, S. 1956. *When Prophecy Fails*. University of Minnesota Press.

Feyerabend, P. K. 1975. *Against Method*. New Left Books.

Flanagan, O. J. 1984. *The Science of the Mind*. MIT Press.

Flavell, J. H., and Wohlwill, J. F. 1969. Formal and functional aspects of cognitive development. In *Studies in Cognitive Development*, ed. D. Elkind and J. Flavell. Oxford University Press.

Fodor, J. A. 1975. *The Language of Thought*. Harvard University Press.

Fodor, J. A. 1980a. Methodological solipsism considered as a research strategy in cognitive psychology. *Behavioral and Brain Sciences* 3: 63–73.

Fodor, J. A. 1980b. Reply to Putnam. In *Language and Learning*, ed. M. Piattelli-Palmarini. Harvard University Press.

Fodor, J. A. 1981a. Introduction. In J. A. Fodor, *Representations*. MIT Press.

Fodor, J. A. 1981b. The present status of the innateness controversy. In J. A. Fodor, *Representations*. MIT Press.

Fodor, J. A. 1983. *The Modularity of Mind*. MIT Press.

Fodor, J. A. 1988. *Psychosemantics: The Problem of Meaning in the Philosophy of Mind*. MIT Press.

Fodor, J. A., Garrett, M., and Brill, S. L. 1975. Pe, ka, pu: The perception of speech sounds in prelinguistic infants. MIT Quarterly Progress Report, January 1975.

Freud, S. 1917. *Introductory Lectures on Psychoanalysis* (Penguin, 1973).

Freud, S. 1933. *New Introductory Lectures on Psychoanalysis* (Penguin, 1973).

Garber, D. 1983. Old evidence and logical omniscience in Bayesian confirmation theory. In *Testing Scientific Theories* (Minnesota studies in the Philosophy of Science, volume 10), ed. J. Earman. University of Minnesota Press.

Gardner, H. 1983. *Frames of Mind: The Idea of Multiple Intelligences*. Basic Books.

Glymour, C. N. 1980. *Theory and Evidence*. Princeton University Press.

Goodman, N. 1954. *Fact, Fiction and Forecast*. Harvard University Press.

Grelling, K., and Nelson, L. 1908. Bemerkungen zu den Paradoxien von Russell und Burali-Forte. *Abhandlungen der Fries'schen Schule neue Folge* 2: 301–334.

Guthrie, E. 1952. *The Psychology of Learning*, revised edition. Harper.

Hacking, I. 1967. Slightly more realistic personal probabilities. *Philosophy of Science* 34: 311–325.

Hall, C. S., and Lindzey, G. 1978. *Theories of personality*. Wiley.

Hanson, N. R. 1961. *Patterns of Discovery*. Cambridge University Press.

Hartmann, H. 1958. *Ego Psychology and the Problem of Adaptation*. International Universities Press.

Heider, F. 1958. *The Psychology of Interpersonal Relations*. Wiley.

Hempel, C. G. 1965. *Aspects of Scientific Explanation*. Free Press.

Hilgard, E. R., and Marquis, D. G. 1940. *Conditioning and Learning*. Appleton-Century-Crofts.

Holland, J. H., Holyoak, K. J., Nisbett, R. E., and Thagard, P. R. 1986. *Induction: Processes of Inference, Learning, and Discovery*. MIT Press.

Horowitz, T. 1985. A priori truth. *Journal of Philosophy* 82: 225–238.

Horwich, P. 1982. *Probability and Evidence*. Cambridge University Press.

Hull, C. 1943. *Principles of Behaviour*. Appleton-Century-Crofts.

Hull, C. 1952. *A Behavior System*. Yale University Press.

Hume, D. 1739. *A Treatise on Human Nature* (Clarendon, 1964).

Kahneman, D., and Tversky, A. 1972. Subjective probability: A judgement of representativeness. *Cognitive Psychology* 3: 430–454.

Kant, I. 1781. *Critique of Pure Reason*. Macmillan, 1929.

Koch, S. 1981. The nature and limits of psychological knowledge: Lessons of a century qua "science." *American Psychologist* 36: 257–269.

Köhler, W. 1947. *Gestalt Psychology: An Introduction to New Concepts in Modern Psychology*. Livewright.

Kripke, S. 1972. *Naming and Necessity*. Harvard University Press.

Kuhn, T. S. 1962. *The Structure of Scientific Revolutions*. University of Chicago Press.

Kuhn, T. S. 1977. *The Essential Tension*. University of Chicago Press.

Kukla, A. 1983. Toward a science of experience. *Journal of Mind and Behavior* 4: 231–246.

Kukla, A. 1989. Nonempirical issues in psychology. *American Psychologist* 44: 785–794.

Kukla, A. 1995a. Amplification and simplification as modes of theoretical analysis in psychology. *New Ideas in Psychology* 13: 201–217.

Kukla, A. 1995b. Is there a logic of incoherence? *International Studies in the Philosophy of Science* 9: 57–69.

Lakatos, I. 1978. *The Methodology of Scientific Research Programmes*. Cambridge University Press.

Langley, P., Simon, H. A., Bradshaw, G. L., and Zytkow, J. M. 1987. *Scientific Discovery: Computational Explorations of the Creative Process*. MIT Press.

Laudan, L. 1977. *Progress and Its Problems: Towards a Theory of Scientific Growth*. University of California Press.

Laudan, L. 1984. *Science and Values*. University of California Press.

Laudan, L. 1996. *Beyond Positivism and Relativism: Theory, Method and Evidence*. Westview.

Locke, J. 1706. *An Essay Concerning Human Understanding* (Everyman's Library, 1961).

Longuet-Higgins, H. C. 1981. Artificial intelligence—a new theoretical psychology? *Cognition* 10: 197–200.

Lyons, W. E. 1986. *The Disappearance of Introspection*. MIT Press.

MacCorquodale, K., and Meehl, P. E. 1948. On a distinction between hypothetical constructs and intervening variables. *Psychological Review* 55: 95–107.

MacIntyre, R. B. 1985. Psychology's fragmentation and suggested remedies. *International Newsletter of Paradigmatic Psychology* 1: 20–21.

Mackay, D. G. 1988. Under what conditions can theoretical psychology survive and prosper? Integrating the rational and empirical epistemologies. *Psychological Review* 95: 559–565.

Maher, B. A. 1985. Underpinnings of today's chaotic diversity. *International Newsletter of Paradigmatic Psychology* 1: 17–19.

Mannheim, K. 1925. *Essays on the Sociology of Knowledge*. Routledge and Kegan Paul.

Marx, M. H., and Hillix, W. A. 1973. *Systems and Theories in Psychology*. McGraw-Hill.

Meehl, P. E. 1950. On the circularity of the law of effect. *Psychological Bulletin* 47: 52–75.

Meehl, P. E. 1967. Theory testing in psychology and physics: A methodological paradox. *Philosophy of Science* 34: 103–115.

Meehl, P. E. 1990. Why summaries of research on psychological theories are often uninterpretable. *Psychological Reports* 66: 195–244.

Michaels, L., and Ricks, C. 1980. *The State of the Language*. University of California Press.

Miller, N. E. 1959. Liberalization of basic S-R concepts: Extensions to conflict behavior, motivation, and social learning. In *Psychology*, volume 2, ed. S. Koch. Ronald.

Nagel, E. 1961. *The Structure of Science*. Hackett.

Newell, A., and Simon, H. A. 1981. Computer science as empirical inquiry: Symbols and search. In *Mind Design*, ed. J. Haugeland. MIT Press.

Nozick, R. 1993. *The Nature of Rationality*. Princeton University Press.

Peirce, C. S. 1901. The logic of abduction. In *Essays in the Philosophy of Science*, ed. V. Tomas (Bobbs-Merrill, 1957).

Piaget, J. 1929. *The Child's Conception of the World*. Harcourt, Brace.

Piaget, J. 1952. *The Origin of Intelligence in Children*. International University Press.

Place, U. T. 1956. Is consciousness a brain process? *British Journal of Psychology* 47: 44–50.

Plato. Phaedo. In *The Collected Dialogues of Plato* (Pantheon, 1961).

Popper, K. R. 1934–35. *The Logic of Scientific Discovery* (Basic Books, 1959).

Price, H. H. 1950. *Perception*, second edition. Methuen.

Putnam, H. 1965. Brains and Behavior. In *Analytical Philosophy*, volume 2, ed. R. J. Butler. Blackwell.

Putnam, H. 1970. Is semantics possible? *Metaphilosophy* 1: 187–201.

Putnam, H. 1975. *Mathematics, Matter, and Method: Philosophical Papers*, Volume 1. Cambridge University Press.

Putnam, H. 1980a. The innateness hypothesis and explanatory models in linguistics. In *Challenges to Empiricism*, ed. H. Morick. Hackett.

Putnam, H. 1980b. What is innate and why: Comments on the debate. In *Language and Learning*, ed. M. Piattelli-Palmarini. Harvard University Press.

Pylyshyn, Z. 1984. *Computation and Cognition: Toward a Foundation for Cognitive Science*. MIT Press.

Quine, W. V. O. 1951. Two dogmas of empiricism. *Philosophical Review* 60: 20–43.

Quine, W. V. O. 1960. *Word and Object*. MIT Press.

Quine, W. V. O. 1966. *The Ways of Paradox*. Random House.

Quine, W. V. O., and Ullian, J. S. 1970. *The Web of Belief*. Random House.

Reichenbach, H. 1963. *The rise of scientific philosophy*. University of California Press.

Rosch, E., and Lloyd, B. B., eds. 1978) *Cognition and Categorization*. Erlbaum.

Rosenkrantz, R. D. 1977. *Inference, Method, and Decision: Toward a Bayesian Philosophy of Science*. Reidel.

Russell, B. 1945. *A History of Western Philosophy*. Simon and Schuster.

Salmon, W. 1966. *Foundations of Scientific Inference*. Pittsburgh University Press.

Salmon, W. 1988. Dynamic Rationality: Propensity, probability, and credence. In *Probability and Causality*, ed. J. Fetzer. Reidel.

Schick, T. W., Jr. 1987. Rorty and Davidson on alternate conceptual schemes. *Journal of Speculative Philosophy* 1: 291–303.

Searle, J. R. 1980. Minds, brains, and programs. *Behavioral and Brain Sciences* 3: 417–424.

Sears, C. E. 1924. *Days of Delusion: A Strange Bit of History*. Houghton Mifflin.

Sheldon, W. H. 1942. *The Varieties of Temperament*. Harper.

Simenon, G. 1971. *Maigret and the Informer*. Harcourt Brace Jovanovich.

Skinner, B. F. 1945. The operational analysis of psychological terms. *Psychological Review* 52: 270–277.

Skinner, B. F. 1950. Are theories of learning necessary? *Psychological Review* 57: 193–216.

Skinner, B. F. 1953. *Science and Human Behavior*. Macmillan.

Skinner, B. F. 1974. *About Behaviorism*. Knopf.

Skyrms, B. 1987. Dynamic coherence and probability kinematics. *Philosophy of Science* 54: 1–20.

Smart, J. J. C. 1959. Sensations and brain processes. *Philosophical Review* 68: 141–156.

Smedslund, J. 1984. What is necessarily true in psychology? In *Annals of Theoretical Psychology*, volume 2, ed. J. R. Royce and L. P. Mos. Plenum.

Spence, K. W. 1936. The nature of discrimination learning in animals. *Psychological Review* 43: 427–449.

Spence, K. W. 1937. The differential response in animals to stimuli varying within a single dimension. *Psychological Review* 44: 430–444.

Spooner, A., and Kellog, W. N. 1947. The backward conditioning curve. *American Journal of Psychology* 60: 321–334.

Staats, A. W. 1983. *Psychology's Crisis of Disunity: Philosophy and Method for a Unified Science*. Praeger.

Staats, A. W. 1991. Unified positivism and unification psychology: Fad or new field? *American Psychologist* 46: 899–912.

Teller, P. 1980. Computer proof. *Journal of Philosophy* 77: 797–803.

Thagard, P. R. 1988. *Computational Philosophy of Science*. MIT Press.

Thorndike, E. L. 1898. Animal intelligence: An experimental study of the associative processes in animals. *Psychological Monographs* 2 (whole no. 8).

Tolman, E, C., and Honzik, C. H. 1930. Introduction and removal of reward, and maze performance in rats. *University of California Publications in Psychology* 4: 257–275.

Tymoczko, T. 1979. The four color map theorem and mathematical proof. *Journal of Philosophy* 76: 57–83.

van Fraassen, B. C. 1980. *The Scientific Image*. Oxford University Press.

van Fraassen, B. C. 1989. *Laws and Symmetry*. Clarendon.

Vollmer, F. 1984. On the limitations of commonsense psychology. *Annals of Theoretical Psychology* 2: 279–286.

Weiner, B., Graham, S., and Chandler, C. 1982. Pity, anger, and guilt: An attributional analysis. *Personality and Social Psychology Bulletin* 8: 226–232.

Wertheimer, M. 1959. On discrimination experiments: I. Two logical structures. *Psychological Review* 66: 252–266.

Wertheimer, M. 1962. *Fundamental Issues in Psychology*. Holt, Rinehart and Winston.

White, R. W. 1959. Motivation reconsidered: The concept of competence. *Psychological Review* 66: 297–333.

Whitehead, A. N., and Russell, B. 1910–1913. *Principia mathematica*. Cambridge University Press, 1963.

Whitt, L. A. 1990. Atoms or affinities? The ambivalent reception of Daltonian theory. *Studies in History and Philosophy of Science* 19: 517–529.

Wolman, B. B. 1981. *Contemporary Theories and Systems in Psychology*. Plenum

Index